KETO DIET
Cookbook for Beginners

550 Recipes
for Busy People on Keto Diet

Elizabeth Cunningham

CONTENTS

PORK, BEEF & LAMB RECIPES 67

SEAFOOD & FISH RECIPES..95

MEATLESS MEALS101

BRUNCH & DINNER 144

DESSERTS & DRINKS 160

INTRODUCTION

The Keto diet is the solution you've always been waiting for.

Here's to shedding weight effortlessly; optimizing your health; and unleashing your inner athlete. The Keto diet will transform your life!

Yes, I know…

These sound like outlandish claims. I'd be the first to agree that I start to sound like some crazy infomercial when I start talking about the Keto diet. But it's not my fault; Keto made me do it!

Jokes aside though, I have real reasons to be this excited; I reaped a ton of benefits.

Bear with me as I take you down a few years of memory lane.

I was in my senior year at college, juggling multiple jobs to keep myself financially afloat; and I was sick. Not sick with a terrible virus but sick not to be as bouncy as I ought to be.

Sick to the bone! Exhausted, overweight, sluggish, depressed, still struggling with acne, and extremely worried about my ever-increasing waistline.

You see, I wasn't your stereotypical college kid. I didn't have terrible eating habits, at least I didn't think I did; I'd always been careful with my diet. Despite my crazy sweet tooth, and my passionate love for cream (mmmm), I'd listened to the health authorities.

I'd stuck to zero-fat foods. Opted for the "diet" versions of foods when available. Tried to live on low-fat pasta dishes, 'slimming' menus of limp boiled fish, boiled potatoes and mushy boiled vegetables. I'd forgone my favorite foods because I was told that healthy people didn't eat those. I was stuck to the foods I hated just because that's what I was told was healthy.

…But, the weight just kept piling on.

So, I slashed my portion sizes. I started to skip meals. I went utterly zero fat. I tried to ignore the fact that my food tasted bland, unappetizing and, at times, even horrible. In my head, it was worth it, so I kept encouraging myself, but my body kept ballooning. Up another clothing size. And another and another.

Would it ever end?…

WHAT IS THE KETO DIET?

Let me cut straight to the chase.

Simply, the Keto diet termed a "low-carb" diet burns fuel from fat in the body instead of carbohydrates. It allows you to shed weight efficiently, enjoy an endless source of energy and carves the body into the best state of health both physically and mentally.

Unlike many other low carb diets, you don't stuff yourself with processed foods, unhealthy fried foods (hello Atkins) and all the junk your body craves, which you know are bad for you.

It is about eating whole foods, which are, as close to their pure state as possible, just like nature intended. It is going back to the basics and enjoying real food. …Real Good Food! The kind that makes you sigh with pleasure feel completely satisfied and causes you to make it repeatedly.

The Keto diet is NOT a hunger strike; you don't need to deprive yourself or limit your food intake in any way. It's about healing your destructive relationship with food, i.e., eating only healthy fun stuff that boosts your self-image and makes you fall in love with exciting food all over again just as you were made to be.

How does the Keto diet work?

While I don't plan to get too deep into the science of the Keto diet, there are a few core principles you should know about.

- Firstly, Dr. Russel Wilder, MD of the Mayo Clinic invented the Keto diet in 1921 as a way to treat epilepsy in kids. It worked! While not recognizing the other benefits it came with at the time; this diet has currently taken the world by storm.

- On a diet, you strictly reduce your carb intake to allow the body to enter into a state called 'Ketosis.' At this point, the body switches from using carbs but fats to produce energy, and that is where the weight loss magic happens. The lipids are shed!

- So, to keep the body pumped with ketones, you ought to ensure a good intake of healthy fats to keep yourself adequately fuelled and healthy.

- Expect to eat around 70%-80% fat, 25% protein, and 5% carbs. For best results, keep your net carbs under 20g per day (although a more conservative aim would be around 50g)

Why no carbs?

I don't hate carbs. They're one of nature's way of fueling our bodies and brains. However, we eat far too much of this stuff by the way we live lately. Mostly, in the form of processed sugars, refined carbs, and other high carb foods.

They spell disaster for your body, and you start piling on weight in those places you hate the most. In your stomach, your hips, your legs, your butt, your arms, your neck. Everywhere that's wrong! It leaves you more vulnerable to health problems such as type 2 diabetes, metabolic syndrome, depression and anxiety, certain cancers and just many more.

Foods that are high in carbs

Before you read this list, prepare not to panic. Seeing what's off the menu, may make you wonder what on earth you'll eat. Take a chill pill; this is normal and shows how addicted to carbs you are!

I'll walk you through the foods you can eat shortly after this list, and you will feel more excited.

Deep breath

Sugar

Sugar is about as high carb as it gets. Avoid it in all forms, including the following foods.

- Soft drinks
- Fruit yogurt
- Premade cereal bars
- Smoothies
- Candy
- Boxed Juice
- Sports drinks
- Chocolate
- Cake
- Buns
- Pastries
- Ice cream
- Donuts
- Cookies
- Breakfast cereals

Grains

Grains are also extremely high in carbs. You'll need to skip the following:

- Wheat
- Barley
- Oats
- Rice
- Rye
- Corn
- Quinoa
- Millet
- Bulgur
- Amaranth
- Sprouted Grains
- Buckwheat

Remember that it's not just about the grains themselves but also the foods made from them, which include:

- Bread
- Pasta
- Rice
- Potatoes
- French fries
- Potato chips
- Porridge
- Muesli

Beans & Lentils

Beans and lentils are another carb offender. Get the following off the menu.

- Red, green, brown and black lentils
- Red Kidney beans
- Black-Eye beans
- Chickpeas
- Black beans
- Green peas
- Lima beans
- Pinto beans
- White beans
- Fava beans

How was it for you? Not as bad as you thought, right?

If I can't eat carbs, what can I eat?

Let's look at the other side of the coin. You're about to be pumped!

Meat, poultry, fish, and seafood

Eat as much as you like. Stick to organic, and grass-fed options if you can afford it. Keep the fat on!

- Beef
- Pork
- Lamb
- Game
- Chicken
- Turkey
- Organ meats
- Salmon
- Mackerel
- Sardines
- Herring
- Cod
- Seafood

Eggs

Eggs are excellent on Keto since they are versatile and rich in nutrients. Enjoy them however you like, and choose free-range, farm-raised types if possible.

Dairy Products

Wave goodbye to those tasteless zero fat products - we're about the whole dairy here! They taste better, they're much more satisfying, and they're exactly what your body needs. This includes:

- Butter
- Cream
- Sour Cream
- Soft/Hard Cheese
- Greek/Bulgarian Yogurt
- Regular Yogurt (sugar-free)

Just a quick word - avoid drinking milk. It's surprisingly high in carbs. Instead, go for nut milk like almond milk and coconut milk.

Fats, oils, and sauces

Awesome! We can include as many fatty foods as we like. Such as:

- Butter
- Cream
- Coconut oil
- Olive oil
- Ghee
- Chicken fat
- Avocados
- Mayonnaise
- High-fat sauces

Please stick to wholefood, healthy fats and avoid those refined polyunsaturated fats and trans fats. They're just not good for you man!

Vegetables

Many veggies are high carb, so you'll need to avoid them. However, there are still much more you can enjoy. They'll bring extra flavor, nutrition and excitement to your meals and help your digestive system to keep working optimally.

Enjoy these:

- Green leafy veggies
- Broccoli/Cabbage
- Brussels sprouts
- Asparagus
- Zucchini
- Eggplant
- Olives
- Mushrooms
- Cucumber
- Lettuce
- Avocado
- Onions & Garlic

Herbs and spices

You can eat as much of these as you like, but please do check the ingredients list on pre-prepared spice blends- they often have some sugar sneaked in.

Sauces and condiments

Certain go-to condiments may be off the menu with Keto, but you can still enjoy the sugar-free versions of the following:

- Soy Sauce
- Lemon and lime juice
- Sriracha Sauce
- Homemade mayo
- Dijon mustard
- Wholegrain mustard (check the label)
- Hot sauces (check the label)
- Salad dressings (homemade only)

Sweeteners

Some Keto purists don't agree that sweeteners should be allowed. For me, a little touch of sweetness can be a welcome treat.

- Erythritol
- Stevia
- Splenda
- Brand-name sugar replacements
- Monk Fruit Sugar & Syrup

Alcoholic and Non-Alcoholic Drinks

There are plenty of great drinks options on the Keto diet.

Start with the basics - tea, coffee, and water. These quench your thirst brilliantly and have zero-carb, provided you avoid non- keto syrups, sugars, and excessive milk. If you like this idea, I'd advise you check out bulletproof coffee. You might have a pleasant surprise!

You'll be happy to know that you can also drink alcohol on the Keto diet, provided you stick with a few safe options, like:

- Champagne (sugar-free)
- Red or white wine
- Whiskey/Brandy
- Tequila
- Vodka Soda
- Dry Martini

Be careful to avoid liquors and alcopops as these are quite high in sugar.

ASK ME ALL YOU WANT

Whenever I tell someone that the Keto diet is the life hack responsible for the impressive changes in me, I usually get bombarded with questions, and that's fine by me.

I'm happy when people are curious, I want them to give it a go themselves, and the more information I can provide the more fulfilled I feel. So, why not you too?

I've gathered some of my most asked questions, and I provide honest answers based on my experience. Let's delve in.

Q: Will I go through detox?

A: Yes, most people experience symptoms when they start the Keto diet, because of your body's transition from using carbs to using fats for fuel. It includes anything from minor headaches and perhaps not feeling like yourself, to more flu-like symptoms. Your experience is very personal and depends on how addicted to carbs you were.

Q: How should I cope with detox symptoms?

A: If you do experience detox symptoms, make sure to slow down, drink plenty of water and sleep as much as you can. Even if you feel rotten for a day or two, remember that it's all for a terrific cause. Today is the first day of a stronger, slimmer and unstoppable you.

Q: Can anyone follow the Keto diet?

A: Yes! Anyone can follow the Keto diet and notice incredible results because it's a healthy and transformative diet and lifestyle. Remember, it was first created for kids with epilepsy, so it's naturally safe. Nevertheless, if you're pregnant, breastfeeding, under 18 years old, diabetic, or have high blood pressure, please consult your doctor first.

Q: I'm morbidly obese. Can I still do the diet?

A: Absolutely! Keto is probably the answer you've been looking for. I'm not going to lie; it will challenge you. You might suffer from regular cravings at the beginning of your journey as you transition to using fats for energy, but it will be worth it. Read the next chapter Obese to Fit: Weight Loss Tips with Keto for more useful tips.

Q: What benefits can I expect from going Keto?

A: There are tons of benefits to reap. I've already shared some of them with you when I spoke about my journey with Keto. But there are many more that I might not have covered. Some are:

- **Weight loss** — No more nibbling lettuce leaves to shed weight. Keep eating the tasty fatty stuff precisely as you want and your body will burn the fats for energy. There'll be no more reserved fats for a bulging stomach.

- **Increased brainpower** — An increase in healthy fat consumption will feed your brain and encourage you to become more productive than ever before, learn new things quickly and get on top of your game.

- **Increased stamina and endurance** — Want to run a marathon? Keto is your diet. Whereas stored sugars will run out on a regular run, this doesn't happen with Keto. Instead, you'll use stored fats, which is fantastic.

- **Healthier hormones** — Whether you're male or female, switching to Keto will help regulate your hormones, help you sleep better and help you feel better 24/7.

- **No more binge eating** — Keto enables you to feel satisfied so you don't find yourself snacking or binge eating all the time.

- **Reduced cholesterol levels** — The Keto diet reduces bad cholesterol and increases the good ones.

- **Eased symptoms of epilepsy** — This diet was designed for you, remember?

- **No more migraines** — Keto works brilliantly for people who suffer from crippling migraines and headaches.

- **Reduced risk of cancer** — Carbs feed cancerous cells in your body, so getting rid of them instantly helps protect you against one of our greatest fears.

Again, I've kept this nice and simple so you can quickly understand Keto and get started righ away!

8 NO-FAIL TIPS TO HELP YOU LIVE A HAPPIER KETO LIFESTYLE

Don't you wish that someone would just hand you a list of Keto lifestyle hacks that would help you get to grips and lose weight, gain energy and feel terrific faster?

Well, today's your lucky day because that's what I've just done for you.

Make Yours!

I feel like a full flute of champagne with an attitude saying this; you've got to make yours!

When you start a Keto diet, it often seems like an easy thing to get the carbs of the menu. Just skip the bread, pasta, potatoes, and rice, and you're done! It isn't that simple; I'm afraid to say. Carbs and more specifically, sugars are in almost every processed food you buy from yogurts, to condiments, to sauces and much more in between.

The best way to beat these carbs is to merely avoid these foods entirely and make your versions. Not only can you control the carbs like this, but you can also tweak the recipe, so it's exactly how you love your food to be. If you absolutely must eat processed food, check your labels!

Counting your macros is essential!

I'm a laid-back kind of a person, and I like to think that once I've understood a concept, I can go ahead without worrying about the details. However, you can't do this when it comes to Keto. As unusual as it might seem, you absolutely must count your macros - your net carb, protein, and fat intake.

Ditch those carb-rich foods before you start

There's nothing worse than feeling like you're comfortable on the Keto diet and super-happy with your progress, only to find a packet of potato chips or long-forgotten cheese fries lurking at the back of the pantry. Bang! There goes your willpower! Even if you have firm resolve, it's quite likely you'll succumb to temptation.

Avoid this problem by thoroughly cleaning your pantry before you get started with Keto.

I understand that if you have a partner or family members around who aren't following the Keto diet, this can be a hard task. In this case, I suggest you grab a large box, place their high-carb foods inside and keep it out of sight!

If you're the one doing the family cooking, a lot of discipline is needed not to have a bite of those pasta dishes when you make them. Let the others do the taste checks when you cook.

Treat yourself!

Just because you're going Keto, doesn't mean you should start eating horrible stodgy foods. Don't follow such boring websites that show these; Keto can be fun-loving. This isn't about eating trash. It's about nourishing your body with exactly what it needs, and that includes your taste buds too.

You absolutely can continue eating like a foodie and enjoy those tender gnocchi in marinara sauce, or fragrant Nasi goreng, or fantastically spiced Indian Lamb Curry. That's exactly why I've written this book; there's a way to go about it.

Greens! Greens! Greens!

It's vital that you eat plenty of green leafy veggies while you're on Keto. They are one of the planet's best sources of minerals and add more fiber, antioxidants and even protein to your healthy diet. I love kale, spring greens, and spinach, but any will do.

Don't be afraid to include plenty of other low carb veggies too. Provided you keep your eye on your macros, they make a very nourishing, healthy addition to your diet that will keep your heart healthy, help prevent cancer and boost your digestive system too.

Get organized

The Organization is key to simplifying your Keto lifestyle, which helps you to stick to the diet. Plan your meals at the start of the week, organize a grocery list and go shopping ideally once to save you some time and energy.

It's also a good idea to cook extra portions of food at once while cooking. Most of the recipes in this book work excellently (and often taste better!) when made in advance. Use your fridge and freezer to store the leftovers, and you'll only have to reheat.

Drink plenty of water & Exercise

As well as eating the right foods, it's also important to stay hydrated. Get a refillable water bottle, fill it up and carry it with you. Aim for a minimum of 2 liters of water per day. Staying active with stressless exercises helps your body get into Ketosis and burns more fat while being excellent for your entire body, mind, and spirit.

Nevertheless, remember, it will take a couple of weeks for your body to adjust to the Keto lifestyle to start seeing the weight loss results you hope for, so don't go too hard on yourself. Slow and steady exercises do the trick.

Make sense of eating out

There's nothing worse than being 'that person' who can't eat a thing on the menu at a restaurant. So, do your homework!

Before you go anywhere, check out your local restaurants and find out if there's anything on the menu that will suit you. Check out the restaurants' online menus or pick up the phone and give them a call.

It is fantastic to find your perfect restaurant; once you do, visit them often for your comfort.

Got it? Awesome! There's just one last topic I'd like to cover before we move forward to the recipes, and that's weight loss. Yes, I know I've talked about it plenty of times already, but it does deserve some space. Because, dare I say it, changing your eating habits isn't enough by itself. You need to do some work on yourself too. Keep reading to learn my Keto weight loss tips.

OBESE TO FIT | MY WEIGHT LOSS TIPS WITH KETO

So, the Keto diet was what helped me to lose weight after a crazy number of times trying. Nothing else ever seemed to work. It didn't matter how determined I felt, or how religiously I stuck to the diet. Nothing worked.

Until Keto!

But, it would be a lie to say that it was Keto alone that helped me to shift the weight.

Because of course, I had a big part to play! It was hard, I needed to be smart, and I knew there'd be a long road ahead of me.

Here's how it happened.

I faced my issues

My weight problem wasn't just because I overate, ate the wrong foods or didn't get enough exercise. It was about what was going on in my head. I started to ask myself why I made the food choices I did, how my weight was benefiting me (really, it was), and how to move through those issues.

So, whatever is the motivation behind the weight gain, even if it's for beauty purposes, you will have to address that issue at mind and make a change because you can still look jaw-dropping gorgeous with weight loss.

I didn't quit

Even with the most amazing diet in the world, you will experience hard times. I bet you, hard times are signs that you are making progress.

You might struggle with food cravings, battle those early detox symptoms and feel desperate when you think of avoiding sugar long-term. I certainly fought along the way.

But I never gave up. I pushed through the difficulties, I held my head high and pushed on through for myself and for everyone that admires me…wink! Looking at myself right now, it paid off!

I retrained my eating habits

I always had a huge appetite. Even in my thinner days, I'd polish off at least twice the amount that everyone else did. When I felt hungry, I ate.

All the diets I'd ever tried before were hard because I was continually feeling either deprived or hungry. But with Keto, I felt satisfied for longer.

I planned my meals

The worst time to decide what to eat is right before your meals when you're feeling hungry. Do this, and you're very likely to make poor food choices and opt for those high-carb, high-sugar, instant 'hit' foods.

That's why, when I got started, I carefully planned my meals throughout the day, compiled my grocery list and made sure I had everything that I needed to be healthy at home and stuck to my Keto lifestyle.

I kept a food diary

It's far too easy to forget what you've eaten and end up overeating in the course of a day. Forgetting to keep track of your macros (your fat, protein, and carbs) and making poor food choices may become inherent in your habits. So, track your food intake and macros by writing them down to give you control over what goes through your lips.

After a while, you'll be disciplined with the routine and will not need to write your intakes down.

I stayed flexible

OK, so this might sound strange for me to say, considering that I'm writing this book. Nevertheless, the truth is, Keto isn't a strict prescription that you need to stick to 100%. We're all different and have varying lifestyles and needs. A specific maximum number of carbs might be best for one person but be crazily high for you. Listen to your own body and give it what it needs.

I failed. But I kept going

I'm only human. I failed.

One day, I went on a date (my first in years, might I add!) and found myself munching on the free bread they provided while the conversation flowed. Eek! I stopped as soon as I realized my fall, but I still felt painfully guilty.

Then, the ultimate question came, should I quit eating now and save the progress, I'd made so far or do I ignore my previous Keto efforts and keep on with my bread? Guess, which option I chose?

I focused on me

About the same time when I went Keto, one of my mother's friends took action to lose weight too. He chose the Keto diet and shifted weight quickly. It was amazing watching him shed those excess pounds and emerge leaner, healthier, more confident, and like a brand-new man.

How about me?

What was happening to my weight loss efforts – so slow? Was I doing something wrong? Should I give up before I make a fool of myself? NO! He had had a different body structure than mine hence the noticeable quick results.

A word of caution: in this age of Instagram, it's easy to forget that we aren't all supposed to be poster boys.

Being different is OK. Instead of thinking about other people and continually comparing my weight loss to theirs, I decided to be bold. I focused on myself instead.

Remember, weight loss isn't always linear. It can be, but more often than not, you might lose four pounds in one week and then gain another the next. Don't panic! It's all part of the journey.

The tips I've shared in this chapter should help you to keep pushing forward and making this shift to a brand new you.

Now that we've got all that out of the way let's talk about food. Sounds good? C'mon then!

TOP 10 KETO RECIPES

Raspberry Almond Pancake with Blackberry Sauce

Ready in about: 40 minutes | **Serves**: 6 | **Per serving**: Kcal 355, Fat 31.2g, Net Carbs 6.8g, Protein 8.8g

INGREDIENTS

Pancakes

2 cups almond flour
½ tsp salt
2 tsp swerve sugar
1 tsp baking soda

1 tsp baking powder
1 ½ cups almond milk
1 tsp almond extract
4 large eggs

¼ cup olive oil
1 tsp raspberry extract
Whole raspberries to garnish

Blackberry sauce

3 cups fresh blackberries
½ cup swerve sugar

½ cup + 1 tbsp water
½ tsp arrowroot starch

A pinch of salt
A squirt of lemon juice

DIRECTIONS

In a bowl, mix almond flour, salt, swerve, baking soda, and baking powder with a whisk; set aside.

In another bowl, whisk almond milk, almond extract, eggs, olive oil, and raspberry extract together. Then, pour the egg mixture into the almond flour mixture and continue whisking until smooth.

Put the mixture in the fridge to set for 5 minutes while you preheat the griddle pan over medium heat.

Once heated, remove the batter from the refrigerator and pour 1 soup spoonful of batter into the greased griddle pan. Cook on one side for 2 minutes, flip the pancake, and cook the other side for 2 minutes. Transfer the pancake to a plate and repeat the cooking process until the batter is exhausted.

Pour the blackberries and half cup of water into a saucepan. Bring the berries to a boil over medium heat. Lower the heat and simmer the berries for 10-12 minutes so that they are soft and exuding juice. Stir in the swerve sugar at this point and cook for 5 more minutes.

Next, stir in salt and lemon juice and while they cook, mix arrowroot starch with the remaining water. Pour the mixture into the berries. Stir and continue cooking the sauce to thicken to your desire. Turn off the heat and let it cool.

Finally, plate the pancakes one on another and generously drizzle the blackberry sauce over them, garnish with the whole raspberries, and serve for breakfast.

Chocolate & Yogurt Egg Muffins

Ready in about: 45 minutes | **Serves**: 6 | **Per serving**: Kcal 187, Fat 11.5g, Net Carbs 2.6g, Protein 3.6g

INGREDIENTS

2 cups almond flour
⅓ cup erythritol
¼ cup unsweetened cocoa powder

2 tsp baking powder
½ tsp salt
1 large egg

1 cup plain yogurt
¼ cup olive oil
¾ cup dark chocolate chips

DIRECTIONS

Preheat the oven to 350°F. In a bowl, whisk almond flour, erythritol, cocoa powder, baking powder, and salt together. In a separate bowl, whisk the egg, yogurt, and olive oil and pour the mixture gradually into the flour mixture while mixing with a spatula just until well incorporated. Try not to over-mix.

Fold in some chocolate chips and fill greased muffin cups with the batter - three-quarter (¾) way up. Top with the remaining chocolate chips, place on a baking tray, and bake for 20 to 25 minutes.

Once they are ready, turn the oven off and let the muffins sit in there to cool for 15 minutes. Remove onto a flat surface to cool completely. Sift a little erythritol over them and serve for breakfast.

Brie & Caramelized Onion Beef Burgers

Ready in about: 35 minutes | **Serves:** 4 | **Per serving:** Kcal 487, Fat 32g, Net Carbs 7.8g, Protein 38g

INGREDIENTS

1 medium white onion, sliced
1 tbsp olive oil

Burgers

1 lb ground beef
2 tbsp olive oil

2 tbsp balsamic vinegar
2 tsp erythritol

Salt and black pepper to taste
4 slices French brie cheese

A pinch of salt

4 low carb hamburger buns, halved
Mayonnaise to serve

DIRECTIONS

Heat the olive oil in a skillet over medium heat. Once it just starts to smoke, reduce the heat to low, and add the onion. Sauté for 15 minutes until golden brown.

Add in erythritol, balsamic vinegar, and salt. Cook for 3 more minutes, turn the heat off and set aside. Make 4 patties out of the ground beef and season with salt and pepper. Heat a skillet over high heat.

When it starts smoking, add the olive oil. Swirl the pan, coat it with the oil, and cook the patties for 4 minutes on each side. Place a brie slice on each patty and top with the caramelized onions. Put the patties with cheese and onions into 2 halves of the buns. Serve with mayonnaise as a snack or for lunch.

Zucchini Parmesan Chips with Greek Yogurt Dip

Ready in about: 50 minutes | **Serves:** 4 | **Per serving:** Kcal 253, Fat 19.4g, Net Carbs 3.8g, Protein 14.5g

INGREDIENTS

½ cup Greek yogurt
½ cup sour cream
1 ½ cups feta cheese, crumbled

¼ cup chopped mint
1 tbsp garlic, minced
2 zucchinis, thinly sliced

⅓ cup coconut flour
½ cup Parmesan cheese, grated
Salt and black pepper to taste

DIRECTIONS

To make the yogurt dip: In the food processor, add the Greek yogurt, sour cream, feta cheese, mint, and garlic. Blend the ingredients on medium speed for 2 minutes. Pour into a bowl and season with salt and pepper. Place the bowl in the refrigerator to chill while you make the chips.

Preheat the oven to 450°F. Mix the coconut flour, Parmesan cheese, salt, and black pepper in a bowl. Dip and press each zucchini slice in the flour mixture on both sides, coating generously. Place on a greased baking sheet and cook in the oven for 25 -30 minutes. Remove and serve with the Greek yogurt dip.

Peanut Butter Pecan Ice Cream

Ready in about: 36 minutes + chilling time | **Serves:** 4 | **Per serving:** Kcal 302, Fat 32g, Net Carbs 2g, Protein 5g

INGREDIENTS

½ cup swerve sweetener confectioners
2 cups heavy cream
1 tbsp erythritol

½ cup smooth peanut butter
1 tbsp olive oil

2 eggs yolks
½ cup pecans, chopped

DIRECTIONS

Warm heavy cream with peanut butter, olive oil, and erythritol in a small pan over low heat without boiling about 3 minutes. Remove from the heat. In a bowl, beat the egg yolks until creamy in color.

Stir the eggs into the cream mixture. Continue stirring until a thick batter has formed, about 3 minutes. Pour the cream mixture into a bowl. Refrigerate for 30 minutes. Stir in sweetener confectioners.

Pour the mixture into the ice cream machine and churn it according to the manufacturer's instructions. Stir in the pecans after and spoon the mixture into loaf pan. Freeze for 2 hours before serving.

Pesto Chicken Pizza

Ready in about: 35 minutes | **Serves**: 6 | **Per serving**: Kcal 497, Fat 32.8g, Net Carbs 3.4g, Protein 25.5g

INGREDIENTS

Pizza bread

3 cups almond flour

3 tbsp butter, melted

3 large eggs

Pesto chicken topping

2 chicken breasts

Salt and black pepper to taste

1 ½ tbsp olive oil

1 green bell pepper, sliced

1 ½ cups olive oil pesto

1 cup mozzarella cheese, grated

1 ½ tbsp Parmesan cheese, grated

2 tbsp pine nuts

A pinch of red pepper flakes

DIRECTIONS

Preheat the oven to 350°F. In a bowl, mix almond flour, butter, and eggs until a dough forms. Mold the dough into a ball and place it in between two full parchment papers on a flat surface. Use a rolling pin to roll it out into a circle of a ¼ -inch thickness. Slide the pizza dough into the pizza pan and remove the parchment paper. Place the pizza pan in the oven and bake for 20 minutes.

Bring a pot of water to simmer on a stovetop, season the chicken with salt and pepper, wrap it in plastic wraps and poach it in the simmering water for 15 minutes. Remove and unwrap the chicken, let rest, then chop it into bite-sized pieces. Once the pizza bread is ready, remove it from the oven.

Fold and seal the extra inch of dough at its edges to make a crust around it. Apply 2/3 of the pesto on it using a spoon and sprinkle half of the mozzarella cheese on it too. Toss the chopped chicken in the remaining pesto and spread it on top of the pizza.

Sprinkle with the remaining mozzarella, bell peppers, and pine nuts and put the pizza back in the oven to bake for 9 minutes. When it is ready, remove from the oven to cool slightly, sprinkle with Parmesan cheese and red pepper flakes. Slice and serve with green salad.

Spicy Ahi Tuna Keto Sushi

Ready in about: 15 minutes | **Serves**: 4 | **Per serving**: Kcal 120, Fat 1.5g, Net Carbs 1.8g, Protein 27g

INGREDIENTS

½ lb ahi tuna, sushi grade

1 ¼ cups cauli rice

1 ½ tsp sugar-free sriracha sauce

1 ½ tbsp mayonnaise

1 nori sheet

Salt to taste

DIRECTIONS

Slice the tuna with a knife into a long tube of a ¼ -inch thickness and set aside. Microwave the cauli rice for 1 minute, pour into a clean kitchen towel, and squeeze as much moisture from it.

Then pour into a bowl and stir in the sriracha and mayonnaise. Lay the nori sheet on a flat surface. Spoon the cauli rice on it ¾ way up, and flatten the cauli evenly with the back of the spoon.

Lay the tuna strip. Sprinkle with salt. Roll the nori sheet with the rice side up and over the tuna, making sure to tuck in as you move, quite firmly too. Once you've reached the empty part of the nori sheet, wet your fingers with water and run along the layer to make it moist. Seal the roll. Cut the sushi into rolls.

Chicken Meatballs with Squash Pasta

Ready in about: 65 minutes | **Serves**: 6 | **Per serving**: Kcal 470, Fat 28g, Net Carbs 2g, Protein 14g

INGREDIENTS

1 cup + 2 tbsp grated Parmesan cheese

1 (2 lb) butternut squash

2 lb ground chicken

Salt and black pepper to taste

1 cup pork rinds, crushed

4 cloves garlic, minced

1 onion, chopped

1 stalk celery, chopped

3 tbsp fresh parsley, chopped

3 tbsp olive oil + extra for brushing

2 eggs, cracked into a small bowl

Grated Parmesan cheese for garnishing

2 cups sugar-free tomato sauce

10 leaves basil, chopped

1 tsp dried oregano

DIRECTIONS

Preheat the oven to 450°F. Cut the squash in half and scoop the seeds out with a spoon. Sprinkle with salt and brush with olive oil. Place in a baking dish and cover with foil. Roast for 20 minutes, then remove the aluminum foil and continue cooking for 35 minutes.

When ready, scrape the pulp into strands. Remove the spaghetti strands to a bowl and toss with 2 tbsp of Parmesan cheese. Season with salt and plate. Add garlic, onion, celery, and parsley to your food processor and blend into a smooth paste for about 2 minutes.

Put the ground chicken in a bowl. Pour in half of the celery puree, pork rinds, eggs, and a cup of Parmesan cheese and mix well. Mold out meatballs from the mixture and place them on a baking sheet. Bake the meatballs for just 10 minutes, but not done.

Place a pot over medium heat and warm 3 tbsp of olive oil. Stir-fry the remaining vegetable paste for 5 minutes. Stir in the tomato sauce, oregano, basil, and salt to taste. Let the sauce cook on low-medium heat for 5 minutes, remove, and add in the meatballs. Continue cooking for 15 minutes. Spoon the meatballs with sauce over the spaghetti, sprinkle with extra Parmesan cheese and serve.

Mocha Mug Cake

Ready in about: 10 minutes | **Serves**: 2 | **Per serving**: Kcal 375, Fat 38g, Net Carbs 2.7g, Protein 12g

INGREDIENTS

6 tbsp almond flour
8 tbsp swerve sugar
4 tbsp unsweetened cocoa powder

4 tsp espresso powder
2 eggs
6 tbsp coconut milk

4 tbsp olive oil
½ tsp baking powder
Whipped cream for topping

DIRECTIONS

Mix almond flour, swerve, cocoa powder, espresso powder, eggs, coconut milk, olive oil, and baking powder in a bowl. Pour the mix into two mugs ¾ way up and cook in a microwave for 70 seconds. Remove and swirl a generous amount of whipping cream on the cakes. *To make more cups, repeat the process.*

Spinach Frittata with Chorizo & Tomato Salad

Ready in about: 60 minutes | **Serves**: 4 | **Per serving**: Kcal 366, Fat 31.5g, Net Carbs 5.2g, Protein 13g

INGREDIENTS

For the frittata

8 eggs
2 tbsp almond milk
Salt and black pepper to taste

10 oz sliced white mushrooms
1 garlic clove, minced
2 tbsp olive oil

6 oz baby spinach, rinsed
¼ cup cheddar cheese, grated

For the salad

4 plum tomatoes, cut into wedges
1 small red onion, thinly sliced

4 oz chorizo, thinly sliced
1 tbsp plain vinegar

2 sprigs thyme, leaves picked
2 tbsp olive oil

DIRECTIONS

Preheat an oven to 350°F and grease a baking dish with cooking spray; set aside.

Heat 1 tbsp of olive oil in a skillet over medium heat and stir-fry the mushrooms to sweat for about 4 minutes. Add garlic, salt, and pepper. Sauté for 30 seconds to make the garlic fragrant. Stir in spinach and cook until wilted, about 5 minutes. Increase the heat and let the excess liquid evaporate.

Beat the eggs in a large bowl and stir in almond milk, salt, pepper, the mushroom/spinach mixture, and cheddar cheese. Pour the mixture into the baking dish and bake in the oven for 25 minutes.

In a salad bowl, add the tomatoes, onion, and thyme. Drizzle the vinegar and a little oil over them, and toss the ingredients with a spoon. Set aside until ready to use.

Heat a skillet over medium heat and fry the chorizo until browned, about 6 minutes. Add the chorizo to the salad, and drizzle a little oil from the pan atop. Slice the frittata into wedges. Serve with the salad.

SMOOTHIES & BREAKFASTS

Morning Berry-Green Smoothie

Ready in about: 5 minutes | **Serves**: 4 | **Per serving**: Kcal 360, Fat 33.3g, Net Carbs 6g, Protein 6g

INGREDIENTS

3 cups mixed blueberries and strawberries

1 avocado, pitted and sliced

2 cups unsweetened almond milk

6 tbsp heavy cream

2 tbsp erythritol

1 cup ice cubes

⅓ cup nuts and seeds mix

DIRECTIONS

Combine the avocado slices, blueberries, strawberries, almond milk, heavy cream, erythritol, ice cubes, nuts, and seeds in a smoothie maker. Blend at high speed until smooth and uniform. Pour the smoothie into drinking glasses and serve immediately.

Breakfast Nut Granola & Smoothie Bowl

Ready in about: 5 minutes | **Serves**: 4 | **Per serving**: Kcal 361, Fat 31.2g, Net Carbs 2g, Protein 13g

INGREDIENTS

6 cups Greek yogurt

4 tbsp almond butter

A handful toasted walnuts

3 tbsp unsweetened cocoa powder

4 tsp swerve brown sugar

2 cups nut granola for topping

DIRECTIONS

Combine the Greek yogurt, almond butter, walnuts, cocoa powder, and swerve brown sugar in a smoothie maker. Puree at high speed until smooth and well mixed. Share the smoothie into four breakfast bowls, top with a half cup of granola each one, and serve.

Morning Almond Shake

Ready in about: 5 minutes | **Serves**: 2 | **Per serving**: Kcal 326, Fat: 27g, Net Carbs: 6g, Protein: 19g

INGREDIENTS

1 ½ cups almond milk

2 tbsp almond butter

½ tsp almond extract

½ tsp cinnamon

2 tbsp flax meal

1 tbsp collagen peptides

A pinch of salt

15 drops of stevia

A handful of ice cubes

DIRECTIONS

Add almond milk, almond butter, flax meal, almond extract, collagen peptides, a pinch of salt, and stevia to a blender bowl. Blitz until uniform and smooth, about 30 seconds.

Then taste and adjust flavor as needed, adding more stevia for sweetness or almond butter to the creaminess. Pour in a smoothie glass, add the ice cubes and sprinkle with cinnamon.

Chocolate Protein Coconut Shake

Ready in about: 5 minutes | **Serves**: 4 | **Per serving**: Kcal 265, Fat: 15.5g, Net Carbs: 4g, Protein: 12g

INGREDIENTS

3 cups flax milk, chilled

3 tsp unsweetened cocoa powder

1 medium avocado, peeled, sliced

1 cup coconut milk, chilled

3 mint leaves + extra to garnish

3 tbsp erythritol

1 tbsp low carb protein powder

Whipping cream for topping

DIRECTIONS

Combine the flax milk, cocoa powder, avocado, coconut milk, 3 mint leaves, erythritol, and protein powder into the smoothie maker, and blend for 1 minute to smooth. Pour the drink into serving glasses, lightly add some whipping cream on top, and garnish with 1 or 2 mint leaves. Serve immediately.

Five Greens Smoothie

Ready in about: 5 minutes | **Serves**: 4 | **Per serving**: Kcal 124, Fat 7.8g, Net Carbs 2.9g, Protein 3.2g

INGREDIENTS

6 kale leaves, chopped
3 stalks celery, chopped

1 ripe avocado, skinned and sliced
2 cups spinach, chopped

1 cucumber, peeled and chopped
Chia seeds to garnish

DIRECTIONS

In a blender, add the kale, celery, avocado, and ice cubes, and blend for 45 seconds. Add the spinach and cucumber, and process for another 45 seconds until smooth. Pour the smoothie into glasses, garnish with chia seeds, and serve the drink immediately.

Dark Chocolate Smoothie

Ready in about: 10 minutes | **Serves**: 2 | **Per serving**: Kcal 335; Fat: 31.7g Net Carbs: 12.7g, Protein: 7g

INGREDIENTS

½ cup pecans
¾ cup coconut milk
¼ cup water

4 oz watercress
1 tsp low carb protein powder
1 tbsp chia seeds

1 tbsp unsweetened cocoa powder
4 fresh dates, pitted

DIRECTIONS

In a blender, add all ingredients and process until creamy and uniform. Chill and serve in glasses.

Bacon & Egg Quesadillas

Ready in about: 30 minutes | **Serves**: 4 | **Per serving**: Kcal 449, Fat 48.7g, Net Carbs 6.8g, Protein 29.1g

INGREDIENTS

8 low carb tortilla shells
6 eggs
1 cup water

3 tbsp butter
1 ½ cups grated cheddar cheese
1 ½ cups grated Swiss cheese

5 bacon slices
1 medium onion, thinly sliced
1 tbsp parsley, chopped

DIRECTIONS

Bring the eggs to a boil in water over medium heat for 10 minutes. Transfer the eggs to an ice water bath, peel the shells, and chop them. Fry the bacon in a skillet over medium heat for 4 minutes until crispy. Remove and chop. Sauté the onion in the remaining grease 2 minutes; set aside.

Melt 1 tablespoon of butter in another skillet over medium heat. Lay one tortilla in a skillet and sprinkle with some Swiss cheese. Add some chopped eggs and bacon over the cheese, top with onion, and sprinkle with some cheddar cheese. Cover with another tortilla shell. Cook for 45 seconds

Carefully flip the quesadilla, and cook the other side too for 45 seconds. Remove to a plate and repeat the cooking process using the remaining tortilla shells. Garnish with parsley and serve warm.

Spicy Egg Muffins with Bacon & Cheese

Ready in about: 30 minutes | **Serves**: 6 | **Per serving**: Kcal 302, Fat 23.7g, Net Carbs 3.2g, Protein 20g

INGREDIENTS

12 eggs
¼ cup coconut milk

Salt and black pepper to taste
1 cup cheddar cheese, grated

12 slices bacon
4 jalapeño peppers, minced

DIRECTIONS

Preheat oven to 370°F. Crack the eggs into a bowl and whisk with coconut milk until combined. Season with salt and pepper, and stir in the cheddar cheese. Line each hole of a muffin tin with a bacon slice.

Fill each one with the egg mixture two-thirds way up. Top with the jalapeno peppers and bake for 20 minutes until puffed and golden. Remove, allow cooling for a few minutes, and serve with arugula salad.

Avocado & Kale Eggs

Ready in about: 20 minutes | **Serves:** 4 | **Per serving:** Kcal 274, Fat 23g, Net Carbs 4g, Protein 13g

INGREDIENTS

2 tbsp ghee
1 red onion, sliced

4 oz chorizo, cut into thin rounds
1 cup kale, chopped

1 ripe avocado, peeled and chopped
4 eggs

DIRECTIONS

Preheat oven to 370°F. Melt ghee in a cast iron pan over medium heat and sauté the onion for 2 minutes. Add the chorizo and cook for 2 minutes more, stirring occasionally. Introduce the kale with a splash of water, stir, and cook for 3 minutes until it is wilted. Mix in the avocado and turn the heat off.

Create four holes in the mixture, crack the eggs into each hole, and slide the pan into the preheated oven. Bake for 6 minutes until the egg whites are set or firm and yolks still runny. Serve right away.

Almond Waffles with Cinnamon Cream

Ready in about: 25 minutes | **Serves:** 6 | **Per serving:** Kcal 307, Fat 24g, Net Carbs 8g, Protein 12g

INGREDIENTS

Cinnamon cream

8 oz cream cheese, softened
1 tsp cinnamon powder

3 tbsp swerve brown sugar
2 tbsp cinnamon

Waffles

5 tbsp butter, melted
1 ½ cups unsweetened almond milk

7 large eggs
¼ tsp liquid stevia

½ tsp baking powder
1 ½ cups almond flour

DIRECTIONS

Combine cream cheese, cinnamon, and swerve with a mixer until smooth. Cover and chill until ready to use.

To make the waffles, whisk the butter, milk, and eggs in a medium bowl. Add the stevia and baking powder and mix. Stir in the almond flour and combine until no lumps exist. Let the batter sit for 5 minutes to thicken. Spritz a waffle iron with a cooking spray.

Ladle a ¼ cup of the batter into the waffle iron and cook according to the manufacturer's instructions until golden, about 10 minutes in total. Repeat with the remaining batter. Slice the waffles into quarters. Apply the cinnamon spread in between each of two waffles and snap. Serve.

Bacon & Cheese Pesto Mug Cakes

Ready in about: 8 minutes | **Serves:** 2 | **Per serving:** Kcal 511, Fat: 38.2g, Net Carbs: 4.5g, Protein: 16.4g

INGREDIENTS

Muffin ingredients

¼ cup flax meal
1 egg

2 tbsp heavy cream
2 tbsp pesto

¼ cup almond flour
Salt and black pepper to taste

Filling

2 tbsp cream cheese

4 slices bacon

½ medium avocado, sliced

DIRECTIONS

Mix together the dry muffin ingredients in a bowl. Add egg, heavy cream, and pesto, and whisk well with a fork. Season with salt and pepper. Divide the mixture between two ramekins. Place in the microwave and cook for 60-90 seconds. Leave to cool slightly before filling.

Meanwhile, in a skillet, over medium heat, cook the bacon slices until crispy. Transfer to paper towels to soak up excess fat; set aside. Invert the muffins onto a plate and cut in half, crosswise. To assemble the sandwiches: spread cream cheese and top with bacon and avocado slices.

Ricotta Cloud Pancakes with Whipped Cream

Ready in about: 20 minutes | Serves: 4 | Per serving: Kcal 407, Fat 30.6g, Net Carbs 6.6g, Protein 11.5g

INGREDIENTS

1 cup almond flour
1 tsp baking powder
2 ½ tbsp erythritol

⅓ tsp salt
1 ¼ cups ricotta cheese
⅓ cup coconut milk

2 large eggs
1 cup heavy whipping cream

DIRECTIONS

In a bowl, whisk the almond flour, baking powder, erythritol, and salt. Crack the eggs into the blender and process for 30 seconds. Add the ricotta cheese, continue processing it, and gradually pour the coconut milk in while you keep on blending. In about 90 seconds, the mixture will be creamy and smooth.

Pour it into the dry ingredients and whisk to combine. Set a skillet over medium heat and let it heat for a minute. Then, fetch a soup spoonful of mixture into the skillet and cook it for 1 minute.

Flip the pancake and cook further for 1 minute. Remove onto a plate and repeat the cooking process until the batter is exhausted. Serve the pancakes with whipping cream.

Kale Frittata with Crispy Pancetta Salad

Ready in about: 25 minutes | Serves: 4 | Per serving: Kcal 453, Fat 30.3g, Net Carbs 4.6g, Protein 26.4g

INGREDIENTS

6 pancetta slices
4 tomatoes, cut into 1-inch chunks
1 large cucumber, seeded and sliced
1 small red onion, sliced

¼ cup balsamic vinegar
8 eggs
1 bunch kale, chopped
Salt and black pepper to taste

6 tbsp grated Parmesan cheese
4 tbsp olive oil
1 large white onion, sliced
1 clove garlic, minced

DIRECTIONS

Place the pancetta in a skillet. Fry over medium heat until crispy, about 4 minutes. Remove and chop it. In a bowl, whisk vinegar, 2 tbsp oil, salt, and pepper to make a dressing. Combine tomatoes, red onion, and cucumber in a salad bowl. Drizzle with the dressing and toss to coat. Top with the pancetta.

Reheat oven to 400°F. Crack the eggs into a bowl and whisk together with half of the Parmesan, salt, and pepper. Set aside. Heat the remaining olive oil in the skillet over medium heat. Sauté the onion and garlic for 3 minutes. Add in the kale, season with salt and pepper, and cook for 2 minutes.

Pour the egg mixture all over, cover, and cook for 4 minutes. Sprinkle the remaining cheese on top and transfer to the oven. Bake for 5 minutes until brown on top. Remove the frittata and slide it onto a warm platter. Cut the frittata into wedges and serve with the pancetta salad.

Giant Egg Quiche

Ready in about: 60 minutes | Serves: 6 | Per serving: Kcal 485, Fat 39.7g, Net Carbs 6.3g, Protein 24.5g

INGREDIENTS

12 eggs, beaten
1 ½ cups cheddar cheese, shredded
1 ½ cups almond milk

½ tsp dried thyme
Salt to taste
¼ cup mushrooms, sliced

½ cup broccoli, chopped
1 clove garlic, minced

Quiche crust

¾ cup almond flour
A pinch of salt

2 oz cold butter
½ tsp baking powder

1 tbsp cold water
2 eggs

DIRECTIONS

Preheat oven to 370°F. In a bowl, mix all the crust ingredients until dough is formed. Press it into a greased baking dish and bake for 20-25 minutes until lightly golden. Spread the cheddar cheese on the crust.

Mix the eggs, almond milk, thyme, salt, mushrooms, broccoli, and garlic in a bowl. Pour the ingredients over the pie crust and bake in the oven for 35 minutes until the quiche is set. Remove and serve sliced.

Zesty Ginger Pancakes with Lemon Sauce

Ready in about: 15 minutes | **Serves**: 4 | **Per serving**: Kcal 324, Fat 24.2g, Net Carbs 5.8g, Protein 7.3g

INGREDIENTS

2 cups almond flour
1 tsp baking powder
1 ½ tsp cinnamon
⅓ cup swerve brown sugar

¼ tsp baking soda
1 tsp ginger powder
⅓ tsp salt
4 eggs

1 ¼ cups almond milk
½ cup lemon juice
½ tsp lemon zest
3 ½ tbsp olive oil

Lemon sauce

½ cup swerve sugar
1 tsp arrowroot starch

1 ¼ cups hot water
2 tbsp lemon juice

2 ½ tbsp butter
1 tbsp lemon zest

DIRECTIONS

In a bowl, mix the almond flour, baking powder, cinnamon, swerve brown sugar, baking soda, ginger powder, salt, eggs, almond milk, lemon juice, lemon zest, and olive oil and stir well. Let sit for 10 minutes.

Heat oil in a skillet over medium heat and spoon 4-5 tablespoons of the mixture into the skillet. Cook the batter for 2 minutes, flip, and cook the other side for another 2 minutes. Remove the pancake onto a plate after and repeat the cooking process until the batter is exhausted.

Mix the swerve sugar and arrowroot starch in a saucepan over medium heat. Gradually stir in the water until it thickens, about 1 minute. Turn the heat off and add the butter, lemon juice, and lemon zest. Stir the mixture until the butter melts. After, drizzle the sauce on the pancakes and serve warm.

Chocolate Crepes with Caramel Cream

Ready in about: 35 minutes | **Serves**: 4 | **Per serving**: Kcal 330, Fat 21g, Net Carbs 5.1g, Protein 11g

INGREDIENTS

1 cup coconut flour
4 tbsp unsweetened cocoa powder

4 egg whites
1 cup + 4 tbsp flax milk

2 tbsp erythritol
2 tbsp olive oil

Caramel cream

½ cup salted butter
4 tbsp swerve brown sugar

1 tsp vanilla extract
1 cup heavy cream

DIRECTIONS

In a bowl, mix coconut flour and cocoa powder. In another bowl, whisk the egg whites, 1 cup flax milk, erythritol, and olive oil. Mix the wet ingredients with the dry ones until smooth.

Set a skillet over medium heat, grease with cooking spray, and pour in a ladleful of the batter. Swirl the pan quickly to spread the dough all around the skillet and cook the crepe for 2-3 minutes.

When it is firm enough to touch and cooked through, slide the crepe into a flat plate. Wipe the pan with a napkin and continue cooking until the remaining batter has finished. Put the butter and brown sugar in a pot and melt the butter over medium heat while stirring continually.

Keep cooking for 4 minutes after the butter has melted; be careful not to burn. Stir in the cream, reduce the heat to low, and let the sauce simmer for 10 minutes while stirring continually. Turn the heat off and stir in the vanilla extract. Once the crepes are ready, drizzle the caramel sauce over them, and serve.

Carrot Zucchini Bread

Ready in about: 70 minutes | **Serves**: 4 | **Per serving**: Kcal 175, Fat 10.5g, Net Carbs 1.8g, Protein 11.6g

INGREDIENTS

1 cup shredded carrots
1 cup shredded zucchini, squeezed
⅓ cup coconut flour
1 tsp vanilla extract

6 eggs
1 tbsp coconut oil
¾ tsp baking soda
1 tbsp cinnamon powder

½ tsp salt
½ cup Greek yogurt
1 tsp apple cider vinegar
½ tsp nutmeg powder

DIRECTIONS

Preheat the oven to 350°F. Mix the carrots, zucchini, coconut flour, vanilla extract, eggs, coconut oil, baking soda, cinnamon, salt, Greek yogurt, vinegar, and nutmeg. Pour the batter into a greased loaf pan.

Bake for 55 minutes. Remove the bread after and let cool for 5 minutes. Preserve the bread and use it for toasts, sandwiches, or served with soups and salads.

Smoked Ham & Egg Muffins

Ready in about: 40 minutes | **Serves:** 6 | **Per serving:** Kcal 367, Fat: 28g, Net Carbs: 1g, Protein: 13.5g

INGREDIENTS

1 cup smoked ham, chopped
⅓ cup grated Parmesan cheese
¼ cup almond flour

6 eggs
⅓ cup mayonnaise, sugar-free
¼ tsp garlic powder

¼ cup chopped onions
Sea salt to taste

DIRECTIONS

Preheat oven to 370°F. Lightly grease a muffin tin with cooking spray and set aside. Place the onions, ham, garlic powder, and salt in a food processor and pulse until ground. Transfer to a bowl and stir in the mayonnaise, almond flour, and Parmesan cheese. Divide the mixture between the muffin cups.

Make sure it goes all the way up the muffin sides to be room for the egg. Bake for 5 minutes. Crack an egg into each muffin cup. Return to the oven and bake for 20 more minutes or until the tops are firm to the touch, and eggs are cooked. Leave to cool slightly before serving.

Smoked Salmon Rolls with Dill Cream Cheese

Ready in about: 10 minutes + time refrigeration | **Serves:** 4 | **Per serving:** Kcal 250, Fat 16g, Net Carbs 7g, Protein 18g

INGREDIENTS

4 tbsp cream cheese, softened
1 small lemon, zested and juiced

2 tsp chopped fresh dill
Salt and black pepper to taste

3 (7-inch) low carb tortillas
6 smoked salmon slices

DIRECTIONS

In a bowl, mix the cream cheese, lemon juice, zest, dill, salt, and black pepper. Lay each tortilla on a plastic wrap (just wide enough to cover the tortilla), spread with cream cheese mixture.

Top each one with two salmon slices. Roll up the tortillas and secure both ends by twisting. Refrigerate for 2 hours. Remove plastic, cut off both ends of each wrap, and cut the wraps into wheels. Serve.

Mushroom & Cheese Lettuce Wraps

Ready in about: 20 minutes | **Serves:** 4 | **Per serving:** Kcal 472; Fat: 44g, Net Carbs: 5.4g, Protein: 19.5g

INGREDIENTS

Wraps

6 eggs
2 tbsp almond milk

1 tbsp olive oil
Sea salt to taste

Filling

2 tbsp olive oil
1 cup mushrooms, sliced

½ tsp cayenne pepper
8 fresh lettuce leaves

4 gruyere cheese slices
2 tomatoes, sliced

DIRECTIONS

Mix all the ingredients for the wraps thoroughly. Set a frying pan over medium heat. Add in ¼ of the mixture and cook for 4 minutes on both sides. Do the same with the remaining mixture. Set aside.

In the same pan, warm the remaining olive oil over medium heat. Cook the mushrooms for 5 minutes until they are browned and softened. Stir in cayenne pepper, black pepper, and salt. Set 2 lettuce leaves onto every egg wrap and top with the mushrooms. Arrange the tomato and cheese slices on top to serve.

Italian Sausage Stacks

Ready in about: 20 minutes | **Serves**: 6 | **Per serving**: Kcal 378, Fat 23g, Net Carbs 5g, Protein 16g

INGREDIENTS

6 Italian sausage patties
4 tbsp olive oil

2 ripe avocados, pitted
Salt and black pepper to taste

6 fresh eggs
Red pepper flakes to garnish

DIRECTIONS

In a skillet, warm the oil over medium heat and fry the sausage patties about 8 minutes until lightly browned and firm. Remove the patties to a plate. Spoon the avocado into a bowl and mash it with a fork. Season with salt and black pepper. Spread the mash on the sausages.

Boil 3 cups of water in a wide pan over high heat and reduce to simmer (don't boil). Crack each egg into a small bowl and gently put the egg into the simmering water. Poach for 2-3 minutes. Use a perforated spoon to remove from the water on a paper towel to dry. Repeat with the other 5 eggs. Top each stack with a poached egg and sprinkle with chili flakes. Serve with turnip wedges.

Coconut Flour Bagels

Ready in about: 25 minutes | **Serves**: 6 | **Per serving**: Kcal 426, Fat 19.1g, Net Carbs 0.4g, Protein 33.1g

INGREDIENTS

½ cup coconut flour
6 eggs, beaten in a bowl
½ cup vegetable broth

¼ cup flaxseed meal
1 tsp onion powder
1 tsp dried parsley

1 tsp chia seeds
1 tsp sesame seeds
1 onion, chopped

DIRECTIONS

Preheat oven to 350°F. Mix the coconut flour, eggs, vegetable broth, flaxseed meal, onion powder, and parsley in a bowl and stir well. Spoon the mixture into a donut tray. Top with onion and sprinkle with chia and sesame seeds. Bake the bagels for 20 minutes. Remove and let cool before serving.

Cheesy Zucchini Balls with Bacon

Ready in about: 20 minutes + chilling time | **Serves**: 6 | **Per serving**: Kcal 407; Fat: 26.8g, Net Carbs: 5.8g, Protein: 33.4g

INGREDIENTS

2 lb zucchinis, chopped
½ lb bacon, chopped
6 oz cottage cheese, crumbled
6 oz cream cheese, softened

1 cup fontina cheese, grated
½ cup dill pickles, chopped
2 cloves garlic, crushed
1 cup Parmesan cheese, grated

½ tsp caraway seeds
¼ cup olive oil
Salt and black pepper to taste
1 cup pork rinds, crushed

DIRECTIONS

In a bowl, mix zucchini, cottage cheese, dill pickles, ½ cup of Parmesan cheese, garlic, cream cheese, bacon, and fontina cheese until well combined. Shape the mixture into balls. Refrigerate for 3 hours. In another bowl, mix the remaining Parmesan cheese, pork rinds, black pepper, caraway seeds, and salt.

Remove the balls from the fridge and roll them in the Parmesan mixture. Warm the olive oil in a skillet over medium heat. Fry the balls until browned on all sides. Set on a paper towel to soak up any excess oil.

Eggs & Crabmeat with Creme Fraiche Salsa

Ready in about: 15 minutes | **Serves**: 3 | **Per serving**: Kcal 334; Fat: 26.2g, Net Carbs: 4.4g, Protein: 21.1g

INGREDIENTS

1 tbsp olive oil
Salsa

6 eggs, whisked

1 (6 oz) can crabmeat, flaked

¾ cup crème fraiche
½ cup scallions, chopped

½ tsp garlic powder
Salt and black pepper to taste

½ tsp fresh dill, chopped

DIRECTIONS

Warm the olive oil a pan over medium heat. Add in the eggs and scramble them. Stir in crabmeat and season with salt and pepper. Cook until cooked thoroughly. In a dish, combine all salsa ingredients. Split the egg/crabmeat mixture among serving plates. Serve alongside the scallions and salsa to the side.

Cheese & Aioli Eggs

Ready in about: 20 minutes | **Serves**: 4 | **Per serving**: Kcal: 355; Fat 22.5g, Net Carbs 1.8g, Protein 29.5g

INGREDIENTS

4 eggs, hard-boiled and chopped
14 oz tuna in brine, drained

¼ lettuce head, torn into pieces
2 green onions, finely chopped

½ cup feta cheese, crumbled
⅓ cup sour cream

Aioli

1 cup mayonnaise
2 cloves garlic, minced

1 tbsp lemon juice
Salt and black pepper to taste

DIRECTIONS

Set the eggs in a serving bowl. Place in tuna, onion, feta cheese, lettuce, and sour cream. In a bowl, mix the mayonnaise, lemon juice, and garlic. Season with salt and pepper. Pour the aioli in the serving bowl and stir to incorporate everything. Serve with pickles.

Kielbasa & Roquefort Waffles

Ready in about: 20 minutes | **Serves**: 2 | **Per serving**: Kcal 470; Fat: 40.3g, Net Carbs: 2.9g, Protein: 24.4g

INGREDIENTS

½ tsp parsley, chopped
½ tsp chili pepper flakes

4 eggs
½ cup Roquefort cheese, crumbled

4 slices kielbasa, chopped
2 tbsp fresh chives, chopped

DIRECTIONS

In a bowl, combine all ingredients except chives. Preheat the waffle iron. Pour in some batter and close the lid. Cook for 5 minutes until golden brown. Repeat with the rest of the batter. Decorate with chives.

Chorizo & Mozzarella Omelet

Ready in about: 15 minutes | **Serves**: 2 | **Per serving**: Kcal 451, Fat: 36.5g, Net Carbs: 3g, Protein: 30g

INGREDIENTS

4 eggs
2 oz mozzarella cheese, sliced

1 tbsp butter
4 thin chorizo slices

1 tomato, sliced
Salt and black pepper to taste

DIRECTIONS

Whisk the eggs with salt and pepper in a bowl. Melt the butter in a skillet over medium heat. Pour the eggs and cook for 1 minute. Top with the chorizo. Arrange the tomato and mozzarella over the chorizo.

Cover the skillet and cook for about 3-5 minutes until the omelet is set. Remove the pan from the heat. Run a spatula around the omelet's edges and flip it onto a plate, folded side down. Serve with salad.

Baked Quail Eggs in Avocados

Ready in about: 15 minutes | **Serves**: 4 | **Per serving**: Kcal 234, Fat 19.1g, Net Carbs 2.2g, Protein 8.2g

INGREDIENTS

2 large avocados, halved and pitted   4 small eggs

Salt and black pepper to taste

DIRECTIONS

Preheat oven to 400°F. Crack the quail eggs into the avocado halves and place them on a greased baking sheet. Bake the filled avocados in the oven for 8-10 minutes until eggs are cooked. Season and serve.

Fontina Cheese & Chorizo Waffles

Ready in about: 30 minutes | **Serves**: 6 | **Per serving**: Kcal 316; Fat: 25g, Net Carbs: 1.5g, Protein: 20.2g

INGREDIENTS

6 eggs
2 tbsp butter, melted

1 cup almond flour
Salt and black pepper to taste

3 chorizo sausages, cooked, chopped
1 cup fontina cheese, shredded

DIRECTIONS

In a shallow bowl, beat the eggs with salt and pepper. Add in the almond milk, butter, fontina cheese, and sausages and stir to combine. Let it sit for 15-20 minutes. Preheat the waffle iron and grease it with cooking spray. Pour in the egg mixture and cook for 5 minutes until golden brown. Serve hot.

Turkey Sausage Egg Cups

Ready in about: 15 minutes | **Serves**: 4 | **Per serving**: Kcal 423; Fat: 34.1g, Net Carbs: 2.2g, Protein: 26.5g

INGREDIENTS

2 tsp butter
8 eggs, beaten

Salt and black pepper to taste
½ tsp dried rosemary

1 cup pecorino romano, grated
4 turkey sausages, chopped

DIRECTIONS

Preheat oven to 400°F. Melt butter in a skillet over medium heat. Cook the turkey sausages for 4-5 minutes. In a bowl, mix 4 eggs, sausages, cheese, and seasonings. Divide between greased muffin cups and bake for 4 minutes. Crack an egg into the middle of each cup. Bake for 4 more minutes. Serve cooled.

Cheese Stuffed Avocados

Ready in about: 20 minutes | **Serves**: 4 | **Per serving**: Kcal 342; Fat: 30.4g, Net Carbs: 7.5g, Protein: 11.1g

INGREDIENTS

3 avocados, halved, pitted, skin on
½ cup feta cheese, crumbled

½ cup cheddar cheese, grated
2 eggs, beaten

Salt and black pepper to taste
1 tbsp fresh basil, chopped

DIRECTIONS

Preheat oven to 360°F. Lay avocado halves in a baking dish. In a bowl, mix both types of cheeses, pepper, eggs, and salt. Split the mixture into the avocado halves. Bake for 15 minutes. Top with basil and serve.

Duo-Cheese Omelet with Pimenta & Basil

Ready in about: 15 minutes | **Serves**: 2 | **Per serving**: Kcal 490; Fat: 44.6g, Net Carbs: 4.5g, Protein: 22.7g

INGREDIENTS

1 tbsp olive oil
4 eggs, beaten
Salt and black pepper to taste

¼ tsp paprika
¼ tsp cayenne pepper
½ cup asiago cheese, shredded

½ cup cheddar cheese, shredded
2 tbsp fresh basil, roughly chopped

DIRECTIONS

Warm the olive oil in a pan over medium. Season the eggs with cayenne pepper, salt, paprika, and pepper. Transfer to the pan and ensure they are evenly spread. Cook for 5 minutes. Top with the asiago and cheddar cheeses. Slice the omelet into two halves. Decorate with fresh basil and serve.

Quick Blue Cheese Omelet

Ready in about: 15 minutes | **Serves**: 2 | **Per serving**: Kcal 307; Fat: 25g, Net Carbs: 2.5g, Protein: 18.5g

INGREDIENTS

4 eggs
Salt to taste

1 tbsp sesame oil
½ cup blue cheese, crumbled

1 tomato, thinly sliced

DIRECTIONS

In a bowl, beat the eggs with salt. Warm the oil in a pan over medium heat. Add in the eggs and cook as you swirl the eggs around the pan. Cook eggs until set. Top with cheese. Decorate with tomato and serve.

Coconut & Walnut Chia Pudding

Ready in about: 10 minutes | **Serves:** 1 | **Per serving:** Kcal 334, Fat: 29g, Net Carbs: 1.5g Protein: 15g

INGREDIENTS

½ tsp vanilla extract
½ cup water
1 tbsp chia seeds

2 tbsp hemp seeds
1 tbsp flaxseed meal
2 tbsp almond meal

2 tbsp shredded coconut
¼ tsp granulated stevia
1 tbsp walnuts, chopped

DIRECTIONS

Put chia seeds, hemp seeds, flaxseed meal, almond meal, stevia, and coconut in a saucepan and pour over the water. Simmer over medium heat, occasionally stirring until creamed and thickened, about 3-4 minutes. Stir in vanilla. When it is ready, spoon into a serving bowl, sprinkle with walnuts, and serve.

Cheese Ciabatta with Pepperoni

Ready in about: 30 minutes | **Serves:** 6 | **Per serving:** Kcal 464, Fat: 33.6g, Net Carbs: 9.1g, Protein: 31.1g

INGREDIENTS

10 oz cream cheese, melted
2 ½ cups mozzarella, shredded
4 large eggs, beaten

3 tbsp Romano cheese, grated
½ cup pork rinds, crushed
2 tsp baking powder

½ cup tomato puree
12 pepperoni slices

DIRECTIONS

In a bowl, combine eggs, mozzarella cheese, cream cheese, baking powder, pork rinds, and Romano cheese. Form into 6 chiabatta shapes. Set a pan over medium heat. Cook each ciabatta for 2 minutes per side. Sprinkle tomato puree over each one and top with pepperoni slices to serve.

Cauliflower & Cheese Burgers

Ready in about: 35 minutes | **Serves:** 6 | **Per serving:** Kcal 416; Fat: 33.8g, Net Carbs: 7.8g, Protein: 13g

INGREDIENTS

3 tbsp olive oil
1 onion, chopped
1 garlic clove, minced

1 lb cauliflower, grated
6 tbsp coconut flour
½ cup gruyere cheese, shredded

1 cup Parmesan cheese, grated
2 eggs, beaten
Sea salt and black pepper to taste

DIRECTIONS

Warm the olive oil in a skillet over medium heat. Add in garlic and onion and cook until soft, about 3 minutes. Stir in cauliflower and cook for a minute. Allow cooling and set aside. Add in the rest of the ingredients. Form balls from the mixture, then press them to form burger patties. Preheat oven to 400°F. Bake the burgers for 20 minutes, flipping once until the top is golden brown. Serve warm.

Mascarpone & Vanilla Breakfast Cups

Ready in about: 20 minutes | **Serves:** 6 | **Per serving:** Kcal 181; Fat: 13.5g, Net Carbs: 3.7g, Protein: 10.5g

INGREDIENTS

¾ cup mascarpone cheese, softened
¼ cup Greek yogurt

3 eggs, beaten
2 tbsp walnuts, ground

4 tbsp erythritol
½ tsp vanilla extract

DIRECTIONS

Preheat oven to 360°F. Mix all ingredients in a bowl. Split the batter into greased muffin cups. Bake for 12-15 minutes. Remove and set on a wire rack to cool slightly before serving.

Mascarpone Snapped Amaretti Biscuits

Ready in about: 25 minutes | **Serves**: 6 | **Per serving**: Kcal 165, Fat 13g, Net Carbs 3g, Protein 9g

INGREDIENTS

6 egg whites
1 egg yolk, beaten
1 tsp vanilla bean paste
4 tbsp swerve sugar

A pinch of salt
¼ cup ground fragrant almonds
1 lemon juice
7 tbsp sugar-free amaretto liquor

¼ cup mascarpone cheese
¼ cup butter, room temperature
¾ cup swerve confectioner's sugar

DIRECTIONS

Preheat oven to 300°F. Line a baking sheet with parchment paper. In a bowl, beat egg whites, salt, and vanilla paste with a hand mixer while you gradually spoon in the swerve sugar until stiff. Add in almonds and fold in the egg yolk, lemon juice, and amaretto liquor. Spoon mixture into a piping bag.

Press out 50 mounds on the baking sheet. Bake the biscuits for 15 minutes until golden brown. Transfer to a wire rack to cool. Whisk the mascarpone cheese, butter, and swerve confectioner's sugar with the cleaned electric mixer. Spread a scoop of mascarpone cream onto the case of half of the biscuits and snap with the remaining biscuits. Dust with some swerve confectioner's sugar and serve.

Breakfast Buttered Eggs

Ready in about: 15 minutes | **Serves**: 2 | **Per serving**: Kcal 321, Fat: 21.5g, Net Carbs: 2.5g, Protein: 12.8g

INGREDIENTS

1 tbsp coconut oil
1 tbsp butter
1 tsp fresh thyme, chopped

4 eggs
1 garlic clove, minced
1 tsp fresh parsley, chopped

¼ tsp cumin
¼ tsp cayenne pepper
Salt and black pepper to taste

DIRECTIONS

Put the coconut oil and butter in a skillet over medium heat. Add in the garlic and thyme and cook for 30 seconds. Sprinkle with parsley and cook for 2 minutes, until crisp.

Carefully crack the eggs into the skillet. Lower the heat and cook for 4-6 minutes. Season with salt, black pepper, cumin, and cayenne pepper. When the eggs are just set, turn the heat off and serve.

Hashed Zucchini & Bacon Breakfast

Ready in about: 25 minutes | **Serves**: 2 | **Per serving**: Kcal 340, Fat: 26.8g, Net Carbs: 6.6g, Protein: 17.4g

INGREDIENTS

1 medium zucchini, diced
2 bacon slices

2 eggs
1 tbsp coconut oil

½ small onion, chopped
1 tbsp fresh parsley, chopped

DIRECTIONS

Place the bacon in a skillet and cook for 5 minutes until crispy. Set aside. Warm the coconut oil and cook the onion until soft for about 3 minutes, stirring occasionally. Add in the zucchini and cook for 10 more minutes until zucchini is brown and tender, but not mushy. Transfer to a plate.

Crack the eggs into the same skillet and fry over medium heat. Top the zucchini mixture with the bacon slices and fried eggs. Serve hot sprinkled with parsley.

Sausage & Squash Omelet with Swiss Chard

Ready in about: 15 minutes | **Serves**: 1 | **Per serving**: Kcal 558, Fat 51.7g, Net Carbs 7.5g, Protein 32.3g

INGREDIENTS

2 eggs
1 cup Swiss chard, chopped
2 oz sausage, chopped

2 tbsp ricotta cheese
4 oz roasted squash
1 tbsp olive oil

Salt and black pepper to taste
Fresh parsley to garnish

Beat the eggs in a bowl, season with salt and pepper, and stir in the Swiss chard and ricotta cheese. In another bowl, mash the squash and add to the egg mixture. Heat the olive oil in a pan over medium heat. Add sausage and cook for 5 minutes until browned, stirring occasionally.

Pour the egg mixture over. Cook for 2 minutes per side until the eggs are thoroughly cooked and lightly browned. Remove and run a spatula around the omelet. Slide it onto a plate. Serve topped with parsley.

Ham & Egg Broccoli Bake

Ready in about: 25 minutes | **Serves**: 4 | **Per serving**: Kcal 344, Fat 28g, Net Carbs 4.2g, Protein 11g

INGREDIENTS

1 head broccoli, cut into florets	¼ cup ham, chopped	Salt and black pepper to taste
2 red bell peppers, chopped	2 tsp ghee	8 eggs

DIRECTIONS

Preheat oven to 425°F. Melt the ghee in a frying pan over medium heat. Brown the ham for about 3 minutes, stirring frequently. Pour the broccoli, bell peppers, and ham on a foil-lined baking sheet and toss to combine. Season with salt and pepper. Bake for 10 minutes until the vegetables have softened.

Remove, create eight indentations with a spoon, and crack an egg into each. Return to the oven and continue to bake for an additional 5-7 minutes until the egg whites are firm. Season with salt and black pepper. Plate the bake and serve with strawberry lemonade (optional).

Broccoli & Colby Cheese Frittata

Ready in about: 20 minutes | **Serves**: 4 | **Per serving**: Kcal 248; Fat: 17.1g, Net Carbs: 6.2g, Protein: 17.6g

INGREDIENTS

2 tbsp olive oil	8 eggs, beaten	¾ cup Colby cheese, grated
½ cup onions, chopped	½ tsp jalapeño pepper, minced	¼ cup fresh cilantro, chopped
1 cup broccoli, chopped	Salt and red pepper, to taste	

DIRECTIONS

Warm the olive oil a frying pan over medium heat. Add onions and sauté until caramelized, about 10 minutes. Place in the broccoli jalapeno pepper and cook for 5 minutes. Pour in the eggs and season with red pepper and salt. Cook until the eggs are set. Scatter Colby cheese over the frittata.

Preheat oven to 370°F. Cook the frittata for approximately 12 minutes until it is set in the middle. Slice into wedges and decorate with fresh cilantro before serving.

Egg Omelet Roll with Cream Cheese & Salmon

Ready in about: 15 minutes | **Serves**: 4 | **Per serving**: Kcal 514, Fat: 47.9g, Net Carbs: 5.8g, Protein: 36.9g

INGREDIENTS

1 avocado, sliced	2 spring onions, sliced	2 tbsp butter
2 tbsp chopped chives	8 eggs	Salt and black pepper to taste
4 oz smoked salmon, cut into strips	4 tbsp cream cheese	

DIRECTIONS

In a small bowl, combine the chives and cream cheese and mix well. Beat the eggs in a large bowl and season with salt and black pepper. Melt the butter in a pan over medium heat. Add the eggs to the pan.

Cook for about 3 minutes. Flip the omelet over and continue cooking for another 2 minutes until golden. Remove the omelet to a plate and spread the chive mixture over. Arrange the salmon, avocado, and onion slices. Slice the omelet and serve immediately.

Prosciutto Frittata with Vegetables

Ready in about: 25 minutes | **Serves**: 4 | **Per serving**: Kcal 310; Fat: 26.2g, Net Carbs: 3.9g, Protein: 15.4g

INGREDIENTS

2 tbsp butter, at room temperature
½ cup green onions, chopped
2 garlic cloves, minced

1 jalapeño pepper, chopped
1 carrot, chopped
8 prosciutto slices

8 eggs, whisked
Salt and black pepper to taste
½ tsp dried thyme

DIRECTIONS

Melt the butter in a pan over medium heat. Stir in green onions and sauté for 4 minutes. Place in garlic, carrot, and jalapeño pepper and cook for 5 more minutes. Remove the mixture to a greased baking pan.

Top with ham slices. Cover with eggs and sprinkle with thyme, black pepper, and salt. Arrange the prosciutto slices on top. Bake in the oven for about 18 minutes at 360°F. Serve sliced.

Cheesy Sausage Quiche

Ready in about: 55 minutes | **Serves**: 6 | **Per serving**: Kcal 340, Fat: 28g, Net Carbs: 3g, Protein: 17g

INGREDIENTS

6 eggs
12 oz raw sausage roll
10 cherry tomatoes, halved

2 tbsp heavy cream
2 tbsp Parmesan cheese
Salt and black pepper to taste

2 tbsp chopped parsley
5 eggplant slices

DIRECTIONS

Preheat oven to 370°F. Press the sausage roll at the bottom of a greased pie dish. Arrange the eggplant slices over the sausage and nd top with cherry tomatoes. Whisk the eggs with heavy cream, salt, Parmesan cheese, and pepper. Spoon the mixture over the sausage. Bake for about 40 minutes until browned around the edges. Serve sprinkled with parsley.

Bacon & Cheese Frittata

Ready in about: 25 minutes | **Serves**: 4 | **Per serving**: Kcal 325, Fat 28g, Net Carbs 2g, Protein 15g

INGREDIENTS

8 bacon slices
8 fresh eggs

2 tbsp butter, melted
½ cup almond milk

1 cup cheddar cheese, shredded
¼ cup green onions, chopped

DIRECTIONS

Preheat oven to 400°F. Cook the bacon in a skillet over medium heat for 6 minutes. Once crispy, remove from the skillet to paper towels to discard grease. Chop into small pieces. Whisk the eggs, butter, and almond milk in a bowl. Mix in the bacon and pour the mixture into a greased baking dish.

Sprinkle with cheddar cheese and green onions and bake in the oven for 10 minutes or until the eggs are thoroughly cooked. Remove, cool the frittata for 3 minutes, and slice into wedges to serve.

Traditional Spinach & Feta Frittata

Ready in about: 30 minutes | **Serves**: 4 | **Per serving**: Kcal 461, Fat: 35g, Net Carbs: 6g, Protein: 26g

INGREDIENTS

10 oz spinach
8 oz feta cheese, crumbled

1 pint cherry tomatoes, halved
10 eggs

4 scallions, diced

DIRECTIONS

Preheat oven to 350°F. In a bowl, whisk the eggs with salt and pepper. Stir in the spinach, feta cheese, and scallions. Pour the mixture into a greased casserole, top with the cherry tomatoes, and bake for 20 minutes until your frittata is set in the middle. Cut the frittata into wedges and serve with salad.

Egg Tofu Scramble with Kale & Mushrooms

Ready in about: 30 minutes | Serves: 4 | Per serving: Kcal 469, Fat 39g, Net Carbs 5g, Protein 25g

INGREDIENTS

2 tbsp ghee
1 cup white mushrooms, sliced

16 oz firm tofu, crumbled
Salt and black pepper to taste

½ cup kale, thinly sliced
6 eggs

DIRECTIONS

Melt the ghee in a skillet over medium heat. Sauté the mushrooms for 5 minutes until they lose their liquid. Add the garlic and cook for 1 minute. Stir in the tofu, season with salt and black pepper, and cook with continuous stirring for 6 minutes. Introduce the kale and cook for about 5 minutes until softened.

Crack the eggs into a bowl, whisk until well combined and creamy in color, and pour all over the kale. Use a spatula to stir the eggs while cooking until scrambled and no more runny, about 5 minutes. Serve.

Breakfast Almond Muffins

Ready in about: 30 minutes | Serves: 4 | Per serving: Kcal 320, Fat 30.6g, Net Carbs 6g, Protein 4g

INGREDIENTS

2 cups almond flour
2 tsp baking powder

8 oz cream cheese, softened
¼ cup butter, melted

1 egg
1 cup unsweetened almond milk

DIRECTIONS

Preheat oven to 400°F. Mix the flour and baking powder in a large bowl. In a separate bowl, beat the cream cheese and butter using a hand mixer and whisk in the egg and milk. Fold in the flour. Spoon the batter into a greased 12-cup muffin tray two-thirds way up. Bake for 20 minutes. Serve cooled.

Egg in a Cheesy Spinach Nests

Ready in about: 35 minutes | Serves: 4 | Per serving: Kcal 230, Fat 17.5g, Net Carbs 4g, Protein 12g

INGREDIENTS

2 tbsp olive oil
2 lb spinach, chopped

Salt and black pepper to taste
2 tbsp Parmesan cheese, shredded

2 tbsp gouda cheese, shredded
4 eggs

DIRECTIONS

Preheat oven to 350°F. Warm the oil in a skillet over medium heat. Add the garlic and sauté until softened, about 2 minutes. Add the spinach and cook for 5 minutes. Season with salt and pepper. Allow cooling.

Mold 4 (firm and separate) spinach nests on a greased baking sheet and crack an egg into each nest. Sprinkle with Parmesan and gouda cheeses. Bake for 15 minutes just until the egg whites have set and the yolks are still runny. Plate the nests and serve right away with low carb toasts and coffee.

Bacon Tomato Cups

Ready in about: 30 minutes | Serves: 6 | Per serving: Kcal 425, Fat 45.2g, Net Carbs 4.3g, Protein 16.2g

INGREDIENTS

12 bacon slices
2 tomatoes, diced

1 onion, diced
1 cup cheddar cheese, shredded

1 cup mayonnaise
12 low carb crepes/pancakes

DIRECTIONS

Fry the bacon in a skillet over medium heat for 5 minutes. Remove and chop with a knife. Transfer to a bowl. Add in cheddar cheese, tomatoes, onion, and mayonnaise. Mix well and set aside. Place the crepes on a flat surface and use rings to cut a circle out of each crepe.

Fit the circled crepes into greased ramekins to make cups. Fill them with 3 tbsp of bacon-tomato mixture and place them on a baking sheet. Bake in the oven for 15 minutes at 350°F. Serve with tomato sauce.

POULTRY RECIPES

Bacon-Wrapped Chicken with Grilled Asparagus

Ready in about: 50 minutes | **Serves**: 4 | **Per serving**: Kcal 468, Fat 38g, Net Carbs 2g, Protein 26g

INGREDIENTS

4 chicken breasts
Pink salt and black pepper to taste
8 bacon slices

2 tbsp olive oil
1 lb asparagus spears
3 tbsp olive oil

2 tbsp fresh lemon juice
2 oz Manchego cheese for topping

DIRECTIONS

Preheat oven to 400°F. Season the chicken breasts with salt and pepper. Wrap 2 bacon slices around each chicken breast. Arrange them on a baking sheet, drizzle with olive oil, and bake for 25-30 minutes until the bacon is brown and crispy. Remove and cover with foil to keep warm.

Preheat grill to high heat. Brush the asparagus with olive oil and season with salt. Grill for 8-10 minutes, frequently turning until slightly charred. Remove to a plate and drizzle with lemon juice. Grate over Manchego cheese to melts a little on contact with the hot asparagus and forms a cheesy dressing. Serve.

Spinach Chicken Cheesy Bake

Ready in about: 45 minutes | **Serves**: 4 | **Per serving**: Kcal 340, Fat 30.2g, Net Carbs 3.1g, Protein 15g

INGREDIENTS

1 lb chicken breasts
1 tsp mixed spice seasoning
Pink salt and black pepper to taste

2 loose cups baby spinach
3 tsp olive oil
4 oz cream cheese

1 ¼ cups mozzarella cheese, grated
4 tbsp water

DIRECTIONS

Preheat oven to 370°F. Season chicken with spice mix, salt, and black pepper. Pat with your hands to have the seasoning stick on the chicken. Put in the casserole dish and layer spinach over the chicken. Mix the oil with cream cheese, mozzarella, salt, and pepper and stir in water a tablespoon at a time.

Pour the mixture over the chicken and cover the casserole dish with aluminium foil. Bake for 20 minutes. Remove the foil and continue cooking for 15 minutes until a nice golden brown color is formed on top. Take out and allow sitting for 5 minutes. Serve warm with braised asparagus.

Cilantro Chicken Breasts with Mayo-Avocado Sauce

Ready in about: 25 minutes | **Serves**: 4 | **Per serving**: Kcal 398, Fat 32g, Net Carbs 4g, Protein 24g

INGREDIENTS

Mayo-avocado sauce

1 avocado, pitted

½ cup mayonnaise

Salt to taste

Chicken

2 tbsp ghee
4 chicken breasts

Pink salt and black pepper to taste
2 tbsp fresh cilantro, chopped

½ cup chicken broth

DIRECTIONS

Spoon the avocado into a bowl and mash with a fork. Add in mayonnaise and salt and stir until a smooth sauce is derived. Pour sauce into a jar and refrigerate. Melt the ghee in a large skillet over medium heat. Season chicken with salt and pepper and fry for 4 minutes on each side until golden brown. Remove.

Pour the broth in the same skillet and add the cilantro. Bring to simmer covered for 3 minutes and return the chicken. Cover and cook on low heat for 5 minutes until the liquid has reduced and chicken is fragrant. Place the chicken only into serving plates and spoon the mayo-avocado sauce over. Serve.

Sweet Garlic Chicken Skewers

Ready in about: 20 minutes + time refrigeration | **Serves**: 4 | **Per serving**: Kcal 225, Fat 17.4g, Net Carbs 2g, Protein 15g

INGREDIENTS

Skewers

3 tbsp soy sauce
1 tbsp ginger-garlic paste

2 tbsp swerve brown sugar
1 tsp chili pepper

2 tbsp olive oil
1 lb chicken breasts, cut into cubes

Dressing

½ cup tahini

½ tsp garlic powder

Pink salt to taste

DIRECTIONS

In a bowl, whisk soy sauce, ginger-garlic paste, swerve brown sugar, chili pepper, and olive oil. Put the chicken in a zipper bag. Pour in the marinade, seal, and shake to coat. Marinate in the fridge for 2 hours.

Preheat grill to 400°F. Thread the chicken on skewers. Cook for 10 minutes in total with three to four turnings until golden brown; remove to a plate. Mix the tahini, garlic powder, salt, and ¼ cup of warm water in a bowl. Pour into serving jars. Serve the chicken skewers and tahini dressing with cauli rice.

Roasted Chicken Breasts with Capers

Ready in about: 65 minutes | **Serves**: 6 | **Per serving**: Kcal 430, Fat 23g, Net Carbs 3g, Protein 33g

INGREDIENTS

2 medium lemons, sliced
3 chicken breasts, halved
Salt and black pepper to taste

¼ cup almond flour
3 tbsp olive oil
2 tbsp capers, rinsed

1 ¼ cups chicken broth
2 tbsp fresh parsley, chopped
1 tbsp butter

DIRECTIONS

Preheat oven to 350°F. Line a baking sheet with parchment paper. Lay the lemon slices on the baking sheet and drizzle with some olive oil. Roast for 25 minutes until the lemon rinds brown.

Cover the chicken with plastic wrap, place them on a flat surface, and gently pound with the rolling pin to flatten to about ½-inch thickness. Remove the plastic wraps and season with salt and pepper. Dredge the chicken in the almond flour on each side, and shake off any excess flour. Set aside.

Heat the remaining olive oil in a skillet over medium heat. Fry the chicken on both sides until golden brown, about 8 minutes. Pour in the broth and let it boil until it becomes thick in consistency, 12 minutes.

Stir in the capers, butter, and roasted lemons and simmer on low heat for 10 minutes. Turn the heat off. Pour the sauce over the chicken and garnish with parsley to serve.

Chicken Drumsticks in Tomato Sauce

Ready in about: 1 ½ hours | **Serves**: 4 | **Per serving**: Kcal 515, Fat 34.2g, Net Carbs 7.3g, Protein 50.8g

INGREDIENTS

8 chicken drumsticks
2 tbsp olive oil
1 medium white onion, chopped
2 medium turnips, peeled and diced

1 medium carrot, chopped
2 green bell peppers, cut into chunks
2 cloves garlic, minced
¼ cup coconut flour

1 cup chicken broth
1 (28 oz) can sugar-free tomato sauce
2 tbsp dried Italian herbs
Salt and black pepper to taste

DIRECTIONS

Preheat oven to 400°F. Heat the olive oil in a skillet over medium heat. Season the drumsticks with salt and pepper and fry for 10 minutes on all sides until brown. Remove to a baking dish. Sauté the onion, turnips, bell peppers, carrot, and garlic in the same oil for 10 minutes with continuous stirring.

In a bowl, combine the broth, coconut flour, tomato paste, and Italian herbs together and pour it over the vegetables in the skillet. Stir and cook for 4 minutes until thickened. Pour the mixture over the chicken in the baking dish. Bake for around 1 hour. Remove from the oven and serve with steamed cauli rice.

Stuffed Chicken Breasts with Cucumber Noodle Salad

Ready in about: 60 minutes | **Serves:** 4 | **Per serving:** Kcal: 453, Fat: 31g, Net Carbs: 6g, Protein: 43g

INGREDIENTS

Chicken

4 chicken breasts
1 cup baby spinach

¼ cup goat cheese
¼ cup cheddar cheese, shredded

4 tbsp butter, melted
Salt and black pepper to taste

Tomato sauce

1 tbsp butter
1 shallot, chopped
2 garlic cloves, chopped

½ tbsp liquid stevia
2 tbsp tomato paste
14 oz canned crushed tomatoes

Salt and black pepper to taste
1 tsp dried basil
1 tsp dried oregano

Salad

2 cucumbers, spiralized

2 tbsp olive oil

1 tbsp white wine vinegar

DIRECTIONS

Preheat oven to 400°F. Place a pan over medium heat. Warm 2 tbsp of butter and sauté spinach until it shrinks. Season with salt and pepper. Transfer to a bowl containing goat cheese, stir, and set aside.

Cut the chicken breasts lengthwise and stuff with the cheese mixture. Set into a baking dish. On top, spread the cheddar cheese and add 2 tbsp of butter. Bake until cooked through for 25-30 minutes.

Warm 1 tbsp of the butter in a pan over medium heat. Add in garlic and shallot and cook for 3 minutes until soft. Stir in herbs, tomato paste, stevia, tomatoes, salt, and pepper and cook for 15 minutes.

Arrange the cucumbers on a serving platter, season with salt, pepper, olive oil, and vinegar. Top with the chicken and pour over the sauce. Serve.

Parmesan Wings with Yogurt Sauce

Ready in about: 25 minutes | **Serves:** 6 | **Per serving:** Kcal 452, Fat 36.4g, Net Carbs 4g, Protein 24g

INGREDIENTS

1 cup Greek-style yogurt
2 tbsp extra-virgin olive oil
1 tsp fresh lemon juice

2 lb chicken wings
Salt and black pepper to taste
½ cup butter, melted

½ cup hot sauce
¼ cup Parmesan cheese, grated
1 tsp dried dill

DIRECTIONS

Preheat oven to 400°F. Mix yogurt, olive oil, dill, salt, and black pepper in a bowl. Chill while making the chicken. Season wings with salt and pepper. Line them on a baking sheet and grease with cooking spray.

Bake for 20 minutes until golden brown. Mix butter, hot sauce, and Parmesan cheese in a bowl. Toss chicken in the sauce to evenly coat and plate. Serve with yogurt dipping sauce.

Creamy Stuffed Chicken with Parma Ham

Ready in about: 40 minutes | **Serves:** 4 | **Per serving:** Kcal 485, Fat 35g, Net Carbs 2g, Protein 26g

INGREDIENTS

4 chicken breasts
2 tbsp olive oil
2 cloves garlic, minced

2 shallots, finely chopped
1 tsp dried mixed herbs
8 slices Parma ham

4 oz cream cheese, softened
1 lemon, zested
Salt to taste

DIRECTIONS

Preheat oven to 350°F. Heat the oil in a skillet over medium heat. Sauté garlic and shallots for 3 minutes. Stir the cream cheese, mixed herbs, salt, and lemon zest for 2 minutes. Remove and let cool.

Score a pocket in each chicken breast, fill the holes with the cheese mixture, and cover with the cut-out chicken. Wrap each breast with 2 ham slices and secure the ends with a toothpick. Lay the chicken parcels on a greased baking sheet. Bake for 20 minutes. Remove and let it rest for 4 minutes. Serve.

Chicken Wings with Herb Chutney

Ready in about: 35 minutes + marinating time | **Serves**: 4 | **Per serving**: Kcal 243, Fat 15g, Net Carbs 3.5g, Protein 22g

INGREDIENTS

12 chicken wings, cut in half
1 tbsp turmeric
1 tbsp cumin
3 tbsp fresh ginger, grated

2 tbsp cilantro, chopped
½ tsp paprika
Salt and black pepper to taste
4 tbsp olive oil

Juice of ½ lime
2 tbsp fresh thyme, chopped
¾ cup cilantro, chopped
1 jalapeño pepper, chopped

DIRECTIONS

In a bowl, stir 1 tbsp ginger, cumin, paprika, salt, 2 tbsp olive oil, black pepper, and turmeric. Place in the chicken wings pieces and toss to coat. Marinate in the fridge for 20 minutes. Remove before grilling.

Heat the grill, place in the marinated wings, and cook for 25 minutes, turning from time to time. Remove and set to a serving plate. Blitz thyme, remaining ginger, salt, jalapeno, black pepper, lime juice, cilantro, remaining olive oil, and 1 tbsp water in a blender. Drizzle the chicken wings with the sauce and serve.

Garlic & Ginger Chicken with Peanut Sauce

Ready in about: 20 minutes + marinating time | **Serves**: 6 | **Per serving**: Kcal 492, Fat: 36g, Net Carbs: 3g, Protein: 35g

INGREDIENTS

Chicken ingredients

1 tbsp wheat-free soy sauce
1 tbsp sugar-free fish sauce
1 tbsp lime juice
1 tsp cilantro, chopped

1 minced garlic
1 tsp minced ginger
1 tbsp olive oil
1 tbsp rice wine vinegar

1 tsp cayenne pepper
1 tbsp erythritol
6 chicken thighs

Peanut sauce

½ cup peanut butter
1 tsp minced garlic
1 tbsp lime juice

2 tbsp water
1 tsp minced ginger
1 tbsp jalapeño pepper, chopped

2 tbsp rice wine vinegar
2 tbsp erythritol
1 tbsp fish sauce

DIRECTIONS

Combine all chicken ingredients in a large Ziploc bag. Seal the bag and shake to combine. Refrigerate for 1 hour. Remove from the fridge about 15 minutes before cooking. Preheat the grill to medium heat.

Cook the chicken for 7 minutes per side until golden brown. Remove to a serving plate. Whisk together all the sauce ingredients in a mixing bowl. Serve the chicken drizzled with peanut sauce.

Chicken Cauliflower Bake

Ready in about: 50 minutes | **Serves**: 6 | **Per serving**: Kcal 390, Fat 27g, Net Carbs 3g, Protein 22g

INGREDIENTS

3 cups cubed leftover chicken
3 cups spinach
2 cauliflower heads, cut into florets

3 eggs, lightly beaten
2 cups grated sharp cheddar cheese
1 cup pork rinds, crushed

½ cup unsweetened almond milk
3 tbsp olive oil
3 cloves garlic, minced

DIRECTIONS

Preheat oven to 350°F. Pour the cauli florets and 3 cups water in a pot over medium heat and bring to a boil. Cover and steam the cauli florets for 8 minutes. Drain through a colander and set aside. Combine the cheddar cheese and pork rinds in a large bowl and mix in the chicken. Set aside.

Heat the olive oil in a skillet and cook the garlic and spinach until the spinach has wilted, about 5 minutes. Add the spinach mixture and cauli florets to the chicken bowl. Add in the eggs and almond milk, mix, and transfer everything to a greased baking dish. Layer the top of the ingredients.

Place the dish in the oven and bake for 30 minutes. By this time, the edges and top must have browned nicely. Remove the chicken from the oven, let rest for 5 minutes, and serve.

Eggplant & Tomato Braised Chicken Thighs

Ready in about: 45 minutes | **Serves**: 4 | **Per serving**: Kcal 468, Fat 39.5g, Net Carbs 2g, Protein 26g

INGREDIENTS

2 tbsp ghee
1 lb chicken thighs

Salt and black pepper to taste
2 garlic cloves, minced

1 (14 oz) can whole tomatoes
1 eggplant, diced

DIRECTIONS

Melt ghee in a saucepan over medium heat. Season the chicken with salt and black pepper and fry for 4 minutes on each side until golden brown. Remove to a plate. Sauté the garlic in the ghee for 2 minutes.

Pour in the tomatoes and cook covered for 8 minutes. Add in the eggplant and sauté for 4 minutes. Adjust the seasoning with salt and black pepper. Stir and add the chicken. Coat with sauce and simmer for 3 minutes. Serve chicken with sauce on a bed of squash pasta.

Lemon-Garlic Chicken Skewers

Ready in about: 20 minutes + marinating time | **Serves**: 4 | **Per serving**: Kcal 350, Fat 11g, Net Carbs 3.5g, Protein 34g

INGREDIENTS

1 lb chicken breasts, cut into cubes
2 tbsp olive oil
2/3 jar preserved lemon, drained

2 garlic cloves, minced
½ cup lemon juice
Salt and black pepper to taste

1 tsp fresh rosemary, chopped
4 lemon wedges

DIRECTIONS

In a wide bowl, mix half of the oil, garlic, salt, pepper, and lemon juice and add the chicken cubes and lemon rind. Let marinate for 2 hours in the refrigerator. Remove the chicken and thread it onto skewers.

Heat a grill pan over high heat. Add in the chicken skewers and sear them for 6 minutes per side. Remove to a plate and serve warm garnished with rosemary and lemons wedges.

Sweet Chili Grilled Chicken

Ready in about: 30 minutes | **Serves**: 6 | **Per serving**: Kcal 265, Fat 9g, Net Carbs 3g, Protein 26g

INGREDIENTS

2 lb chicken breasts
4 cloves garlic, minced
2 tbsp fresh oregano, chopped

½ cup lemon juice
2/3 cup olive oil
1 tbsp erythritol

Salt and black pepper to taste
3 small chilies, minced

DIRECTIONS

Preheat grill to high heat. In a bowl, mix the garlic, oregano, lemon juice, olive oil, chilies, and erythritol. Cover the chicken with plastic wraps and use the rolling pin to pound to ½-inch thickness.

Remove the wrap and brush the spice mixture on the chicken on all sides. Place on the grill and cook for 15 minutes, flip, and continue cooking for 10 more minutes. Remove to a plate and serve with salad.

Chicken & Squash Traybake

Ready in about: 50 minutes | **Serves**: 4 | **Per serving**: Kcal: 411, Fat: 15g, Net Carbs: 5.5g, Protein: 31g

INGREDIENTS

1 ½ lb chicken thighs
1 lb butternut squash, cubed

½ cup black olives, pitted
¼ cup olive oil

5 garlic cloves, sliced
¼ tbsp dried oregano

DIRECTIONS

Preheat oven to 400°F. Place the chicken in a greased baking dish with the skin down. Place the garlic, olives, and butternut squash around the chicken. Drizzle with olive oil. Sprinkle with black pepper, salt, and oregano. Bake in the oven for 45 minutes until golden brown. Serve warm.

Cheese & Spinach Stuffed Chicken Breasts

Ready in about: 50 minutes | Serves: 4 | Per serving: Kcal 491, Fat. 36g, Net Carbs: 3.5g, Protein: 38g

INGREDIENTS

4 chicken breasts	⅓ cup Parmesan cheese	2 cups spinach, chopped
½ cup mozzarella cheese, grated	6 oz cream cheese, softened	½ tsp ground nutmeg

Breading

2 eggs	2 tbsp olive oil	⅓ cup Parmesan cheese
⅓ cup almond flour	½ tsp parsley	1 tsp onion powder

DIRECTIONS

Pound the chicken until it doubles in size. Mix the cream cheese, spinach, mozzarella cheese, nutmeg, salt, black pepper, and Parmesan cheese in a bowl. Divide the mixture between the chicken breasts. Close the chicken around the filling. Wrap the breasts with cling film. Refrigerate for 15 minutes.

Preheat oven to 370°F. Beat the eggs in a shallow dish. Combine all other breading ingredients in a bowl. Dip the chicken in egg first, then in the breading mixture. Heat the olive oil in a pan over medium heat. Cook chicken for 3-5 minutes on all sides. Transfer to a baking sheet. Bake for 20 minutes. Serve.

Bacon & Chicken Cottage Pie Cups

Ready in about: 55 minutes | Serves: 4 | Per serving: Kcal 571, Fat 45g, Net Carbs 8.2g, Protein 41g

INGREDIENTS

1 onion, chopped	3 garlic cloves, minced	12 oz chicken breasts, cubed
4 bacon slices, chopped	Salt and black pepper to taste	2 tbsp Dijon mustard
3 tbsp butter	¾ cup crème fraîche	¾ cup cheddar cheese, shredded
1 carrot, chopped	½ cup chicken stock	

For the dough

¾ cup almond flour	1 ½ cups mozzarella cheese, grated	1 tsp onion powder
3 tbsp cream cheese, softened	1 egg	1 tsp garlic powder

DIRECTIONS

Melt the butter in a pan over medium heat. Sauté the onion, garlic, salt, pepper, bacon, and carrot for 5 minutes. Add in the chicken and cook for 3 minutes. Stir in the crème fraîche, mustard, and stock and cook for 7 minutes. Mix in the cheddar cheese. Microwave mozzarella and cream cheeses for 1 minute.

Stir in the garlic powder, salt, pepper, almond flour, onion powder, and egg. Knead the dough well, split into 4 pieces, and flatten each one into a circle. Set the chicken mixture into 4 greased ramekins, top with dough circles, and place in the oven. Cook for 25 minutes at 370° F. Serve chilled.

Easy Chicken Chili

Ready in about: 30 minutes | Serves: 4 | Per serving: Kcal: 421, Fat: 21g, Net Carbs: 5.6g, Protein: 45g

INGREDIENTS

4 chicken breasts	2 tbsp tomato puree	1 serrano pepper, minced
2 tbsp butter	½ tsp chili powder	½ cup cheddar cheese, shredded
1 onion, chopped	½ tsp cumin	Salt and black pepper to taste
8 oz diced tomatoes	½ tsp garlic powder	

DIRECTIONS

Put a large saucepan over medium heat and add the chicken. Cover with water and bring to a boil. Cook for 10 minutes. Transfer the chicken to a flat surface and shred with forks. Reserve 2 cups of the broth.

Melt the butter in a large pot over medium heat. Sauté onion until transparent for 3 minutes. Stir in the chicken, tomatoes, cumin, serrano pepper, garlic powder, tomato puree, broth, and chili powder. Adjust the seasoning and let the mixture boil. Simmer for 10 minutes. Top with shredded cheese and serve.

Chicken in White Wine Sauce

Ready in about: 40 minutes | **Serves**: 4 | **Per serving**: Kcal 345, Fat 12g, Net Carbs 4g, Protein 24g

INGREDIENTS

1 ½ chicken thighs
Salt and black pepper to taste
2 shallots, chopped

2 tbsp canola oil
4 pancetta strips, chopped
2 garlic cloves, minced

10 oz white mushrooms, halved
1 cup white wine
1 cup whipping cream

DIRECTIONS

Warm the canola oil a pan over medium heat. Cook the pancetta for 3 minutes. Add in the chicken, sprinkle with pepper and salt, and cook until brown, about 5 minutes. Remove to a plate. In the same pan, sauté shallots, mushrooms, and garlic for 6 minutes. Return the pancetta and chicken to the pan.

Stir in the white wine and 1 cup of water and bring to a boil. Reduce the heat and simmer for 20 minutes. Pour in the whipping cream and warm without boiling. Serve with steamed asparagus.

Poulet en Papillote

Ready in about: 60 minutes | **Serves**: 4 | **Per serving**: Kcal 364, Fat 16.5g, Net Carbs 4.8g, Protein 25g

INGREDIENTS

4 chicken breasts, scored
4 tbsp white wine
1 tbsp olive oil
4 tbsp butter, sliced

3 cups mixed mushrooms, teared up
1 medium celeriac, peeled and sliced
3 cloves garlic, minced
4 sprigs thyme, chopped

3 lemons, juiced
Salt and black pepper to taste
2 tbsp Dijon mustard

DIRECTIONS

Preheat oven to 450°F. Arrange the celeriac on a baking sheet, drizzle it with olive oil, and bake for 20 minutes; set aside. In a bowl, mix the chicken, roasted celeriac, mushrooms, garlic, thyme, lemon juice, salt, pepper, and mustard. Make 4 large cuts of foil, fold them in half, and fold them in half again.

Tightly fold the two open edges together to create bags. Distribute the chicken mixture among the bags, top with white wine and butter. Seal the last open end securely, making sure not to pierce the bags. Put them on a baking tray and bake for 25 minutes. Remove the chicken from the bags and serve.

Chicken & Broccoli Stir-Fry

Ready in about: 30 minutes | **Serves**: 4 | **Per serving**: Kcal 286, Fat 10.1g, Net Carbs 3.4g, Protein 17.3g

INGREDIENTS

2 chicken breasts, cut into strips
2 tbsp olive oil

1 cup unsalted cashew nuts
2 cups broccoli florets

1 white onion, thinly sliced
Salt and black pepper to taste

DIRECTIONS

Toast the cashew nuts in a dry skillet over medium heat for 2-3 minutes, shaking occasionally. Remove to a plate. Heat the olive oil in the pan and sauté the onion for 4 minutes until soft; set aside.

Add the chicken to the pan. Cook for 4 minutes. Include the broccoli, salt, and black pepper. Stir and cook for 5-6 minutes until tender and add in the onion. Stir once more, cook for 1 minute, and turn the heat off. Serve the chicken stir-fry topped with the cashew nuts.

Fried Chicken with Coconut Sauce

Ready in about: 30 minutes | **Serves**: 6 | **Per serving**: Kcal 491, Fat 35g, Net Carbs 3.2g, Protein 58g

INGREDIENTS

3 tbsp coconut oil
2 lb chicken breasts
1 cup chicken stock

1 ¼ cups leeks, chopped
1 tbsp lime juice
¼ cup coconut cream

1 tsp red pepper flakes
2 tbsp green onions, chopped
Salt and black pepper to taste

Put a pan over medium heat and warm oil. Add in the chicken and cook each side for 2 minutes. Set aside. Place the leeks in the pan and cook for 4 minutes. Stir in stock, pepper flakes, salt, pepper, coconut cream, and lime juice. Take the chicken back to the pan and cook covered for 15 minutes. Serve warm.

Spanish Chicken

Ready in about: 50 minutes | **Serves**: 4 | **Per serving**: Kcal 415, Fat 33g, Net Carbs 4g, Protein 25g

INGREDIENTS

½ cup mushrooms, chopped
1 lb chorizo, chopped
2 tbsp avocado oil
4 cherry peppers, chopped
1 red bell pepper, seeded, chopped

1 onion, peeled and sliced
2 garlic cloves, minced
2 cups tomatoes, chopped
4 chicken thighs
Salt and black pepper to taste

1 cup chicken stock
1 tsp turmeric
1 tbsp white wine vinegar
1 tsp dried oregano
2 tbsp fresh parsley, chopped

DIRECTIONS

Warm the avocado oil in a pan over medium heat. Stir in the chorizo and cook for 5-6 minutes until browned; remove to a bowl. Place the chicken thighs in the chorizo fat and cook each side for 3 minutes. Season with salt and black pepper and set aside on a bowl.

In the same pan, add the onion, garlic, bell pepper, cherry peppers, and mushrooms and cook for 4 minutes. Pour in the stock, turmeric, tomatoes, vinegar, and oregano. Return the chorizo and chicken and place the pan in the oven. Bake for 30 minutes at 400°F. Garnish with chopped parsley and serve.

Chicken in Creamy Tomato Sauce

Ready in about: 25 minutes | **Serves**: 6 | **Per serving**: Kcal 456, Fat 38.2g, Net Carbs 2g, Protein 24g

INGREDIENTS

3 tbsp butter
6 chicken thighs
Salt and black pepper to taste

14 oz canned tomato sauce
2 tsp Italian seasoning
½ cup heavy cream

1 cup mozzarella cheese, shredded
½ cup Parmesan cheese, grated

DIRECTIONS

In a saucepan, melt the butter over medium heat. Season the chicken with salt and black pepper and brown for 5 minutes on each side. Plate the chicken. Pour the tomato sauce and Italian seasoning in the pan and cook for 8 minutes. Adjust the taste with salt and black pepper.

Stir in the heavy cream and mozzarella cheese. Once the cheese has melted, return the chicken to the pot and simmer for 4 minutes. Remove to a plate, garnish with Parmesan cheese, and serve.

Cheesy Chicken Bake with Zucchini

Ready in about: 40 minutes | **Serves**: 6 | **Per serving**: Kcal: 489, Fat: 37g, Net Carbs: 4.5g, Protein: 21g

INGREDIENTS

2 lb chicken breasts, cubed
3 tbsp butter
1 cup green bell peppers, sliced
1 cup yellow onions, sliced

1 zucchini, cubed
2 garlic cloves, minced
1 tsp dried dill
Salt and black pepper to taste

8 oz cream cheese, softened
½ cup mayonnaise
2 tbsp Worcestershire sauce
2 cups cheddar cheese, shredded

DIRECTIONS

Preheat oven to 370°F. Melt the butter in a pan over medium heat. Add in the chicken and cook until lightly browned, about 5 minutes. Put in onions, zucchini, garlic, and bell peppers and sauté for 5-6 minutes until tender, stirring occasionally. Season with salt, black pepper, and dill, stir, and set aside.

In a bowl, mix cream cheese, mayonnaise, and Worcestershire sauce. Stir in the chicken-vegetable mix. Transfer to a greased baking dish. Sprinkle with the cheddar cheese and bake for 30 minutes. Serve.

Spicy Chicken Kebabs

Ready in about: 20 minutes + marinade time | **Serves**: 6 | **Per serving**: Kcal 198, Fat: 13.5g, Net Carbs: 3.1g, Protein: 17.5g

INGREDIENTS

2 lb chicken breasts, cubed
3 tbsp sesame oil

1 cup red bell peppers, chopped
2 tbsp five-spice powder

2 tbsp granulated sweetener
1 tbsp fish sauce

DIRECTIONS

Combine the sesame oil, fish sauce, five-spice powder, and granulated sweetener in a bowl and mix well. Add in the chicken and toss to coat. Let marinate for 1 hour in the fridge. Preheat the grill. Thread the chicken and bell peppers onto skewers. Grill for 3 minutes per side. Serve warm with steamed broccoli.

Roasted Stuffed Chicken with Tomato Basil Sauce

Ready in about: 35 minutes | **Serves**: 6 | **Per serving**: Kcal 338, Fat: 28g, Net Carbs: 2.5g, Protein: 37g

INGREDIENTS

4 oz cream cheese
3 oz mozzarella slices, sliced
10 oz spinach

⅓ cup shredded mozzarella cheese
2 tbsp olive oil
1 cup tomato-basil sauce

3 whole chicken breasts
Salt and black pepper to taste

DIRECTIONS

Preheat oven to 400°F. Combine the cream cheese, shredded mozzarella, and spinach in a bowl. Microwave for 90 seconds. Cut the chicken a couple of times horizontally and stuff with the mixture.

Brush with olive oil. Place on a lined baking dish and bake in the oven for 25 minutes. Pour the tomato-basil sauce over and top with mozzarella slices. Return to the oven and cook for an additional 5 minutes.

Roasted Chicken Kabobs with Celery Fries

Ready in about: 50 minutes | **Serves**: 4 | **Per serving**: Kcal: 579, Fat: 43g, Net Carbs: 6g, Protein: 39g

INGREDIENTS

1 lb chicken breasts, cubed
4 tbsp olive oil

1 cup chicken broth
1 head celery root, sliced

2 tbsp olive oil
Salt and black pepper to taste

DIRECTIONS

Preheat oven to 400°F. In a bowl, mix 2 tbsp of the olive oil, salt, and pepper. Add in the chicken and toss to coat. Cover with foil and place in the fridge. Arrange the celery slices in a baking tray in an even layer and coat with the remaining olive oil. Season with salt and black pepper and place in the oven.

Bake for 10 minutes. Take out the chicken of the refrigerator and thread it onto skewers. Place over the celery, pour in the chicken broth, and roast in the oven for 30 minutes. Serve warm in plates.

Chicken with Creamed Turnip Greens

Ready in about: 35 minutes | **Serves**: 4 | **Per serving**: Kcal 446, Fat: 38g, Net Carbs: 2.6g, Protein: 18g

INGREDIENTS

1 lb chicken thighs
2 tbsp coconut oil
2 tbsp coconut flour

12 oz turnip greens, chopped
1 tsp oregano
1 cup heavy cream

1 cup chicken broth
2 tbsp butter

DIRECTIONS

Warm the coconut oil in a skillet over medium heat. Brown the chicken on all sides, about 6-8 minutes. Set aside. Add and melt the butter and whisk in the flour. Whisk in heavy cream and chicken broth.

Bring to a boil. Stir in oregano. Add the turnip greens to the skillet and cook until wilted, about 3-4 minutes. Add the thighs in the skillet and cook for an additional 15 minutes. Serve warm.

Chicken Garam Masala

Ready in about: 35 minutes | **Serves**: 4 | **Per serving**: Kcal: 564, Fat: 50g, Net Carbs: 5g, Protein: 33g

INGREDIENTS

1 lb chicken breasts, cut lengthwise
2 tbsp butter
Salt and pepper, to taste

1 tbsp olive oil
1 yellow bell pepper, finely chopped

1 ¼ cups heavy whipping cream
1 tbsp fresh cilantro, finely chopped

Garam masala

1 tsp ground cumin
2 tsp ground coriander
1 tsp ground cardamom

1 tsp turmeric
1 tsp ginger
1 tsp paprika

1 tsp cayenne, ground
1 pinch ground nutmeg

DIRECTIONS

Preheat oven to 400°F. In a bowl, mix the garam masala spices. Coat the chicken with half of the mixture. Heat the olive oil and butter in a frying pan over medium heat. Brown the chicken for 3 minutes per side.

Transfer to a baking dish. To the remaining masala, add heavy cream, bell pepper, salt, and pepper. Pour over the chicken. Bake for 20 minutes until the mixture starts to bubble. Garnish with cilantro to serve.

Lemon Chicken Bake

Ready in about: 55 minutes | **Serves**: 6 | **Per serving**: Kcal 274, Fat 9g, Net Carbs 4.5g, Protein 25g

INGREDIENTS

6 chicken breasts
1 parsnip, cut into wedges

Salt and black pepper to taste
2 lemons, juiced and zested

Lemon rinds from 2 lemons
1 cup chicken stock

DIRECTIONS

In a baking dish, add the chicken alongside pepper and salt. Sprinkle with lemon juice and broth. Toss to coat. Add in parsnip, lemon rinds, and lemon zest and put in the oven. Bake for 45 minutes at 370°F. Get rid of the lemon rinds, split the chicken onto plates, sprinkle sauce from the baking dish over. Serve.

Yummy Chicken Nuggets

Ready in about: 25 minutes | **Serves**: 2 | **Per serving**: Kcal 417, Fat 37g, Net Carbs 4.3g, Protein 35g

INGREDIENTS

½ cup almond flour
1 egg, beaten

½ tsp garlic powder
2 chicken breasts, cut into chunks

Salt and black pepper to taste
½ cup butter

DIRECTIONS

In a bowl, mix salt, garlic powder, flour, and pepper and stir. Dip the chicken chunks in egg, then in the flour mixture. Warm butter in a pan over medium heat. Add in the chicken nuggets and cook for 6 minutes on each side. Remove to paper towels, drain the excess grease, and serve with your favorite dip.

Sticky Cranberry Chicken Wings

Ready in about: 50 minutes | **Serves**: 6 | **Per serving**: Kcal 152, Fat 8.5g, Net Carbs 1.6g, Protein 17.6g

INGREDIENTS

2 lb chicken wings
4 tbsp unsweetened cranberry puree

3 tbsp olive oil
Salt to taste

4 tbsp chili sauce
Lemon juice from 1 lemon

DIRECTIONS

Preheat oven to 400°F. In a bowl, mix cranberry puree, olive oil, salt, chili sauce, and lemon juice. Add in the wings and toss to coat. Place the chicken under the broiler, and cook for 45 minutes, turning once halfway. Remove the chicken after and serve warm with a cranberry dipping sauce.

Grilled Chicken Wings

Ready in about: 15 minutes + chilling time | **Serves**: 4 | **Per serving**: Kcal 216, Fat 11.5g, Net Carbs 4.3g, Protein 18.5g

INGREDIENTS

2 lb chicken wings
Juice from 1 lemon
½ cup fresh parsley, chopped

2 garlic cloves, minced
1 serrano pepper, chopped
3 tbsp olive oil

Salt and black pepper to taste
½ cup ranch dip
1 tsp fresh cilantro, chopped

DIRECTIONS

In a bowl, stir together lemon juice, garlic, salt, serrano pepper, cilantro, olive oil, and black pepper. Place in the chicken wings and toss to coat. Refrigerate for 2 hours. Preheat grill to high heat. Add in the chicken wings. Cook each side for 6 minutes. Remove to a plate and serve with ranch dip.

Lemon & Rosemary Chicken in a Skillet

Ready in about: 20 minutes + marinating time | **Serves**: 4 | **Per serving**: Kcal 477, Fat: 31g, Net Carbs: 2.5g, Protein: 31g

INGREDIENTS

8 chicken thighs
Salt and black pepper to taste

1 lemon, juiced and zested
4 tbsp olive oil

1 tbsp fresh rosemary, chopped
1 garlic clove, minced

DIRECTIONS

Combine 2 tbsp of the olive oil, lemon juice, lemon zest, garlic, rosemary, salt, and pepper in a bowl. Add in the chicken thighs and toss to coat. Place in the fridge to marinate for at least 1 hour.

Heat the remaining olive oil in a skillet over medium heat. Add the chicken along with the juices and cook until crispy, about 4-5 minutes per side. Remove to a plate and serve with green salad

Greek Chicken with Capers

Ready in about: 30 minutes | **Serves**: 4 | **Per serving**: Kcal 387, Fat 21g, Net Carbs 2.2g, Protein 25g

INGREDIENTS

½ cup Kalamata olives, pitted and chopped
¼ cup olive oil
1 onion, chopped
4 chicken breasts

2 garlic cloves, minced
Salt and black pepper to taste
1 tbsp capers

1 lb tomatoes, chopped
½ tsp red chili flakes

DIRECTIONS

Sprinkle black pepper and salt on the chicken and brush with some olive oil. Add it to a pan set over high heat and cook for 2 minutes. Flip to the other side and cook for 2 more minutes. Transfer the chicken breasts to the oven and bake for 8 minutes at 450°F. Split the chicken into serving plates.

Put the same pan over medium heat and warm the remaining oil. Place in the onion, olives, capers, garlic, and chili flakes and cook for 1 minute. Stir in the tomatoes, black pepper, and salt, and cook for 2 minutes. Sprinkle over the chicken breasts and serve.

Stuffed Avocados with Chicken

Ready in about: 10 minutes | **Serves**: 2 | **Per serving**: Kcal 511, Fat 40, Net Carbs 5g, Protein 24g

INGREDIENTS

2 avocados, cut in half and pitted
¼ cup pesto
2 tbsp cream cheese

1 ½ cups chicken, cooked, shredded
¼ tsp cayenne pepper
½ tsp onion powder

½ tsp garlic powder
Salt and black pepper to taste
2 tbsp lemon juice

DIRECTIONS

Scoop the insides of the avocado halves, and place the flesh in a bowl. Add in the chicken and stir in the remaining ingredients. Stuff the avocado cups with chicken mixture and enjoy.

Homemade Chicken Pizza Calzone

Ready in about: 60 minutes | Serves: 4 | Per serving: Kcal 425, Fat 15g, Net Carbs 4.6g, Protein 28g

INGREDIENTS

2 eggs
1 low carb pizza crust
½ cup Pecorino cheese, grated
½ lb chicken breasts, halved

½ cup sugar-free marinara sauce
1 tsp Italian seasoning
1 tsp onion powder
Salt and black pepper to taste

¼ cup flax seed, ground
1 cup provolone cheese, grated

DIRECTIONS

In a bowl, combine the Italian seasoning with onion powder, salt, Pecorino cheese, pepper, and flaxseed. In a separate bowl, beat the eggs with pepper and salt. Dip the chicken pieces in eggs and then in cheese mixture. Lay them on a lined baking sheet and bake for 25 minutes in the oven at 390°F.

Remove the chicken from the oven and leave it to cool slightly before chopping. Place the pizza dough on a lined baking sheet. Spread ½ cup of the provolone cheese on 1 half of the crust, leaving a ⅓ inch edge around the trim. Scatter the chopped chicken over the cheese and top with marinara sauce.

Sprinkle with the remaining cheese. Fold the other half of the dough over the filling. Seal the edges, set in the oven, and bake for 20 minutes. Allow the calzone to cool down before slicing. Serve.

Easy Chicken Meatloaf

Ready in about: 50 minutes | Serves: 6 | Per serving: Kcal 273, Fat 14g, Net Carbs 4g, Protein 28

INGREDIENTS

1 cup sugar-free marinara sauce
2 lb ground chicken

2 garlic cloves, minced
2 tsp onion powder

1 tsp Italian seasoning
Salt and black pepper to taste

Filling

½ cup ricotta cheese
1 cup Grana Padano cheese, grated

1 cup Colby cheese, shredded
2 tsp fresh chives, chopped

2 tbsp fresh parsley, chopped

DIRECTIONS

In a bowl, combine the ground chicken with half of the marinara sauce, pepper, onion powder, Italian seasoning, salt, and garlic. In a separate bowl, mix the ricotta cheese with half of the Grana Padano cheese, chives, pepper, half of the Colby cheese, salt, and parsley.

Place half of the chicken mixture into a loaf pan and spread evenly. Top with the cheese filling. Cover with the rest of the chicken mixture and spread again. Set the meatloaf in the preheated to 380°F oven.

Bake for 25 minutes. Remove meatloaf and spread the rest of the marinara sauce, Grana Padano cheese, and Colby cheese. Bake for 18 minutes. Allow meatloaf cooling and serve in sliced.

Chicken in Creamy Mushroom Sauce

Ready in about: 40 minutes | Serves: 4 | Per serving: Kcal 448, Fat 38.2g, Net Carbs 2g, Protein 22g

INGREDIENTS

2 tbsp ghee
4 chicken breasts, cut into chunks
Salt and black pepper to taste

1 packet white onion soup mix
2 cups chicken broth
15 baby Bella mushrooms, sliced

1 cup heavy cream
2 tbsp fresh parsley, chopped

DIRECTIONS

Melt ghee in a saucepan over medium heat, season the chicken with salt and black pepper, and brown on all sides for 6 minutes in total. Put on a plate. In a bowl, stir the onion soup mix and chicken broth. Add the mixture to the saucepan and simmer for 3 minutes. Add in the mushrooms and chicken. Cover.

Simmer for another 20 minutes. Stir in heavy cream and cook for 3 minutes. Adjust the seasoning. Ladle the chicken with creamy sauce and mushrooms over bed of cauli mash. Garnish with parsley and serve.

Thyme Chicken Thighs

Ready in about: 30 minutes | **Serves**: 4 | **Per serving**: Kcal 528, Fat: 42g, Net Carbs: 4g, Protein: 33g

INGREDIENTS

½ cup chicken stock
2 tbsp olive oil
1 onion, chopped

4 chicken thighs
¼ cup heavy cream
2 tbsp Dijon mustard

1 tsp thyme
1 tsp garlic powder

DIRECTIONS

Heat the olive oil in a pan over medium heat. Cook the chicken for about 4 minutes per side. Set aside. Sauté the onion in the same pan for 3 minutes, add the stock, and simmer for 5 minutes. Stir in mustard, heavy cream, thyme, and garlic powder. Pour the sauce over the chicken and serve.

Lime Chicken Wings

Ready in about: 30 minutes | **Serves**: 4 | **Per serving**: Kcal 365, Fat: 25g, Net Carbs: 4g, Protein: 21g

INGREDIENTS

1 tsp garlic powder
1 lime, zested and juiced
½ tsp ground cilantro

1 tbsp fish sauce
2 tbsp butter
¼ tsp xanthan gum

3 tbsp swerve sweetener
20 chicken wings
Salt and black pepper to taste

DIRECTIONS

Combine lime juice and zest, fish sauce, cilantro, swerve sweetener, garlic powder, and 1 cup of water in a saucepan over medium heat. Bring to a boil. Cover, lower the heat, and let simmer for 10 minutes.

Stir in the butter and xanthan gum. Set aside. Season the wings with salt and pepper. Preheat the grill and cook for 5 minutes per side. Serve topped with the sauce.

One-Pot Chicken with Mushrooms

Ready in about: 35 minutes | **Serves**: 6 | **Per serving**: Kcal 447, Fat: 37g, Net Carbs: 1g, Protein: 31g

INGREDIENTS

2 cups mushrooms, sliced
½ tsp onion powder
½ tsp garlic powder

¼ cup butter
1 tsp Dijon mustard
1 tbsp tarragon, chopped

2 lb chicken thighs
Salt and black pepper to taste

DIRECTIONS

Season the thighs with salt, pepper, garlic and onion powders. Melt the butter in a skillet over medium heat. Cook the chicken until browned; set aside. Add mushrooms to the same fat and cook for 5 minutes.

Stir in Dijon mustard and ½ cup of water. Return the chicken to the skillet. Season with salt and pepper, reduce the heat, and cover with a lid. Let simmer for 15 minutes. Stir in tarragon. Serve warm.

Grilled Paprika Chicken with Steamed Broccoli

Ready in about: 17 minutes | **Serves**: 6 | **Per serving**: Kcal 422, Fat 35.3g, Net Carbs 2g, Protein 26g

INGREDIENTS

1 tsp smoked paprika
Salt and black pepper to taste

1 tsp garlic powder
3 tbsp olive oil

6 chicken breasts
1 head broccoli, cut into florets

DIRECTIONS

Place broccoli florets onto the steamer basket over the boiling water and steam for 8 minutes or until crisp-tender. Set aside. Preheat grill to high and grease the grate with cooking spray

Mix paprika, salt, pepper, and garlic powder in a bowl. Brush chicken with olive oil, sprinkle spice mixture over, and massage with hands. Grill chicken for 7 minutes per side until well-cooked. Serve warm.

Baked Chicken with Parmesan Topping

Ready in about: 45 minutes | Serves: 4 | Per serving: Kcal 361, Fat 15g, Net Carbs 5g, Protein 25g

INGREDIENTS

4 chicken breast halves
Salt and black pepper to taste
¼ cup green chilies, chopped
4 bacon slices, chopped

4 oz cream cheese, softened
1 onion, chopped
½ cup mayonnaise
½ cup Grana Padano cheese, grated

1 cup cheddar cheese, grated
2 oz pork rinds, crushed
2 tbsp olive oil
½ cup Parmesan cheese, shredded

DIRECTIONS

Season the chicken with salt and pepper. Heat the olive oil in a pan over medium heat and fry the chicken for about 4-6 minutes until cooked through with no pink showing. Remove to a baking dish.

In the same pan, fry bacon until crispy and remove to a plate. Sauté the onion in the same fat for 3 minutes until soft. Remove from heat, add in the fried bacon, cream cheese, 1 cup of water, Grana Padano cheese, mayonnaise, chilies, and cheddar cheese and spread over the chicken.

Bake in the oven for 10-15 minutes at 370°F. Remove and sprinkle with mixed Parmesan cheese and pork rinds and return to the oven. Bake for another 10-15 minutes until the cheese melts. Serve immediately.

Chicken with Baked Cheese Slices

Ready in about: 30 minutes | Serves: 4 | Per serving: Kcal 445, Fat 34g, Net Carbs 4g, Protein 39g

INGREDIENTS

2 tbsp butter
1 tsp garlic, minced
1 lb chicken breasts
1 tsp creole seasoning
¼ cup scallions, chopped

½ cup tomatoes, chopped
½ cup chicken stock
¼ cup whipping cream
½ cup Monterey Jack cheese, grated
¼ cup fresh cilantro, chopped

Salt and black pepper to taste
4 oz cream cheese, softened
8 eggs
1 tsp garlic powder

DIRECTIONS

Set a pan over medium heat and warm 1 tbsp butter. Add chicken, sprinkle with creole seasoning, and cook each side for 2 minutes; remove to a plate. Melt the rest of the butter, stir in garlic and tomatoes, and cook for 4 minutes. Return the chicken to the pan and pour in the stock. Simmer for 15 minutes. Place in the whipping cream, scallions, salt, Monterey Jack cheese, and pepper and cook for 2 minutes.

In a blender, combine the cream cheese with garlic powder, salt, eggs, and pepper and pulse until smooth. Spread the mixture on a lined baking sheet and bake in the oven for 10 minutes at 325°F. Allow the cheese sheet to cool down, place on a cutting board, roll, and cut into medium slices. Split them among bowls and top with chicken mixture. Sprinkle with chopped cilantro and serve.

Chicken Goujons with Tomato Sauce

Ready in about: 50 minutes | Serves: 6 | Per serving: Kcal 415, Fat 36g, Net Carbs 5g, Protein 28g

INGREDIENTS

1 ½ lb chicken breasts, cubed
Salt and black pepper to taste
1 egg, beaten in a bowl
1 cup almond flour

¼ cup Parmesan cheese, grated
½ tsp garlic powder
½ tsp dried parsley
½ tsp dried basil

4 tbsp avocado oil
4 cups butternut squash spirals
6 oz Gruyere cheese, shredded
1½ cups tomato sauce

DIRECTIONS

In a bowl, combine the almond flour, Parmesan cheese, pepper, and garlic powder. Dip the chicken in the egg first, and then in the almond flour mixture. Set a pan over medium heat and warm 3 tablespoons avocado oil. Add in the chicken and cook until golden, about 5-6 minutes. Remove to paper towels.

In a bowl, combine the butternut squash spirals with salt, dried basil, remaining avocado oil, and black pepper. Transfer to a baking dish and top with the chicken pieces, followed by the tomato sauce. Scatter shredded Gruyere cheese on top and bake for 30 minutes at 360°F. Remove and serve.

Chicken Paella with Chorizo

Ready in about: 65 minutes | **Serves**: 6 | **Per serving**: Kcal 440, Fat 28g, Net Carbs 3g, Protein 22g

INGREDIENTS

2 lb chicken drumsticks
12 oz chorizo, chopped
1 onion, chopped
4 oz jarred piquillo peppers, diced
2 tbsp olive oil

½ cup chopped parsley
1 tsp smoked paprika
2 tbsp tomato puree
½ cup white wine
1 cup chicken broth

4 cups cauli rice
1 cup green beans, chopped
1 lemon, cut in wedges
Salt and black pepper to taste

DIRECTIONS

Preheat oven to 350°F. Heat the olive oil in a pan over medium heat. Season the chicken with salt and pepper and fry on both sides for 8-10 minutes until lightly brown. Remove to a plate. Add the chorizo and onion to the hot oil and sauté for 4 minutes. Include in tomato puree, piquillo peppers, and paprika.

Let simmer for 2 minutes. Add in the broth and cook for 6 minutes until it is slightly reduced. Stir in cauli rice, white wine, green beans, and parsley, and lay the chicken on top. Transfer the pan to the oven and bake for 20-25 minutes. Let the paella to sit for 10 minutes. Arrange the lemon wedges on top and serve.

Fried Chicken Breasts

Ready in about: 20 minutes + marinating time| **Serves**: 4 | **Per serving**: Kcal 387, Fat 16g, Net Carbs 2.5g, Protein 23g

INGREDIENTS

2 chicken breasts, cut into strips
1 cup pork rinds, crushed

4 tbsp coconut oil
16 oz jarred pickle juice

2 eggs, whisked

DIRECTIONS

In a bowl, combine chicken with pickle juice. Refrigerate for 2 hours. Set the eggs in one bowl and pork rinds in a separate one. Dip the chicken in the eggs and then in pork rinds. Put a pan over medium heat and warm oil. Fry the chicken for 3 minutes per side and remove to a plate. Serve.

Chicken Breasts with Walnut Crust

Ready in about: 30 minutes | **Serves**: 4 | **Per serving**: Kcal 322, Fat 18g, Net Carbs 1.5g, Protein 35g

INGREDIENTS

1 egg, whisked
Salt and black pepper to taste

2 tbsp coconut oil
1 ½ cups walnuts, ground

1 lb chicken breast halves
1 lemon, sliced

DIRECTIONS

Season the chicken with salt and pepper. Dip in the egg first and then in walnuts. Warm the coconut oil in a pan over medium heat and brown the chicken for 5-6 minutes in total. Remove to a baking sheet, set in the oven, and bake for 10 minutes at 350° F. Serve topped with lemon slices.

Ranch Chicken Meatballs

Ready in about: 25 minutes | **Serves**: 4 | **Per serving**: Kcal 456, Fat 31g, Net Carbs 2.1g, Protein 32g

INGREDIENTS

1 lb ground chicken
Salt and black pepper to taste
2 tbsp ranch dressing

½ cup almond flour
¼ cup mozzarella cheese, grated
1 tbsp Italian seasoning

¼ cup hot sauce
1 egg

DIRECTIONS

In a bowl, combine chicken, pepper, ranch dressing, Italian seasoning, almond flour, mozzarella cheese, salt, and egg and mix well. Form into golf ball-sized meatballs. Arrange them on a lined baking tray and bake in the oven for 16 minutes at 480°F. Remove to a bowl and serve with hot sauce.

Chicken with Anchovy Tapenade

Ready in about: 30 minutes | Serves: 2 | Per serving: Kcal 155, Fat 13g, Net Carbs 3g, Protein 25g

INGREDIENTS

1 chicken breast, cut into 4 pieces

Anchovy tapenade

½ cup black olives, pitted
1 oz anchovy fillets, rinsed

1 tbsp coconut oil

1 garlic clove, crushed
Salt and black pepper to taste

2 garlic cloves, crushed

1 tbsp olive oil
1 tbsp lemon juice

DIRECTIONS

Blend the tapenade ingredients in a food processor until smooth and set aside. Warm the coconut oil in a pan over medium heat. Stir in the garlic and sauté for 1 minute. Add in the chicken pieces and cook each side for 4 minutes. Top the chicken with the anchovy tapenade and serve.

Cheddar Chicken Tenders

Ready in about: 35 minutes | Serves: 4 | Per serving: Kcal 507, Fat 54g, Net Carbs 1.3g, Protein 42g

INGREDIENTS

2 eggs
2 tbsp butter, melted

3 cups cheddar cheese, crushed
½ cup pork rinds, crushed

1 lb chicken tenders
Pink salt to taste

DIRECTIONS

Preheat oven to 350°F. Line a baking sheet with parchment paper. Whisk the eggs with butter in a bowl. Mix the cheese and pork rinds in another bowl. Season the chicken with salt. Dip it in the egg mixture.

Coat with the cheddar mixture. Place on the baking sheet, cover with aluminium foil, and bake for 15 minutes. Remove foil and bake for 10 more minutes until golden brown. Serve chicken with mustard dip.

Chicken & Green Cabbage Casserole

Ready in about: 50 minutes | Serves: 4 | Per serving: Kcal 231, Fat 15g, Net Carbs 6g, Protein 25g

INGREDIENTS

3 cups cheddar cheese, grated
10 oz green cabbage, shredded
1 lb chicken breasts, cubed

1 cup mayonnaise
1 tbsp coconut oil, melted
1 cup chicken stock

Salt and black pepper to taste
Juice of 1 lemon

DIRECTIONS

Apply oil to a baking dish and set the chicken pieces to the bottom. Spread green cabbage, followed by half of the cheddar cheese. In a bowl, combine the mayonnaise with pepper, stock, lemon juice, and salt.

Pour the mixture over the chicken, spread the rest of the cheese, and cover with aluminum foil. Bake for 30 minutes in the oven at 350°F. Open the aluminum foil and cook for 10 more minutes. Serve.

Habanero Chicken Wings

Ready in about: 40 minutes | Serves: 4 | Per serving: Kcal 416, Fat 25g, Net Carbs 2g, Protein 26g

INGREDIENTS

2 lb chicken wings
Salt and black pepper to taste
3 tbsp coconut aminos

3 tbsp rice vinegar
1 tbsp stevia
¼ cup chives, chopped

½ tsp xanthan gum
2 dried habanero peppers, chopped

DIRECTIONS

Spread the chicken wings on a lined baking sheet and sprinkle with 2 tbsp water, pepper and salt. Bake in the oven for 30 minutes at 370°F. Put a pan over medium heat and add in the remaining ingredients. Bring to a boil and cook for 2 minutes. Pour the sauce over the chicken and bake for 10 minutes. Serve.

Bacon & Cheese Chicken

Ready in about: 30 minutes | **Serves:** 4 | **Per serving:** Kcal 423, Fat 21g, Net Carbs 3.3g, Protein 34g

INGREDIENTS

4 bacon strips
4 chicken breasts

2 tbsp avocado jalapeño sauce
1 oz coconut aminos

2 tbsp coconut oil
4 oz Monterey Jack cheese, grated

DIRECTIONS

Heat a pan over medium heat and add in the bacon. Cook for 5 minutes until crispy. Remove to paper towels, drain the grease, and crumble. To the pan, add and warm the coconut oil. Place in the chicken breasts, cook for 4 minutes, flip, and cook for an additional 4 minutes. Transfer to a baking dish.

Top with the coconut aminos, Monterey Jack cheese, and crumbled bacon. Insert in the oven, turn on the broiler, and cook for 5 minutes. Serve topped with avocado jalapeño sauce.

Chicken Gumbo

Ready in about: 40 minutes | **Serves:** 4 | **Per serving:** Kcal 361, Fat 22g, Net Carbs 6g, Protein 26g

INGREDIENTS

2 sausages, sliced
2 chicken breasts, cubed
1 celery stalk, chopped
½ tsp dried oregano
2 bell peppers, seeded and chopped

1 onion, chopped
2 cups tomatoes, chopped
4 cups chicken broth
½ tsp dried thyme
2 garlic cloves, minced

1 tsp dry mustard
1 tsp cayenne pepper
Salt and black pepper to taste
½ tsp cajun seasoning
2 tbsp olive oil

DIRECTIONS

In a pot over medium heat, warm the olive oil. Add the sausages and chicken and cook for 5-6 minutes; set aside. Add the onion, garlic, celery, and bell peppers and sauté for 5 minutes. Stir in dry mustard, oregano, thyme, cayenne pepper, and cajun seasoning for 1 minute. Pour in the broth and tomatoes.

Cook for 10 minutes. Return the sausages and chicken, adjust the seasoning with salt and pepper and bring to a boil. Reduce the heat and simmer for 20 minutes covered. Serve hot divided between bowls.

Chicken Breasts with Cheddar & Pepperoni

Ready in about: 40 minutes | **Serves:** 4 | **Per serving:** Kcal 387, Fat 21g, Net Carbs 4.5g, Protein 32g

INGREDIENTS

12 oz canned tomato sauce
2 tbsp olive oil
4 chicken breast halves

Salt and black pepper to taste
½ tsp dried oregano
4 oz cheddar cheese, sliced

1 tsp garlic powder
2 oz pepperoni, sliced

DIRECTIONS

Preheat oven to 390°F. In a bowl, mix chicken with oregano, salt, garlic, and pepper. Heat the olive oil in a pan over medium heat. Add in the chicken and cook each side for 2 minutes. Remove to a baking dish. Top with the cheddar cheese, spread the sauce, and cover with pepperoni slices. Bake for 30 minutes.

Roasted Chicken with Tarragon

Ready in about: 50 minutes | **Serves:** 4 | **Per serving:** Kcal: 415, Fat: 23g, Net Carbs: 5.5g, Protein: 42g

INGREDIENTS

1 lb chicken thighs
1 lb radishes, sliced

2 oz butter, sliced
1 tbsp tarragon

Salt and black pepper to taste
1 cup mayonnaise

DIRECTIONS

Preheat oven to 400°F. Place the chicken on a greased baking dish. Add in radishes and season with tarragon, pepper, and salt. Top with butter and bake in the oven for 40 minutes. Serve with mayonnaise.

Baked Chicken with Acorn Squash & Goat's Cheese

Ready in about: 60 minutes | **Serves**: 6 | **Per serving**: Kcal 235, Fat 16g, Net Carbs 5g, Protein 12g

INGREDIENTS

6 chicken breasts, butterflied
1 lb acorn squash, cubed

Salt and black pepper to taste
1 cup goat's cheese, crumbled

½ tsp dried parsley
3 tbsp olive oil

DIRECTIONS

Arrange the chicken breasts and squash in a baking dish. Season with salt, black pepper, and parsley. Drizzle with olive oil and pour a cup of water. Cover with aluminium foil and bake in the oven for 30 minutes at 420°F. Discard the foil, scatter goat's cheese, and bake for 15-20 minutes. Serve and enjoy!

Quattro Formaggi Stuffed Chicken Breasts

Ready in about: 40 minutes | **Serves**: 6 | **Per serving**: Kcal 565, Fat 37g, Net Carbs 2g, Protein 51g

INGREDIENTS

2 lb chicken breasts
2 oz mozzarella cheese, cubed
2 oz mascarpone cheese, softened

4 oz cheddar cheese, cubed
2 oz provolone cheese, cubed
1 zucchini, shredded

Salt and black pepper to taste
1 garlic clove, minced
2 oz smoked bacon slices, chopped

DIRECTIONS

Sprinkle black pepper and salt to the zucchini, squeeze well, and place in a bowl. Stir in the smoked bacon, mascarpone, cheddar cheese, provolone cheese, mozzarella cheese, black pepper, and garlic.

Cut slits into chicken breasts, apply black pepper and salt, and stuff with the zucchini and cheese mixture. Set on a lined baking sheet, place in the oven at 400°F, and bake for 45 minutes. Serve

Pancetta & Chicken Casserole

Ready in about: 40 minutes | **Serves**: 4 | **Per serving**: Kcal 313, Fat 18g, Net Carbs 3g, Protein 26g

INGREDIENTS

8 pancetta strips, chopped
⅓ cup Dijon mustard
Salt and black pepper to taste

1 onion, chopped
2 tbsp olive oil
1 ½ cups chicken stock

1 lb chicken breasts
¼ tsp sweet paprika

DIRECTIONS

In a bowl, combine paprika, salt, pepper, and mustard. Massage the chicken with the mixture. Set a pan over medium heat, stir in the pancetta, and cook until it browns, about 5 minutes. Remove to a plate. Place oil in the same pan and add the chicken breasts. Cook each side for 2 minutes and set aside.

Pour the stock in the pan and bring to a simmer. Stir in black pepper, pancetta, salt, and onion. Return the chicken to the pan, stir gently, and simmer for 20 minutes over medium heat, turning the meat halfway through. Split the chicken on serving plates, sprinkle the sauce over it, and serve.

Chicken & Bacon Rolls

Ready in about: 45 minutes | **Serves**: 4 | **Per serving**: Kcal 623, Fat 48g, Net Carbs 5g, Protein 38g

INGREDIENTS

1 tbsp fresh chives, chopped
8 oz blue cheese, crumbled

1 lb chicken breasts, halved
12 bacon slices

2 tomatoes, chopped
Salt and black pepper to taste

DIRECTIONS

Set a pan over medium heat. Add in the bacon and cook until halfway done; remove to a plate. In a bowl, stir blue cheese, chives, tomatoes, pepper, and salt. Use a meat tenderizer to flatten the chicken breasts, season, and lay blue cheese mixture on top. Roll them up and wrap in bacon slices. Place the wrapped chicken breasts in a greased baking dish and roast in the oven for 30 minutes at 370°F. Serve warm.

Pacific Chicken

Ready in about: 50 minutes | **Serves**: 6 | **Per serving**: Kcal: 465, Fat: 31g, Net Carbs: 2.6g, Protein: 33g

INGREDIENTS

4 chicken breasts
Salt and black pepper to taste
½ cup mayonnaise
1 tbsp Dijon mustard

1 tsp xylitol
¾ cup pork rinds, crushed
¾ cup Grana Padano cheese, grated
1 tsp garlic powder

1 tsp onion powder
Salt and black pepper to taste
8 pieces ham, sliced
4 Gruyere cheese slices

DIRECTIONS

Set oven to 350°F. In a bowl, mix mustard, mayonnaise, and xylitol. Rub the mixture onto the chicken. In another bowl, combine the pork rinds, garlic and onion powders, salt, pepper, and Grana Padano cheese.

Pour half of the mixture in a greased baking dish. Add the chicken to the top. Cover with the remaining pork rind mixture. Roast for 40 minutes until the chicken is cooked thoroughly. Take out from the oven and top with Gruyere cheese and ham. Place back in the oven and cook until golden brown. Serve warm.

Slow Cooker Chicken Stroganoff

Ready in about: 4 hours 15 minutes | **Serves**: 4 | **Per serving**: Kcal 365, Fat 22g, Net Carbs 4g, Protein 26g

INGREDIENTS

2 garlic cloves, minced
8 oz mushrooms, chopped
¼ tsp celery seeds, ground
1 cup chicken stock

1 cup sour cream
1 cup leeks, chopped
1 lb chicken breasts
½ tsp dried thyme

2 tbsp fresh parsley, chopped
Salt and black pepper to taste
4 zucchinis, spiralized
2 tbsp olive oil

DIRECTIONS

Place the chicken in the slow cooker. Season with salt and pepper and add in the leeks, sour cream, parsley, celery seeds, garlic, mushrooms, stock, and thyme. Cover and cook on high for 4 hours on High.

Heat the olive oil in a pan over medium heat. Add in the zucchini pasta and cook for 1-2 minutes until tender. Divide the zucchini between serving plates, top with the chicken mixture, and serve.

Chicken with Asparagus & Root Vegetables

Ready in about: 35 minutes | **Serves**: 4 | **Per serving**: Kcal 497, Fat 31g, Net Carbs 7.4g, Protein 37g

INGREDIENTS

2 cups whipping cream
1 lb chicken breasts, chopped
3 tbsp butter
1 onion, chopped

1 carrot, chopped
4 cups chicken stock
Salt and black pepper to taste
1 bay leaf

1 turnip, chopped
1 parsnip, chopped
17 oz asparagus, trimmed
2 tsp fresh thyme, chopped

DIRECTIONS

Put a pan over medium heat and warm butter. Sauté the onion, carrot, turnip, parsnip, and chicken for 5-6 minutes. Pour in the chicken stock and bay leaf. Bring to a boil and simmer for 20 minutes.

Add in the asparagus and cook for 7 minutes. Discard the bay leaf. Stir in the whipping cream and adjust the seasoning with salt and pepper. Scatter with fresh thyme and serve.

One-Pot Chicken with Mushrooms & Spinach

Ready in about: 40 minutes | **Serves**: 4 | **Per serving**: Kcal 453, Fat 23g, Net Carbs 1g, Protein 32g

INGREDIENTS

1 lb chicken thighs
1 cup mushrooms, sliced
2 cups spinach, chopped

¼ cup butter
Salt and black pepper to taste
½ tsp onion powder

½ tsp garlic powder
1 tsp Dijon mustard
1 tbsp fresh tarragon, chopped

DIRECTIONS

Melt the butter a pan over medium heat. Add in the thighs, onion powder, pepper, garlic powder, and salt. Cook each side for 3 minutes. Set aside. To the same pan, add the mushrooms and cook for 5 minutes. Place in ½ cup water and mustard, take the chicken pieces back to the pan, and cook for 15 minutes while covered. Stir in the tarragon and spinach and cook for 5 minutes. Serve warm.

Chicken Stew with Sun-Dried Tomatoes

Ready in about: 60 minutes | **Serves**: 4 | **Per serving**: Kcal 224, Fat 11g, Net Carbs 6g, Protein 23g

INGREDIENTS

1 carrot, chopped
2 tbsp olive oil
1 celery stalk, chopped
2 cups chicken stock
1 shallot, chopped

1 lb chicken thighs
2 garlic cloves, minced
½ tsp dried rosemary
2 oz sun-dried tomatoes, chopped
1 cup spinach

¼ tsp dried thyme
½ cup heavy cream
Salt and black pepper to taste
A pinch of xanthan gum

DIRECTIONS

In a pot, heat the olive oil over medium heat and add garlic, carrot, celery, and shallot. Season with salt and pepper and sauté for 5-6 minutes until tender. Stir in the chicken and cook for 5 minutes.

Pour in the stock, tomatoes, rosemary, and thyme and simmer for 30 minutes covered. Stir in xanthan gum, cream, and spinach and cook for 5 minutes. Adjust the seasonings. Serve the stew into bowls.

Coconut Chicken Soup

Ready in about: 30 minutes | **Serves**: 4 | **Per serving**: Kcal 387, Fat 23g, Net Carbs 5g, Protein 31g

INGREDIENTS

2 tbsp coconut oil
1-inch piece peeled ginger, grated
2 chicken breasts, diced
4 cups chicken stock

½ cup coconut cream
¼ cup celery, chopped
1 cup mushrooms, sliced
1 tbsp lime juice

½ tsp red pepper flakes
2 tbsp fresh cilantro, chopped
2 tbsp fish sauce
Salt and black pepper to taste

DIRECTIONS

Warm the coconut oil in a large saucepan over medium heat. Add in the chicken, ginger, mushrooms, and celery and sauté for 3-4 minutes, stirring occasionally. Pour in the chicken stock, fish sauce, lime juice, and pepper flakes and bring to a boil. Reduce the heat and simmer for 18-20 minutes.

Whisk in the coconut cream and season with salt and pepper. Continue cooking for about 5 minutes. Garnish with cilantro, spoon onto soup bowls, and serve.

Kale & Ricotta Stuffed Chicken Breasts

Ready in about: 25 minutes | **Serves**: 4 | **Per serving**: Kcal 305, Fat 12g, Net Carbs 4g, Protein 23g

INGREDIENTS

10 oz kale, trimmed and chopped
4 chicken breasts
Salt and black pepper to taste

4 oz cream cheese, softened
½ cup ricotta cheese, crumbled
1 garlic clove, minced

2 tbsp avocado oil
½ cup white wine
2 tbsp butter

DIRECTIONS

Warm avocado oil in a pan over medium heat. Add in kale, garlic, salt, and pepper and sauté for 5 minutes until wilted. Remove to a bowl and let it cool. Add in the ricotta cheese and cream cheese and stir well. Put the chicken breasts on a working surface, cut a pocket in each one, and stuff them with the mixture.

Melt the butter in the pan over medium heat and add the stuffed chicken. Cook each side for 5 minutes. Transfer to a baking tray, drizzle with white wine and 2 tablespoons of water, and place in the preheated to 420°F oven. Bake for 10 minutes. Remove and arrange on a serving plate. Serve sliced.

Chicken & Zucchini Bake

Ready in about: 45 minutes | **Serves:** 4 | **Per serving:** Kcal 235, Fat 11g, Net Carbs 2g, Protein 35g

INGREDIENTS

1 zucchini, chopped
Salt and black pepper to taste
1 tsp garlic powder

2 tbsp avocado oil
1 lb chicken breasts, sliced
1 tomato, cored and chopped

½ tsp dried oregano
½ tsp dried basil
½ cup mozzarella cheese, shredded

DIRECTIONS

Apply pepper, garlic powder, and salt to the chicken. Set a pan over medium heat and warm avocado oil. Add in the chicken slices and cook until golden, 5 minutes. Remove to a baking dish. To the same pan, add zucchini, tomato, pepper, basil, oregano, and salt and cook for 2 minutes. Spread over the chicken.

Bake in the oven for 20 minutes at 330°F. Sprinkle the mozzarella over the chicken, return to the oven, and bake for 5 minutes until the cheese is melted and bubbling. Serve with green salad.

Almond-Crusted Chicken Breasts

Ready in about: 60 minutes | **Serves:** 4 | **Per serving:** Kcal 485, Fat 32g, Net Carbs 1g, Protein 41g

INGREDIENTS

4 bacon slices, cooked and crumbled
4 chicken breasts
1 tbsp water

½ cup olive oil
1 egg, whisked
Salt and black pepper to taste

1 cup asiago cheese, shredded
¼ tsp garlic powder
1 cup ground almonds

DIRECTIONS

In a bowl, combine almonds with pepper, salt, and garlic. Place egg in a separate bowl and mix with the water. Season with pepper and salt. Dip each piece into the egg and then into the almond mixture.

Warm oil a pan and cook the chicken breasts until golden-brown. Remove to a baking pan. Bake in the oven for 20 minutes at 360°F. Scatter with cheese and bacon and roast for 5-10 minutes. Serve warm

Chicken Thighs with Broccoli & Green Onions

Ready in about: 25 minutes | **Serves:** 2 | **Per serving:** Kcal 387, Fat 23g, Net Carbs 5g, Protein 27g

INGREDIENTS

2 boneless chicken thighs, cut into strips
1 tbsp olive oil
1 tsp red pepper flakes
½ tsp onion powder

½ tbsp fresh ginger, grated
¼ cup tamari sauce
½ tsp garlic powder

½ tsp xanthan gum
½ cup green onions, chopped
1 small head broccoli, cut into florets

DIRECTIONS

Warm the oil in a pan over medium heat. Add in chicken, green onions, and ginger and sauté for 4 minutes. Stir in the onion powder, pepper flakes, garlic powder, xanthan gum, and erythritol for 1 minute. Pour in 1 cup water and tamari sauce. Simmer for 15 minutes. Add in broccoli. Cook for 6 minutes. Serve.

Baked Pecorino Toscano Chicken

Ready in about: 50 minutes | **Serves:** 4 | **Per serving:** Kcal 346, Fat 24g, Net Carbs 6g, Protein 20g

INGREDIENTS

4 chicken breasts, halved
½ cup mayonnaise

½ cup buttermilk
Salt and black pepper to taste

¾ cup Pecorino cheese, grated
8 mozzarella cheese slices

DIRECTIONS

Place the chicken in a greased baking dish. In a bowl, mix mayonnaise, buttermilk, cheese, salt, and pepper. Spread half of the mixture over the chicken. Arrange the mozzarella slices over, and finish with a layer of the remaining mixture. Pour in ½ cup of water. Bake in the oven for 35-40 minutes at 370°F.

Chicken with Green Sauce

Ready in about: 35 minutes | Serves: 4 | Per serving: Kcal 236, Fat 9g, Net Carbs 2.3g, Protein 18g

INGREDIENTS

2 tbsp butter
4 scallions, chopped

4 chicken breasts
Salt and black pepper to taste

6 oz sour cream
2 tbsp fresh dill, chopped

DIRECTIONS

Melt butter in a pan with the butter over medium heat. Add in the chicken, season with pepper and salt, and fry for 2-3 per side until golden. Transfer to a baking dish. Cook in the oven for 15 minutes at 390°F.

To the pan, add scallions and cook for 2 minutes. Pour in the sour cream, warm through without boil. Slice the chicken and place on a platter with green sauce spooned over. Top with fresh dill and serve..

Paprika Chicken with Cream Sauce

Ready in about: 50 minutes | Serves: 4 | Per serving: Kcal 381, Fat 33g, Net Carbs 2.6g, Protein 31.3g

INGREDIENTS

1 lb chicken thighs
Salt and black pepper to taste

1 tsp onion powder
¼ cup heavy cream

2 tbsp butter
2 tbsp sweet paprika

DIRECTIONS

In a bowl, combine paprika with onion powder, pepper, and salt. Rub the chicken with the mixture and lay on a lined baking sheet. Bake for 40 minutes in the oven at 400°F. Set aside. Add the cooking juices to a skillet over medium heat, and mix with the heavy cream and butter. Cook for 5-6 minutes until the sauce is thickened. Sprinkle the sauce over the chicken and serve.

Stuffed Mushrooms with Chicken

Ready in about: 40 minutes | Serves: 4 | Per serving: Kcal 261, Fat 16g, Net Carbs 6g, Protein 14g

INGREDIENTS

8 portobello mushrooms, stems removed
3 cups cauliflower florets
Salt and black pepper to taste

1 onion, chopped
1 lb ground chicken

2 tbsp butter
½ cup vegetable broth

DIRECTIONS

In a food processor, add the cauliflower florets, pepper, and salt and blend until it has rice texture. Transfer to a plate. Warm the butter in a pan over medium heat. Stir in onion and cook for 3 minutes.

Add in the cauliflower rice and ground chicken and cook for 5 minutes. Stir in the broth, salt, and pepper and cook for further 2 minutes. Arrange the mushrooms on a lined baking sheet, stuff each one with chicken mixture, put in the oven, and bake for 30 minutes at 350°F. Place on serving plates and enjoy!

Roasted Chicken with Herbs

Ready in about: 50 minutes | Serves: 6 | Per serving: Kcal 367, Fat 15g, Net Carbs 1.1g, Protein 33g

INGREDIENTS

1 (4-pound) whole chicken
½ tsp onion powder
Salt and black pepper to taste

2 tbsp olive oil
1 tsp dry thyme
1 tsp dry rosemary

1 ½ cups chicken broth
2 tsp guar gum
2 tbsp fresh parsley, chopped

DIRECTIONS

Rub chicken with oil, salt, rosemary, thyme, pepper, and onion powder. Place it in a baking dish and pour in the stock. Bake for 40 minutes at 380°F. Remove the chicken to a platter. Add the guar gum and 1 cup water in a pan over medium heat. Cook for 2-3 minutes until thickened. Season with salt and black pepper and stir in the parsley. Carve the chicken and top with the sauce to serve.

Roast Chicken with Herb Stuffing

Ready in about: 120 minutes | **Serves**: 6 | **Per serving**: Kcal 432, Fat: 32g, Net Carbs: 5.1g, Protein: 30g

INGREDIENTS

5-pound whole chicken
1 tbsp fresh oregano, chopped
1 tbsp fresh thyme, chopped

Salt and black pepper to taste
1 tbsp fresh parsley, chopped
2 tbsp olive oil

2 lb Brussels sprouts
1 lemon, cut into wedges
4 tbsp butter, softened

DIRECTIONS

Preheat oven to 420°F. Season the chicken with salt and pepper and brush with some butter. Stuff it with oregano, thyme, and lemon. Place ina greased baking dish, pour in 1 cup water, and roast for 15 minutes. Reduce the heat to 325°F, spread the remaining butter all over, and bake for 40 more minutes.

Warm the olive oil in a pan over medium heat and add the Brussels sprouts. Season with salt and pepper and sauté for 8-10 minutes until tender. Sprinkle with parsley. Remove the chicken from the oven and let sit for 10 minutes. Carve and place on a serving platter. Serve with Brussels sprouts.

Chicken Breasts with Spinach & Artichoke

Ready in about: 40 minutes | **Serves**: 4 | **Per serving**: Kcal 431, Fat 21g, Net Carbs 3.5g, Protein 36g

INGREDIENTS

4 oz cream cheese, softened
4 chicken breasts
8 oz canned artichoke hearts

1 cup spinach
½ cup Pecorino cheese, grated
½ tsp onion powder

½ tbsp garlic powder
Salt and black pepper to taste
4 oz Monterrey Jack cheese, grated

DIRECTIONS

Lay the chicken breasts on a lined baking sheet, season with pepper and salt, and set in the preheated oven at 350°F. Bake for 25 minutes. Chop the artichoke hearts and place them in a bowl. Add in onion powder, Pecorino cheese, salt, spinach, cream cheese, garlic powder, and pepper and toss to combine.

Remove the chicken from the oven and cut each piece in half lengthwise. Divide the artichokes mixture on top, sprinkle with Monterrey cheese, and return in the oven. Bake for 10 minutes. Serve warm.

Zesty Grilled Chicken

Ready in about: 20 minutes + marinating time | **Serves**: 6 | **Per serving**: Kcal 375, Fat 12g, Net Carbs 3g, Protein 42g

INGREDIENTS

2 lb chicken thighs and drumsticks
1 tbsp coconut aminos
1 tbsp apple cider vinegar

A pinch of red pepper flakes
Salt and black pepper to taste
½ tsp ground ginger

3 tbsp butter
1 garlic clove, minced
1 tsp lime zest

DIRECTIONS

In a blender, combine the butter, ½ cup water, salt, ginger, vinegar, garlic, pepper, lime zest, aminos, and pepper flakes and pulse until smooth. Transfer to a bowl and stir in the chicken. Refrigerate for 1 hour.

Set the chicken pieces skin side down on a preheated grill pan over medium heat. Cook for 5 minutes, turn, and cook for 5 more minutes. Split among serving plates and enjoy!

Turkey Enchilada Bowl

Ready in about: 30 minutes | **Serves**: 4 | **Per serving**: Kcal: 568, Fat: 40.2g, Net Carbs: 5.9g, Protein: 38g

INGREDIENTS

1 lb boneless, skinless turkey thighs, cut into pieces
2 tbsp coconut oil
¾ cup red enchilada sauce
1 onion, chopped

3 oz canned diced green chiles
1 avocado, diced
1 cup mozzarella cheese, shredded

¼ cup pickled jalapeños, chopped
½ cup sour cream
1 tomato, diced

DIRECTIONS

Warm the coconut oil in a large pan over medium heat. Add in the turkey and cook until browned on the outside, about 5-6 minutes. Stir in onion, chiles, ¼ cup water, and enchilada sauce. Cover with a lid.

Allow simmering for 20 minutes until the turkey is cooked through. Spoon the turkey onto a serving bowl and top with the sauce, mozzarella cheese, sour cream, tomato, and avocado. Serve.

Red Wine Chicken

Ready in about: 40 minutes | **Serves**: 4 | **Per serving**: Kcal 314, Fat 12g, Net Carbs 4g, Protein 27g

INGREDIENTS

2 tbsp butter
1 lb chicken breasts, halved
2 garlic cloves, minced

Salt and black pepper to taste
1 cup chicken stock
1 tbsp stevia

½ cup red wine
2 tomatoes, sliced
6 mozzarella cheese slices

DIRECTIONS

Set a pan over medium heat and warm butter. Add the chicken, season with pepper and salt, and cook until brown, 5-6 minutes. Stir in the stevia, garlic, chicken stock, and red wine and cook for 10 minutes.

Remove to a lined baking sheet and arrange mozzarella cheese slices on top. Bake in the preheated to 370°F oven for 20 minutes until the cheese melts. Lay tomato slices over chicken pieces and serve.

Turkey & Bell Pepper One-Pan

Ready in about: 25 minutes | **Serves**: 4 | **Per serving**: Kcal 448, Fat 32g, Net Carbs 5g, Protein 45g

INGREDIENTS

1 lb turkey breast, skinless, boneless
1 tsp garlic powder
1 tsp chili powder
1 tsp cumin
2 tbsp lime juice

Salt and black pepper to taste
1 tsp sweet paprika
2 tbsp coconut oil
1 tsp ground coriander
1 green bell pepper, seeded, sliced

1 red bell pepper, seeded, sliced
1 onion, sliced
1 tbsp fresh cilantro, chopped
1 avocado, sliced
2 limes, cut into wedges

DIRECTIONS

In a bowl, mix the lime juice, cumin, garlic powder, coriander, paprika, salt, chili powder, and black pepper. Slice the turkey into strips and add them to the bowl. Toss to coat and let sit for 10 minutes.

Warm the coconut oil in a pan over medium heat. Add the turkey and cook each side for 3-5 minutes; remove to a plate. In the same pan, stir the bell peppers and onion and cook for 6 minutes. Take the turkey back to the pan and stir well. Sprinkle with cilantro. Serve topped with lime wedges and avocado.

Chili Turkey Patties with Cucumber Salsa

Ready in about: 30 minutes | **Serves**: 4 | **Per serving**: Kcal 475, Fat: 38g, Net Carbs: 5g, Protein: 26g

INGREDIENTS

Turkey

2 spring onions, thinly sliced
1 lb ground turkey

1 egg
2 garlic cloves, minced

1 chili pepper, deseeded and diced
2 tbsp ghee

Cucumber salsa

1 tbsp apple cider vinegar
1 tbsp chopped dill

2 cucumbers, grated
1 cup sour cream

1 jalapeño pepper, minced
2 tbsp olive oil

DIRECTIONS

Place all turkey ingredients except the ghee in a bowl. Mix to combine. Make patties out of the mixture. Melt the ghee in a skillet over medium heat. Cook the patties for 3 minutes per side; remove to a plate. Place all salsa ingredients in a bowl and mix to combine. Serve the cakes topped with salsa.

Chicken & Eggplant Gruyere Gratin

Ready in about: 55 minutes | **Serves**: 4 | **Per serving**: Kcal 412, Fat 37g, Net Carbs 5g, Protein 34g

INGREDIENTS

3 tbsp butter
1 eggplant, chopped

2 tbsp gruyere cheese, grated
Salt and black pepper to taste

2 garlic cloves, minced
1 lb chicken thighs

DIRECTIONS

Warm butter in a pan over medium heat. Add in the chicken thighs, season with pepper and salt, and cook for 6 minutes on all sides. Lay them in a baking dish. In the same, add garlic and cook for 1 minute.

Stir in the eggplant, pepper, and salt and cook for 10 minutes. Pour the mixture over the chicken, top with the gruyere cheese, and set in the preheated to 350°F oven. Bake for 30 minutes. Turn on the oven's broiler, and broil everything for 2 minutes. Split among serving plates and enjoy!

Pressure Cooker Mexican Turkey Soup

Ready in about: 35 minutes | **Serves**: 4 | **Per serving**: Kcal 387, Fat 24g, Net Carbs 6g, Protein 38g

INGREDIENTS

½ lb turkey breast, cubed
4 cups chicken stock
1 onion, chopped

1 cup canned chunky salsa
8 oz cheddar cheese, shredded
¼ tsp cayenne red pepper

4 oz canned diced green chilies
1 tsp fresh cilantro, chopped
2 tbsp olive oil

DIRECTIONS

Set the pressure cooker to Sauté and warm the olive oil. Cook the turkey and onion for 5-6 minutes, stirring occasionally. Stir in the salsa, green chilies, cayenne pepper, and chicken stock and seal the lid.

Press Pressure Cook and set the cooking time to 15 minutes. When ready, do a quick pressure release. Stir in the cheddar cheese until it is melted, about 2 minutes. Sprinkle with cilantro and serve.

Turkey & Cheese Stuffed Peppers

Ready in about: 40 minutes | **Serves**: 4 | **Per serving**: Kcal 486, Fat 17g, Net Carbs 8.6g, Protein 51g

INGREDIENTS

4 bell peppers, tops removed
3 oz cream cheese, softened
1 carrot, chopped

2 tbsp olive oil
1 tbsp hot sauce
¾ cup blue cheese, crumbled

1 onion, chopped
1 lb ground turkey
Salt and black pepper to taste

DIRECTIONS

Warm the olive oil in a saucepan over medium heat and sauté the onion and carrot for 3-4 minutes. Stir in the ground turkey and cook for 5-6 minutes. Season with salt and pepper and remove to a bowl. Let it cool slightly. Add in the hot sauce and cream cheese and stir well. Stuff the peppers with the mixture.

Arrange them on a lined baking sheet. Place in the preheated to 425°F oven and bake for 20 minutes. Top with the blue cheese and add back to the oven. Bake for 5 minutes until the cheese melts. Serve.

Rosemary Turkey Pie

Ready in about: 40 minutes +chilling time | **Serves**: 4 | **Per serving**: Kcal 325, Fat 23g, Net Carbs 5.6g, Protein 21g

INGREDIENTS

2 cups chicken stock
1 cup turkey meat, cooked, chopped
Salt and black pepper to taste

1 tbsp fresh rosemary, chopped
½ cup kale, chopped
½ cup butternut squash, chopped

½ cup Monterey jack cheese, grated
¼ tsp smoked paprika
¼ tsp xanthan gum

For the crust

¼ cup butter
¼ tsp xanthan gum

2 cups almond flour
A pinch of salt

1 egg
¼ cup cheddar cheese

DIRECTIONS

Set a greased pot over medium heat. Place in the turkey and squash and cook for 10 minutes. Stir in stock, Monterey Jack cheese, rosemary, black pepper, smoked paprika, kale, and salt. In a bowl, combine ½ cup stock from the pot with ¼ teaspoon xanthan gum, and transfer everything to the pot; set aside.

In a separate bowl, stir flour, ¼ teaspoon xanthan gum, and salt. Whisk in the butter, cheddar cheese, and egg until a pie crust dough forms. Shape into a ball, wrap in plastic foil, and refrigerate for 30 minutes. Spray a baking dish with cooking spray and sprinkle pie filling on the bottom. Set the dough on a working surface and roll into a circle. Top the filling with the circle. Ensure well pressed and seal edges, set in an oven at 350°F, and bake for 35 minutes. Allow the pie to cool, and enjoy.

Turkey Cakes with Sautéed Green Cabbage

Ready in about: 30 minutes | **Serves**: 4 | **Per serving**: Kcal: 443, Fat: 25g, Net Carbs: 5.8g, Protein: 31g

INGREDIENTS

1 lb ground turkey	Salt and black pepper to taste	½ head green cabbage, shredded
1 egg	1 tsp dried thyme	½ cup almond flour
1 onion, chopped	3 tbsp butter	2 tbsp fresh parsley, chopped

DIRECTIONS

Combine the ground turkey, egg, almond flour, thyme, salt, and pepper in a mixing bowl. Mix well and create cakes from the mixture. Melt the butter in a large pan over medium heat and fry the cakes on all sides until cooked thoroughly, about 6-8 minutes. Place on a plate and cover with foil to keep warm.

In the same pan, add and sauté the green cabbage for 8-10 minutes until tender. Season with salt and pepper. Sprinkle with parsley. Plate the turkey cakes and cabbage and serve.

Chipotle Turkey Meatballs

Ready in about: 15 minutes | **Serves**: 4 | **Per serving**: Kcal 310, Fat: 26g, Net Carbs: 2g, Protein: 22g

INGREDIENTS

1 lb ground turkey	½ tsp garlic powder	¼ cup almond flour
2 tbsp sun-dried tomatoes, chopped	1 egg	2 tbsp olive oil
2 tbsp chipotle hot sauce	Salt and black pepper to taste	½ cup mozzarella cheese, shredded

DIRECTIONS

Mix everything except the olive oil and chipotle sauce with your hands in a bowl. Form the mixture into 16 small balls. Heat the olive oil in a skillet over medium heat. Cook the meatballs for 4-5 minutes per each side. Place on paper towels to remove excess fat. Serve drizzled with chipotle sauce.

Turkey Salad with Spinach & Raspberries

Ready in about: 25 minutes | **Serves**: 4 | **Per serving**: Kcal 451, Fat 33g, Net Carbs 6g, Protein 28g

INGREDIENTS

1 tbsp swerve sugar	¼ cup water	10 oz baby spinach
1 red onion, chopped	1 ¾ cups raspberries	1 lb turkey breast, boneless, halved
¼ cup vinegar	1 tbsp Dijon mustard	4 oz goat cheese, crumbled
¼ cup olive oil	Salt and black pepper to taste	½ cup pecans, halved

DIRECTIONS

In a blender, combine swerve sugar, vinegar, 1 cup of the raspberries, black pepper, mustard, water, onion, half of the olive oil, and salt and pulse until smooth. Strain the dressing into a bowl and set aside.

Warm the remaining oil in a pan over medium heat. Season the turkey with salt and pepper. Place it skin-side down into the pan. Cook for 12-14 minutes, flipping once. Place the spinach in a platter and top with the remaining raspberries, pecans, goat cheese, and dressing. Slice the turkey and put over the salad.

Broccoli & Turkey Bacon Crepes

Ready in about: 40 minutes | **Serves**: 6 | **Per serving**: Kcal 371, Fat 32g, Net Carbs 7g, Protein 25g

INGREDIENTS

6 eggs
1 cup cream cheese
1 tsp erythritol
1 ½ tbsp coconut flour
⅓ cup Parmesan cheese, grated
½ tsp xanthan gum
1 cup broccoli florets

1 cup mushrooms, sliced
8 oz turkey bacon, cubed
8 oz cheese blend
1 garlic clove, minced
1 onion, chopped
2 tbsp red wine vinegar
2 tbsp butter

½ cup heavy cream
1 tsp Worcestershire sauce
¼ cup chicken stock
½ tsp nutmeg
2 tbsp fresh parsley, chopped
Salt and black pepper to taste

DIRECTIONS

In a bowl, combine 3/4 cup of cream cheese, eggs, erythritol, coconut flour, xanthan gum, Parmesan cheese, and stir until you obtain a crepe batter. Set a pan sprayed with cooking spray over medium heat. Pour some of the batter, spread well into the pan, cook for 2 minutes, flip, and cook for 40 seconds until golden. Do the same with the rest of the batter. Stack all the crepes on a serving plate.

In the same pan, melt the butter and sauté onion, garlic, and mushrooms for 3 minutes until tender. Add in the turkey bacon, salt, vinegar, heavy cream, 6 ounces of the cheese blend, remaining cream cheese, nutmeg, black pepper, broccoli, stock, and Worcestershire sauce. Cook for 7 minutes.

Fill each crepe with the mixture, roll up each one, and arrange on a baking dish. Scatter over the remaining cheese blend and cook under the broiler for 5 minutes. Arrange the crepes on serving plates, garnish with chopped parsley, and serve.

Turkey & Green Bean Stew with Salsa Verde

Ready in about: 30 minutes | **Serves**: 6 | **Per serving**: Kcal 193, Fat 11g, Net Carbs 2g, Protein 27g

INGREDIENTS

4 cups leftover turkey, chopped
2 cups green beans
2 garlic cloves, minced

Salt and black pepper to taste
2 tbsp olive oil
½ cup salsa verde

1 tsp red pepper flakes
1 onion, chopped
1 tbsp fresh cilantro, chopped

DIRECTIONS

Warm the olive oil in a pan over medium heat. Add in the onion and garlic and sauté for 3 minutes until soft, stirring occasionally. Stir in red pepper flakes, salsa verde, salt, and black pepper for 1 minute.

Pour in 2 cups of water and bring to a boil. Simmer for 10 minutes. Add in the turkey and green beans and cook for 10 more minutes. Spoon the stew onto bowls. Top with cilantro and serve.

Mushroom & Cabbage Turkey Au Gratin

Ready in about: 55 minutes | **Serves**: 6 | **Per serving**: Kcal 351, Fat 15.8g, Net Carbs 8.2g, Protein 36.9g

INGREDIENTS

1 lb mushrooms, sliced
3 cups green cabbage, shredded
2 lb turkey breast, skinless, boneless

3 tbsp olive oil
1 tsp fresh dill, chopped
1 onion, chopped

1 cup Parmesan cheese, grated
Salt and black pepper to taste
2 garlic cloves, minced

DIRECTIONS

Set a saucepan over medium heat. Add in the turkey and cover with salted water. Bring to a boil and simmer for 20 minutes. Remove to a baking dish and let it sit for a few minutes. Cut it and set aside.

Warm the olive oil in a pan over medium heat and sauté the onion and garlic for 3 minutes. Stir in mushrooms, green cabbage, dill, salt, and pepper for 5 minutes. Pour the mixture into the baking dish and stir to combine. Top with Parmesan cheese. Place in the oven. Bake for 20 minutes at 390°F. Serve.

Zucchini Spaghetti with Turkey Bolognese Sauce

Ready in about: 30 minutes | Serves: 6 | Per serving: Kcal 273, Fat: 16g, Net Carbs: 3.8g, Protein: 19g

INGREDIENTS

2 cups sliced mushrooms
2 tsp olive oil
1 lb ground turkey

3 tbsp pesto sauce
1 cup diced onion
2 cups broccoli florets

6 cups zucchini, spiralized
Salt and black pepper to taste

DIRECTIONS

Heat the olive oil in a skillet. Add zucchini and cook for 2-3 minutes, stirring continuously; set aside. Add turkey to the skillet and cook until browned, about 7-8 minutes. Transfer to a plate. Add onion, broccoli, and mushrooms in the turkey fat and sauté for 5-6 minutes until tender. Return the turkey to the skillet, and stir in the pesto, salt, and pepper. Simmer for 15 minutes. Stir in zucchini pasta and serve.

Spicy Eggs with Turkey Ham

Ready in about: 15 minutes | Serves: 2 | Per serving: Kcal 462; Fat: 40.6g, Net Carbs: 7.1g, Protein: 16.9g

INGREDIENTS

2 tbsp olive oil
½ cup onions, chopped
1 tsp garlic, minced

1 tsp serrano pepper, minced
Salt and black pepper to taste
5 oz turkey ham, chopped

4 eggs, whisked
1 thyme sprig, chopped
½ cup olives, pitted and sliced

DIRECTIONS

Over medium heat, set a skillet and warm oil. Add in onion and sauté for 4 minutes until tender. Stir in garlic, salt, ham, black pepper, and serrano pepper and cook for 5-6 more minutes. Add in eggs and sprinkle with thyme. Cook for 5 minutes. Garnish with sliced olives before serving.

Turkey Pastrami & Mascarpone Pinwheels

Ready in about: 40 minutes | Serves: 4 | Per serving: Kcal 266, Fat 24g, Net Carbs 0g, Protein 13g

INGREDIENTS

10 canned pepperoncini peppers, sliced and drained
Cooking spray

8 oz mascarpone cheese

10 oz turkey pastrami, sliced

DIRECTIONS

Lay a 12 x 12 plastic wrap on a flat surface and arrange the pastrami all over slightly overlapping each other. Spread the cheese on top of the salami layers and arrange the pepperoncini on top. Hold two opposite ends of the plastic wrap and roll the pastrami. Twist both ends to tighten and refrigerate for 2 hours. Unwrap the salami roll and slice into 2-inch pinwheels. Serve.

Buttered Duck Breast

Ready in about: 30 minutes | Serves: 2 | Per serving: Kcal 547, Fat 46g, Net Carbs 2g, Protein 35g

INGREDIENTS

1 medium duck breast, skin scored
1 tbsp heavy cream

2 tbsp butter
Salt and black pepper to taste

1 cup kale
¼ tsp fresh sage

DIRECTIONS

Warm half of the butter in a pan over medium heat. Add in sage and heavy cream and cook for 2 minutes. Stir in the kale and cook for 1 minute. Melt the remaining butter in another pan over medium heat.

Add in the duck as the skin side faces down. Cook for 4 minutes, flip, and cook for 3 minutes. Set the duck breast on a flat surface and slice. Arrange the slices on a platter and drizzle over the sauce to serve.

Duck & Vegetable Casserole

Ready in about: 20 minutes | **Serves:** 2 | **Per serving:** Kcal 433, Fat 21g, Net Carbs 8g, Protein 53g

INGREDIENTS

½ lb duck breast, skin on and sliced
2 zucchinis, sliced
1 tbsp coconut oil

2 green onions, chopped
1 carrot, chopped
1 green bell pepper, chopped

Salt and black pepper to taste
1 garlic clove, minced

DIRECTIONS

Warm the coconut oil in a pan over medium heat. Add in the duck and cook each side for 3 minutes. Remove to a plate. To the pan, add the green onions and garlic and cook for 2 minutes. Place in the zucchini, bell pepper, salt, pepper, and carrot and cook for 10 minutes. Pour over the duck and serve.

Cheesy Turkey & Broccoli Traybake

Ready in about: 30 minutes | **Serves:** 4 | **Per serving:** Kcal: 365, Fat: 28g, Net Carbs: 2.6g, Protein: 29g

INGREDIENTS

1 lb turkey breast, cooked, shredded
2 tbsp olive oil
1 head broccoli, cut into florets

½ cup sour cream
½ cup heavy cream
1 cup Monterrey Jack cheese, grated

4 tbsp pork rinds, crushed
Salt and black pepper to taste
½ tsp paprika

DIRECTIONS

Preheat oven to 450°F. Boil water in a pan. Add in broccoli and cook for 8 minutes. In a bowl, mix the ground turkey, sour cream, olive oil, and broccoli and stir. Transfer the mixture to a greased baking tray. Sprinkle heavy cream over the dish, top with seasonings, and coat with the Monterrey Jack cheese. Cover with pork rinds. Place in the oven and cook for 20-25 minutes. Place on a plate and serve.

Coconut Turkey Chili with Kale

Ready in about: 30 minutes | **Serves:** 4 | **Per serving:** Kcal 295, Fat 15.2g, Net Carbs 4.2g, Protein 25g

INGREDIENTS

1 lb turkey breast, cubed
1 cup kale, chopped
20 oz canned diced tomatoes
2 tbsp coconut oil

2 tbsp coconut cream
2 garlic cloves, minced
1 onion, sliced
1 tsp ground coriander

1 tbsp fresh ginger, grated
1 tbsp turmeric
Salt and black pepper to taste
½ tsp chili powder

DIRECTIONS

Warm the olive oil in a pan over medium heat and. Add in the turkey, onion, garlic, and ginger and cook for 5 minutes. Stir in tomatoes, turmeric, coriander, salt, pepper, and chili powder and for 10 minutes. Pour in the coconut cream and kale and simmer for 5 more minutes. Serve warm.

Turkey & Leek Soup

Ready in about: 45 minutes | **Serves:** 4 | **Per serving:** Kcal 305, Fat 11g, Net Carbs 3g, Protein 15g

INGREDIENTS

1 celery stalk, chopped
2 leeks, chopped
2 tbsp butter

4 cups chicken stock
Salt and black pepper to taste
¼ cup fresh parsley, chopped

3 cups zoodles
½ lb turkey breast, skinless, boneless

DIRECTIONS

Melt the butter in a pot over medium heat. Chop the turkey into cubes and add it to the pot along with leeks and celery. Cook for 5 minutes. Pour in the stock, season with salt and pepper, and cook for 30 minutes. Mix in the zoodles and cook for 5 more minutes. Serve topped with parsley in bowls and enjoy!

PORK, BEEF & LAMB RECIPES

Baked Pork Meatballs in Pasta Sauce

Ready in about: 45 minutes | Serves: 6 | Per serving: Kcal 590, Fat 46.8g, Net Carbs 4.1g, Protein 46.2g

INGREDIENTS

2 lb ground pork
1 tbsp olive oil
1 cup pork rinds, crushed
2 cloves garlic, minced

½ cup coconut milk
2 eggs, beaten
½ cup Parmesan cheese, grated
½ cup asiago cheese, grated

Salt and black pepper to taste
2 jars sugar-free marinara sauce
1 cup Italian blend kinds of cheeses
3 tbsp fresh basil, chopped

DIRECTIONS

Preheat oven to 400°F. Combine the coconut milk and pork rinds in a bowl. Mix in the ground pork, garlic, asiago cheese, Parmesan cheese, eggs, salt, and pepper and stir. Form balls of the mixture and place them in a greased baking pan. Bake in the oven for 20 minutes. Transfer the meatballs to a plate.

Pour half of the marinara sauce in the baking pan. Place the meatballs back in the pan and pour in the remaining marinara sauce. Sprinkle with the Italian blend cheeses and drizzle with the olive oil.

Cover the pan with foil and put it back in the oven. Bake for 10 minutes. After, remove the foil, and cook for 5 minutes. Once ready, take out the pan and garnish with basil. Serve on a bed of squash spaghetti.

Grilled Pork Loin Chops with Barbecue Sauce

Ready in about: 15 minutes + marinating time | Serves. 4 | Per serving: Kcal 363, Fat 26.6g, Net Carbs 0g, Protein 34.1g

INGREDIENTS

4 thick-cut pork loin chops, boneless
½ cup sugar-free BBQ sauce

1 tsp black pepper
1 tbsp erythritol

½ tsp ginger powder
2 tsp sweet paprika

DIRECTIONS

In a bowl, mix pepper, erythritol, ginger powder, and sweet paprika, and rub the pork on all sides with the mixture. Cover the pork chops with plastic wrap and place them in the fridge to marinate for 2 hours.

Preheat the grill to 450°F. Unwrap the meat, place on the grill grate, and cook for 2 minutes per side. Reduce the heat and brush the BBQ sauce on the meat, cover, and grill for 5 minutes. Open the lid, turn the meat, and brush again with barbecue sauce. Continue cooking covered for 5 minutes. Serve.

Pork Pie with Cauliflower

Ready in about: 1 hour and 30 minutes | Serves: 6 | Per serving: Kcal 485, Fat: 41g, Net Carbs: 4g, Protein: 29g

INGREDIENTS

Crust

1 egg
¼ cup butter

2 cups almond flour
¼ tsp xanthan gum

¼ cup shredded mozzarella
A pinch of salt

Filling

2 lb ground pork
⅓ cup pureed onion

¾ tsp allspice
1 cup mashed cauliflower

1 tbsp ground sage
2 tbsp butter

DIRECTIONS

Preheat oven to 350°F. Whisk together all the crust ingredients in a bowl. Make two balls out of the mixture and refrigerate for 10 minutes. Combine ½ cup water, meat, and salt, in a pot over medium heat.

Cook for about 15 minutes. Place the meat along with the other ingredients in a bowl. Mix with your hands to combine. Roll out the pie crusts and place one at the bottom of a greased pie pan. Spread the filling over the crust. Top with the other coat. Bake in the oven for 50 minutes. Serve.

Pork Sausage Bake

Ready in about: 50 minutes | **Serves**: 4 | **Per serving**: Kcal 465, Fat 41.6g, Net Carbs 4.4g, Protein 15.1g

INGREDIENTS

1 lb pork sausages
4 large tomatoes, cut in rings
1 red bell pepper, sliced
1 yellow bell pepper, sliced

1 green bell pepper, sliced
1 sprig thyme, chopped
1 sprig rosemary, chopped
2 cloves garlic, minced

2 bay leaves
2 tbsp olive oil
2 tbsp balsamic vinegar

DIRECTIONS

Preheat oven to 350°F. In a greased baking pan, arrange the tomatoes and bell peppers. Sprinkle with thyme, rosemary, garlic, olive oil, and balsamic vinegar. Top with the sausages.

Put the pan in the oven and bake for 20 minutes. After, remove the pan, shake it a bit, and turn the sausages over with a spoon. Continue cooking for 25 minutes or until the sausages have browned to your desired color. Serve with the veggie and cooking sauce with cauli rice.

Pork Osso Bucco

Ready in about: 1 hour 55 minutes | **Serves**: 6 | **Per serving**: Kcal 590, Fat 40g, Net Carbs 6.1g, Protein 34g

INGREDIENTS

3 tbsp butter, softened
6 (16 oz) pork shanks
2 tbsp olive oil
2 cloves garlic, minced

1 cup diced tomatoes
Salt and black pepper to taste
1 onion, chopped
½ celery stalk, chopped

½ cup chopped carrots
1 cups Cabernet Sauvignon wine
3 cups vegetable broth
2 tsp lemon zest

DIRECTIONS

Melt the butter in a large saucepan over medium heat. Season the pork with salt and black pepper and brown it for 12 minutes; remove to a plate. In the same pan, sauté the onion for 3 minutes. Return the pork shanks. Stir in the wine, carrots, celery, tomatoes, broth, salt, and pepper and cover the pan.

Let simmer on low heat for 1 ½ hours, basting the pork every 15 minutes with the sauce. In a bowl, mix the garlic, parsley, and lemon zest to make a gremolata, and stir the mixture into the sauce when it is ready. Turn the heat off and dish the Osso Bucco. Serve with creamy turnip mash.

Charred Tenderloin with Lemon Chimichurri

Ready in about: 64 minutes | **Serves**: 4 | **Per serving**: Kcal 388, Fat 18g, Net Carbs 2.1g, Protein 28g

INGREDIENTS

Lemon Chimichurri

1 lemon, juiced
¼ cup mint leaves, chopped

¼ cup fresh oregano, chopped
2 cloves garlic, minced

¼ cup olive oil
Salt to taste

Pork

1 (4 lb) pork tenderloin

Salt and black pepper to taste

1 tbsp olive oil

DIRECTIONS

Make the lemon chimichurri to have the flavors incorporate while the pork cooks. In a bowl, mix the mint, oregano, and garlic. Then, add the lemon juice, olive oil, and salt, and combine well. Set aside.

Preheat the charcoal grill to 450°F, creating a direct heat area and indirect heat area. Rub the pork with olive oil and season with salt and pepper. Place the meat over direct heat and sear for 3 minutes on each side, moving to the indirect heat area. Close the lid and cook for 25 minutes on one side

Next, open, turn the meat, and grill for 20 minutes on the other side. Remove the pork from the grill and let it sit for 5 minutes before slicing. Spoon lemon chimichurri over the pork and serve with fresh salad.

Spiced Pork Roast with Collard Greens

Ready in about: 60 minutes | **Serves:** 4 | **Per serving:** Kcal 430, Fat 23g, Net Carbs 3g, Protein 45g

INGREDIENTS

2 tbsp olive oil
Salt and black pepper to taste
1 ½ lb pork loin

A pinch of dry mustard
1 tsp red pepper flakes
½ tsp ginger, minced

1 cup collard greens, chopped
2 garlic cloves, minced
½ lemon, sliced

DIRECTIONS

In a bowl, combine the ginger with mustard, salt, and pepper. Add in the meat and toss to coat. Heat the oil in a saucepan over medium heat. Brown the pork on all sides, about 5 minutes. Transfer to the oven.

Pour in ¼ cup water and roast for 40 minutes at 390°F. To the saucepan, add collard greens, lemon slices, garlic, and ¼ cup water. Simmer for 10 minutes. Slice the loin and top with the sauce to serve.

BBQ Pork Pizza with Goat Cheese

Ready in about: 30 minutes | **Serves:** 4 | **Per serving:** Kcal 344, Fat 24g, Net Carbs 6,5g, Protein 18g

INGREDIENTS

1 low carb pizza bread
1 tbsp olive oil

1 cup Manchego cheese, grated
2 cups leftover pulled pork

½ cup sugar-free BBQ sauce
1 cup goat cheese, crumbled

DIRECTIONS

Preheat oven to 400°F. Put the pizza bread on a pizza pan. Brush with olive oil and sprinkle the Manchego cheese all over. Mix the pork with BBQ sauce and spread over the cheese. Drop goat cheese on top and bake for 25 minutes until the cheese has melted. Slice the pizza with a cutter and serve.

Oregano Pork Chops with Spicy Tomato Sauce

Ready in about: 50 minutes | **Serves:** 4 | **Per serving:** Kcal 410, Fat 21g, Net Carbs 3.6g, Protein 39g

INGREDIENTS

4 pork chops
1 tbsp fresh oregano, chopped
2 garlic cloves, minced

2 tbsp canola oil
15 oz canned diced tomatoes
1 tbsp tomato paste

Salt and black pepper to taste
¼ cup tomato juice
1 red chili, finely chopped

DIRECTIONS

Warm the olive oil a pan over medium heat. Season the pork with salt and pepper. Add it to the pan and cook for 6 minutes on both sides; remove to a bowl. Sauté the garlic in the same fat for 30 seconds. Stir in tomato paste, tomatoes, tomato juice, and chili. Bring to a boil and reduce the heat. Place in the pork chops and simmer everything for 30 minutes. Sprinkle with fresh oregano and serve.

Peanut Butter Pork Stir-Fry

Ready in about: 23 minutes | **Serves:** 4 | **Per serving:** Kcal 571, Fat 49g, Net Carbs 1g, Protein 22.5g

INGREDIENTS

2 tbsp ghee
2 lb pork loin, cut into strips
Pink salt to taste

2 tsp ginger-garlic paste
¼ cup chicken broth
5 tbsp peanut butter, softened

2 cups mixed stir-fry vegetables
½ tsp chili pepper

DIRECTIONS

Melt the ghee in a wok over high heat. Rub the pork with salt, chili pepper, and ginger-garlic paste. Place it into the wok and cook for 6 minutes until no longer pink. Mix peanut butter and broth until smooth.

Pour in the wok and stir for 6 minutes. Add in the mixed veggies and simmer for 5 minutes. Adjust the taste with salt and black pepper and spoon the stir-fry to a side of cilantro cauli rice.

Pork Casserole

Ready in about: 35 minutes | **Serves**: 4 | **Per serving**: Kcal 495, Fat 29g, Net Carbs 2.7g, Protein 36.5g

INGREDIENTS

1 lb ground pork
1 large yellow squash, thinly sliced
Salt and black pepper to taste
1 clove garlic, minced

4 green onions, chopped
1 cup chopped cremini mushrooms
1 (15 oz) can diced tomatoes
½ cup pork rinds, crushed

2 tbsp fresh parsley, chopped
1 cup cottage cheese, crumbled
1 cup Mexican cheese blend
3 tbsp olive oil

DIRECTIONS

Preheat oven to 370°F. Heat the olive oil in a skillet over medium heat. Add in the pork, season with salt and black pepper, and cook for 3 minutes or until no longer pink. Stir occasionally while breaking any lumps apart. Add the garlic, half of the green onions, mushrooms, and 2 tablespoons of pork rinds.

Cook for 3 minutes. Stir in the tomatoes and ⅓ cup water. Cook for 3 minutes. Remove the pan. Mix the parsley, cottage cheese, and Mexican cheese blend in a bowl. Sprinkle the bottom of a baking dish with some pork rinds, top with half of the squash, and season with salt. Top with 2/3 of the pork mixture and 2/3 of the cheese mixture. Repeat the layering process a second time to exhaust the ingredients.

Cover the baking dish with foil and bake for 20 minutes. After, remove the foil and brown the top of the casserole with the oven's broiler side for 2 minutes. Remove the dish when ready and serve warm.

Pork Wraps

Ready in about: 40 minutes | **Serves**: 6 | **Per serving**: Kcal 435, Fat 37g, Net Carbs 2g, Protein 34g

INGREDIENTS

6 bacon slices
2 tbsp fresh parsley, chopped
1 lb pork tenderloin, sliced
⅓ cup ricotta cheese

3 tbsp coconut oil
¼ cup onions, chopped
3 garlic cloves, minced
2 tbsp Parmesan cheese, grated

15 oz canned diced tomatoes
⅓ cup vegetable stock
Salt and black pepper to taste
½ tsp Italian seasoning

DIRECTIONS

Use a meat pounder to flatten the pork pieces. Set the bacon slices on top of each piece and divide the parsley, ricotta cheese, and Parmesan cheese between them. Roll each pork piece and secure it with a toothpick. Set a pan over medium heat and warm oil. Cook the pork rolls until browned. Remove.

Add onions and garlic in the pan and cook for 5 minutes. Place in the stock and cook for 3 minutes. Get rid of the toothpicks from the rolls and return to the pan. Stir in pepper, salt, tomatoes, and Italian seasoning. Bring to a boil, reduce the heat, and cook for 20 minutes covered. Split among bowls to serve.

Spicy Pork Ribs

Ready in about: 8 hours 45 minutes | **Serves**: 6 | **Per serving**: Kcal 580, Fat 36.6g, Net Carbs 0g, Protein 44.5g

INGREDIENTS

3 racks pork ribs, silver lining removed
2 cups sugar-free BBQ sauce
2 tbsp erythritol

2 tsp chili powder
2 tsp cumin powder
2 tsp smoked paprika

2 tsp garlic powder
Salt and black pepper to taste
1 tsp mustard powder

DIRECTIONS

Preheat a smoker to 400°F, using mesquite wood to create flavor in the smoker. In a bowl, mix the erythritol, chili powder, cumin powder, black pepper, smoked paprika, garlic powder, salt, and mustard powder. Rub the ribs and let marinate for 30 minutes.

Place on the grill grate and cook at reduced heat of 225°F for 4 hours. Flip the ribs after and continue cooking for 4 hours. Brush the ribs with bbq sauce on both sides and sear them in increased heat for 3 minutes per side. Remove and let sit for 4 minutes before slicing. Serve with red cabbage coleslaw.

Zoodle & Bacon Halloumi Gratin with Spinach

Ready in about: 35 minutes | **Serves:** 4 | **Per serving:** Kcal 350, Fat 27g, Net Carbs 5.3g, Protein 16g

INGREDIENTS

2 large zucchinis, spiralized
4 slices bacon, chopped
2 cups baby spinach

4 oz halloumi cheese, cut into cubes
2 cloves garlic, minced
1 cup heavy cream

½ cup sugar-free tomato sauce
1 cup mozzarella cheese, grated
½ tsp dried Italian herbs

DIRECTIONS

Preheat oven to 350°F. Place a pan over medium heat and fry the bacon for 4 minutes. Add in the garlic and cook for 1 minute. In a bowl, mix heavy cream, tomato sauce, and 1/6 cup water and add it to the pan.

Stir in zucchini, spinach, halloumi, Italian herbs, salt, and pepper. Sprinkle the mozzarella cheese on top and transfer the pan to the oven. Bake for 20 minutes or until the cheese is golden. Serve warm.

Pork Lettuce Cups

Ready in about: 20 minutes | **Serves:** 6 | **Per serving:** Kcal 311, Fat 24.3g, Net Carbs 1g, Protein 19g

INGREDIENTS

2 lb ground pork
1 tbsp ginger-garlic paste
Pink salt and black pepper to taste

3 tbsp butter
Leaves from 1 head Iceberg lettuce
2 green onions, chopped

1 red bell pepper, chopped
½ cucumber, finely chopped
½ tsp cayenne pepper

DIRECTIONS

Melt butter in a pan over medium heat. Rub the pork with ginger-garlic paste, salt, pepper, and cayenne pepper and add it to the pan. Cook for 10 minutes until the pork is no longer pink. Remove and let it cool.

Pat the lettuce leaves dry with paper towels. Spoon two to three tablespoons of the pork mixture in each leaf. Top with green onions, bell pepper, and cucumber. Serve with soy drizzling sauce.

Swiss-Style Italian Sausage

Ready in about: 25 minutes | **Serves:** 6 | **Per serving:** Kcal 567, Fat 45g, Net Carbs 7.6g, Protein 34g

INGREDIENTS

¼ cup olive oil
2 lb Italian pork sausage, chopped
1 onion, sliced

4 sun-dried tomatoes, sliced thin
Salt and black pepper to taste
½ lb Gruyere cheese, grated

3 yellow bell peppers, chopped
3 orange bell peppers, chopped
1 tsp red pepper flakes

DIRECTIONS

Set a pan over medium heat and warm oil. Place in the sausage slices and cook each side for 3 minutes. Remove to a bowl and set aside. Stir tomatoes, bell peppers, and onion in the pan and cook for 5 minutes. Season with black pepper, pepper flakes, and salt and mix well. Cook for 1 minute and remove from heat.

Lay sausage slices onto a baking dish, place the bell pepper mixture on top and scatter with the Gruyere cheese. Place in the preheated to 340°F oven. Bake for 10 minutes until the cheese melts. Serve warm.

Pork & Mushroom Bake

Ready in about: 1 hour 15 minutes | **Serves:** 6 | **Per serving:** Kcal 403, Fat: 32.6g, Net Carbs: 8g, Protein: 19.4g

INGREDIENTS

1 onion, chopped
2 (10.5-oz) cans mushroom soup

6 pork chops
½ cup sliced mushrooms

Salt and black pepper to taste

DIRECTIONS

Preheat oven to 370°F. Season the pork with salt and pepper. Place on a baking dish. Combine the mushroom soup, mushrooms, and onion in a bowl and stir. Pour it over the pork. Bake for 45 minutes.

Pork Chops with Mint & Parsley Pesto

Ready in about: 3 hours 10 minutes | **Serves**: 4 | **Per serving**: Kcal 567, Fat 40g, Net Carbs 5.5g, Protein 37g

INGREDIENTS

1 cup parsley
1 cup mint
1 ½ onions, chopped

⅓ cup pistachios, chopped
3 tbsp avocado oil
Salt to taste

4 pork chops
2 garlic cloves, minced
1 lemon, juiced and zested

DIRECTIONS

In a food processor, combine the parsley with avocado oil, mint, pistachios, salt, lemon zest, and half of the onions. Rub the pork with this mixture, place in a bowl, and refrigerate for 1 hour while covered.

Remove the chops and set them to a baking dish. Top with the remaining onions and garlic. Sprinkle with lemon juice. Pour in 1 cup of water. Bake for 2 hours in the oven at 250°F. Serve warm.

Jamaican Pork Oven Roast

Ready in about: 4 hours and 20 minutes | **Serves**: 4 | **Per serving**: Kcal 282, Fat: 24g, Net Carbs: 0g, Protein: 23g

INGREDIENTS

2 lb pork roast
1 tbsp olive oil

1 tsp jerk spice blend
2 cups chicken stock

Salt and black pepper to taste

DIRECTIONS

Rub the pork with olive oil, spice blend, salt, and pepper. Heat a dutch oven over medium heat and sear the meat well on all sides. Add in the chicken stock. Cover the pot and cook for 4 hours on low heat. Shred the pork with 2 forks and serve with green salad.

Hot Pork with Dill Pickles

Ready in about: 20 minutes + marinating time | **Serves**: 4 | **Per serving**: Kcal 315, Fat 18g, Net Carbs 2.3g, Protein 36g

INGREDIENTS

¼ cup lime juice
4 pork chops
2 tbsp coconut oil, melted

2 garlic cloves, minced
½ tsp chili powder
1 tsp ground cinnamon

Salt and black pepper to taste
½ tsp hot pepper sauce
4 dill pickles, cut into spears

DIRECTIONS

In a bowl, combine the lime juice with coconut oil, salt, hot pepper sauce, black pepper, cinnamon, garlic, and chili powder. Place in the pork chops, toss to coat, and refrigerate for 4 hours.

Arrange the pork on the preheated grill over medium heat and cook for 7 minutes. Turn, add in the dill pickles, and cook for another 7 minutes. Split among serving plates and serve.

Bacon Smothered Pork Chops

Ready in about: 25 minutes | **Serves**: 6 | **Per serving**: Kcal 435, Fat 37g, Net Carbs 3g, Protein 22g

INGREDIENTS

6 strips bacon, chopped
6 pork chops

Pink salt and black pepper to taste
2 sprigs fresh thyme

¼ cup chicken broth
½ cup heavy cream

DIRECTIONS

Cook bacon in a large skillet on medium heat for 5 minutes. Remove with a slotted spoon onto a paper towel-lined plate to soak up excess fat. Season the pork chops with salt and black pepper and brown in the bacon fat for 4 minutes on each side. Remove to the bacon plate.

Stir the thyme, chicken broth, and heavy cream in the skillet and simmer for 5 minutes. Return the chops and bacon and cook further for another 2 minutes. Serve chops with a generous ladle of sauce.

Mustardy Pork Chops

Ready in about: 15 minutes | **Serves**: 4 | **Per serving**: Kcal 382, Fat 21.5g, Net Carbs 1.2g, Protein 38g

INGREDIENTS

4 pork loin chops
1 tsp Dijon mustard
1 tbsp soy sauce

1 tsp lemon juice
1 tbsp water
Salt and black pepper to taste

2 tbsp butter
A bunch of scallions, chopped

DIRECTIONS

In a bowl, combine the water with lemon juice, mustard, and soy sauce. Set aside. Set a pan over medium heat and melt the butter. Add in the pork chops and season with salt and black pepper.

Cook for 4 minutes, turn, and cook for an additional 4 minutes. Remove to a plate. In the same pan, pour mustard sauce and simmer for 5 minutes. Drizzle the sauce over the pork, top with scallions, and serve.

Pork Goulash with Cauliflower

Ready in about: 15 minutes | **Serves**: 4 | **Per serving**: Kcal 475, Fat 37g, Net Carbs 4.5g, Protein 44g

INGREDIENTS

1 red bell pepper, chopped
2 tbsp olive oil
1 ½ lb ground pork

Salt and black pepper to taste
2 cups cauliflower florets
1 onion, chopped

14 oz canned diced tomatoes
¼ tsp garlic powder
1 tbsp tomato puree

DIRECTIONS

Heat olive oil in a pan over medium heat. Add in the pork and brown for 5 minutes. Mix in the bell pepper and onion and cook for 4 minutes. Stir in 1 cup water, tomatoes, and cauliflower. Bring to a simmer and cook for 5 minutes. Pour in tomato paste, salt, pepper, and garlic powder and stir for 5 minutes. Serve.

Creamy Pork Chops

Ready in about: 50 minutes | **Serves**: 4 | **Per serving**: Kcal 612, Fat 40g, Net Carbs 6.8g, Protein 42g

INGREDIENTS

8 oz mushrooms, sliced
1 tsp garlic powder

1 onion, chopped
1 cup heavy cream

4 pork chops, boneless
¼ cup coconut oil

DIRECTIONS

Set a pan over medium heat and warm the oil. Add in the onion and mushrooms and cook for 4 minutes. Stir in the pork chops, season with garlic powder, and sear until browned. Put the pan in the oven.

Bake for 30 minutes at 350°F. Remove the pork chops. Place the pan over medium heat, pour the heavy cream over the mushroom mixture, and cook for 5 minutes. Top the pork chops with the sauce to serve.

Juicy Pork Medallions

Ready in about: 30 minutes | **Serves**: 4 | **Per serving**: Kcal 325, Fat 18g, Net Carbs 6g, Protein 36g

INGREDIENTS

1 lb pork tenderloin, cut into medallions
2 onions, chopped

6 bacon slices, chopped

½ cup vegetable stock

DIRECTIONS

Set a pan over medium heat. Add in the bacon and cook until crispy, about 5 minutes; remove to a plate. Add onions to the pan and cook for 3 minutes; set aside. Add the pork medallions to the pan

Brown for 3 minutes on each side, turn, and reduce the heat. Add in the vegetable stock and cook for 10 minutes. Return the bacon and onions to the pan and cook for 1 minute. Serve warm.

Lemon Pork Chops with Buttered Brussels Sprouts

Ready in about: 35 minutes | **Serves**: 6 | **Per serving**: Kcal 549, Fat 48g, Net Carbs 2g, Protein 26g

INGREDIENTS

3 tbsp lemon juice
3 cloves garlic, pureed
2 tbsp olive oil

6 pork loin chops
1 tbsp butter
1 lb Brussels sprouts, trimmed, halved

2 tbsp white wine
Salt and black pepper to taste

DIRECTIONS

Preheat oven to 400°F. Mix the lemon juice, garlic, salt, black pepper, and oil in a bowl. Brush the pork with the mixture. Place in a baking sheet and brown in the oven for 15 minutes, turning once. Remove.

Melt butter in a small wok and cook the Brussels sprouts for 5 minutes until tender. Drizzle with white wine, sprinkle with salt and black pepper, and cook for another 5 minutes. Serve them with the chops.

Pancetta & Kale Pork Sausages

Ready in about: 30 minutes | **Serves**: 4 | **Per serving**: Kcal 386, Fat 29g, Net Carbs 5.4g, Protein2 1g

INGREDIENTS

2 cups kale
4 cups chicken broth
2 tbsp olive oil
1 cup heavy cream

3 pancetta slices, chopped
½ lb radishes, chopped
2 garlic cloves, minced
Salt and black pepper to taste

½ tsp red pepper flakes
1 onion, chopped
1 ½ lb hot pork sausage, chopped

DIRECTIONS

Warm the olive oil in a pot over medium heat. Stir in garlic, onion, pancetta, and sausage and cook for 5 minutes. Pour in the broth, radishes, and kale and simmer for 10 minutes. Sprinkle with salt, red pepper flakes, and black pepper. Add in the heavy cream, stir, and cook for about 5 minutes. Serve.

Pulled Pork with Avocado

Ready in about: 2 hours 55 minutes | **Serves**: 6 | **Per serving**: Kcal 567, Fat 42.6g, Net Carbs 4.1g, Protein 42g

INGREDIENTS

2 lb pork shoulder
1 tbsp avocado oil

½ cup vegetable stock
1 tsp taco seasoning

1 avocado, sliced

DIRECTIONS

Preheat oven to 350°F. Rub the pork with taco seasoning and set in a greased baking dish. Pour in the vegetable stock. Place in the oven, cover with aluminium foil, and cook for 1 hour 45 minutes.

Discard the foil and cook for another 10-15 minutes until brown on top. Leave to rest for 15-20 minutes. Shred it with 2 forks. Serve topped with avocado slices.

Smoked Pork Sausages with Mushrooms

Ready in about: 1 hour 10 minutes | **Serves**: 6 | **Per serving**: Kcal 525, Fat 32g, Net Carbs 7.3g, Protein 29g

INGREDIENTS

3 yellow bell peppers, chopped
2 lb smoked sausage, sliced
Salt and black pepper to taste

2 lb portobello mushrooms, sliced
2 sweet onions, chopped
1 tbsp swerve sugar

2 tbsp olive oil
Arugula to garnish

DIRECTIONS

Preheat oven to 320°F. In a baking dish, combine the sausages with swerve, olive oil, black pepper, onion, bell peppers, salt, and mushrooms. Pour in 1 cup of water and toss to ensure everything is coated. Bake for 1 hour. Remove and let sit for 5 minutes. Serve scattered with arugula.

Stuffed Pork with Red Cabbage Salad

Ready in about: 40 minutes + marinating time | **Serves**: 4 | **Per serving**: Kcal 413, Fat 37g, Net Carbs 3g, Protein 26g

INGREDIENTS

Zest and juice from 2 limes
2 garlic cloves, minced
¾ cup + 3 tbsp olive oil
1 cup fresh cilantro, chopped
1 tsp dried oregano

Salt and black pepper to taste
1 tsp cumin
4 pork loin steaks
2 pickles, chopped
4 ham slices

6 Swiss cheese slices
2 tbsp mustard
1 head red cabbage, shredded
2 tbsp vinegar
Salt to taste

DIRECTIONS

In a food processor, blitz lime zest, ¾ cup oil, oregano, cumin, cilantro, lime juice, garlic, salt, and pepper. Rub the steaks with the mixture and toss to coat. Place in the fridge for 2 hours. Arrange the steaks on a working surface. Split the pickles, mustard, cheese, and ham on them, roll, and secure with toothpicks.

Heat a pan over medium heat. Add in the pork rolls, cook each side for 2 minutes and remove to a baking sheet. Bake in the oven at 350°F for 25 minutes. In a bowl, mix the cabbage with the remaining olive oil, vinegar, and salt. Serve with the meat.

Paprika Pork Chops

Ready in about: 25 minutes | **Serves**: 4 | **Per serving**: Kcal 349, Fat 18.5g, Net Carbs 4g, Protein 41.8g

INGREDIENTS

4 pork chops
Salt and black pepper to taste

3 tbsp paprika
¾ cup cumin powder

1 tsp chili powder

DIRECTIONS

In a bowl, combine the paprika with black pepper, cumin, salt, and chili. Place in the pork chops and toss to coat. Heat a grill to medium heat. Add in the pork chops and cook for 5 minutes. Flip and cook for 5 minutes. Serve with steamed vegetables.

Greek Pork with Olives

Ready in about: 35 minutes | **Serves**: 4 | **Per serving**: Kcal 415, Fat 25.2g, Net Carbs 2.2g, Protein 36g

INGREDIENTS

4 pork chops, bone-in
Salt and black pepper to taste

2 garlic cloves, minced
½ cup Kalamata olives, pitted, sliced

2 tbsp olive oil
1 cup vegetable broth

DIRECTIONS

Season pork chops with black pepper and salt. Add them to a roasting pan. Add in garlic, olives, olive oil, and vegetable broth. Roast in the oven for 10 minutes at 425°F. Serve warm.

Garlicky Pork with Bell Peppers

Ready in about: 40 minutes | **Serves**: 4 | **Per serving**: Kcal 456, Fat 25g, Net Carbs 6g, Protein 40g

INGREDIENTS

1 tbsp butter
4 pork steaks, bone-in
1 cup chicken stock

Salt and black pepper to taste
½ tsp lemon pepper
2 tbsp olive oil

6 garlic cloves, minced
4 bell peppers, sliced
1 lemon, sliced

DIRECTIONS

Heat a pan with the olive oil and butter over medium heat. Add in the pork steaks, season with black pepper and salt, and cook until browned; remove to a plate. In the same pan, add garlic and bell peppers. Cook for 4 minutes. Pour in the chicken stock, lemon slices, salt, lemon pepper, and pepper and stir for 5 minutes. Return the pork steaks and cook for 10 minutes. Pour the sauce over the steaks and serve.

Pork Chops with Cranberry Sauce

Ready in about: 2 hours 40 minutes | **Serves**: 4 | **Per serving**: Kcal 450, Fat 34g, Net Carbs 6g, Protein 26g

INGREDIENTS

4 pork chops
1 tsp garlic powder
Salt and black pepper to taste
3 tsp fresh basil, chopped
2 tbsp olive oil

1 shallot, chopped
1 cup white wine
1 bay leaf
2 cups vegetable stock
1 cup dried cranberries, soaked

½ tsp fresh rosemary, chopped
½ cup swerve sugar
Juice of 1 lemon
1 cup water
1 tsp harissa paste

DIRECTIONS

In a bowl, combine the pork chops with basil, salt, garlic powder, and black pepper. Heat the olive oil in a pan over medium heat. Add in the pork and cook until browned, about 6 minutes; set aside.

Stir the shallot in the same pan and cook for 2 minutes. Pour in the wine and bay leaf and cook for 4 more minutes. Stir in juice from ½ lemon and vegetable stock and simmer for 5 minutes. Return the pork and simmer for 10 minutes. Cover the pan with foil and place it in the oven. Bake at 350°F for 2 hours.

Set a pan over medium heat. Add in the cranberries, rosemary, harissa paste, water, swerve sugar, and remaining lemon juice and simmer for 15 minutes. Take out the pork chops from the oven. Remove and discard the bay leaf. Pour the cranberry sauce over the chops. Sprinkle with parsley and serve.

Pork Nachos

Ready in about: 15 minutes | **Serves**: 4 | **Per serving**: Kcal 452, Fat 25g, Net Carbs 9.3g, Protein 22g

INGREDIENTS

1 bag low carb tortilla chips
2 cups leftover pulled pork

1 red bell pepper, chopped
1 red onion, diced

2 cups Monterey Jack cheese, grated

DIRECTIONS

Preheat oven to 350°F. Arrange the chips on a baking pan, scatter pork over, followed by red bell pepper and onion, and sprinkle with the cheese. Place the pan in the oven and cook for 10 minutes until the cheese has melted. Allow cooling for 3 minutes and serve.

Pork in White Wine Sauce

Ready in about: 1 hour 25 minutes | **Serves**: 6 | **Per serving**: Kcal 514, Fat 32.5g, Net Carbs 6g, Protein 43g

INGREDIENTS

2 tbsp olive oil
2 lb pork stew meat, cubed
Salt and black pepper to taste
2 tbsp butter

4 garlic cloves, minced
¾ cup vegetable stock
½ cup white wine
3 carrots, chopped

1 cabbage head, shredded
½ cup scallions, chopped
1 cup heavy cream

DIRECTIONS

Warm the butter and olive in a pan over medium heat. Sear the pork until brown, about 5-6 minutes. Add in garlic, scallions, and carrots and sauté for 5 minutes. Pour in the cabbage, vegetable stock, and wine.

Stir and bring to a boil. Reduce the heat to low heat and cook for 1 hour covered. Add in heavy cream and stir for 1 minute. Adjust the seasoning with salt and pepper and serve.

Balsamic Grilled Pork Chops

Ready in about: 20 minutes + marinating time | **Serves**: 6 | **Per serving**: Kcal 418, Fat 26.8g, Net Carbs 1.5g, Protein 38g

INGREDIENTS

6 pork loin chops, boneless
1 tsp erythritol

¼ cup balsamic vinegar
3 cloves garlic, minced

¼ cup olive oil
Salt and black pepper to taste

Put the pork in a plastic bag. In a bowl, mix the erythritol, balsamic vinegar, garlic, olive oil, salt, pepper, and pour the mixture over the pork. Seal the bag, shake it, and place it in the refrigerator for 2 hours.

Preheat the grill to medium heat, remove the pork when ready, and grill covered for 10 minutes on each side. Remove and let sit for 4 minutes. Serve with sautéed parsnips.

Herby Pork Chops with Berry Sauce

Ready in about: 17 minutes | **Serves**: 4 | **Per serving**: Kcal 413, Fat 32.5g, Net Carbs 1.1g, Protein 26.3g

INGREDIENTS

1 tbsp olive oil + extra for brushing	2 cups raspberries	3 tbsp balsamic vinegar
2 lb pork chops	¼ cup water	2 tsp sugar-free Worcestershire sauce
Pink salt and black pepper to taste	1 ½ tbsp Italian Herb mix	

DIRECTIONS

Heat the olive oil in a skillet over medium heat, season the pork with salt and black pepper, and cook for 5 minutes on each side. Put on serving plates and reserve the pork drippings.

Mash the raspberries with a fork in a bowl until jam-like. Pour into a saucepan, add the water, and herb mix. Bring to boil on low heat for 4 minutes. Stir in pork drippings, vinegar, and Worcestershire sauce. Simmer for 1 minute. Spoon sauce over the pork chops and serve with braised rapini.

Pork Burgers with Caramelized Onion Rings

Ready in about: 20 minutes | **Serves**: 6 | **Per serving**: Kcal 445, Fat 32g, Net Carbs 7.6g, Protein 26g

INGREDIENTS

2 lb ground pork	1 tbsp butter	3 drops liquid stevia
Pink salt and chili pepper to taste	1 white onion, sliced into rings	6 zero carb burger buns, halved
3 tbsp olive oil	1 tbsp balsamic vinegar	2 firm tomatoes, sliced into rings

DIRECTIONS

Combine the pork, salt, and chili pepper in a bowl and mold out 6 patties. Heat the olive oil in a skillet over medium heat. Fry the patties for 4-5 minutes on each side until golden brown. Remove to a plate.

Melt butter in a skillet over medium heat, sauté onions for 2 minutes, and stir in the balsamic vinegar and liquid stevia. Cook for 30 seconds, stirring once or twice until caramelized. In each bun, place a patty, top with some onion rings and 2 tomato rings. Serve the burgers with cheddar cheese dip.

Beef Mushroom Meatloaf

Ready in about: 1 hour and 15 minutes | **Serves**: 12 | **Per serving**: Kcal 294, Fat: 19g, Net Carbs: 6g, Protein: 23g

INGREDIENTS

3 pounds ground beef	1 cup sliced mushrooms	¼ cup chopped bell peppers
½ cup chopped onions	3 eggs	⅓ cup grated Parmesan cheese
½ cup almond flour	¼ tsp pepper	1 tsp balsamic vinegar
2 garlic cloves, minced	2 tbsp chopped parsley	1 tsp salt

Glaze

2 cups balsamic vinegar	1 tbsp sweetener	2 tbsp sugar-free ketchup

DIRECTIONS

Combine all meatloaf ingredients in a large bowl. Press this mixture into a greased loaf pans. Bake in the oven for 30 minutes at 370°F. Combine all the glaze ingredients in a saucepan over medium heat.

Simmer for 20 minutes until the glaze is thickened. Pour ¼ cup of the glaze over the meatloaf. Save the extra for future use. Put the meatloaf back in the oven and cook for 20 more minutes.

Sausage Links with Tomato & Spinach Salad

Ready in about: 15 minutes | **Serves**: 4 | **Per serving**: Kcal 365, Fat 26g, Net Carbs 6.8g, Protein 18g

INGREDIENTS

4 pork sausage links, sliced
½ lb mixed cherry tomatoes, halved
2 cups baby spinach

2 tbsp olive oil
4 oz Monterrey Jack cheese, cubed
1 tbsp lemon juice

1 cup basil pesto
Salt and black pepper to taste

DIRECTIONS

Warm the olive oil in a pan over medium heat. Cook the sausage links for 4 minutes per side. In a salad bowl, combine spinach, cheese, salt, pesto, pepper, cherry tomatoes, and lemon juice and toss to coat. Mix in the sausage. Serve.

Pork Stew with Bacon & Cauliflower

Ready in about: 40 minutes | **Serves**: 6 | **Per serving**: Kcal 331, Fat 14.2g, Net Carbs 2.9g, Protein 43.8g

INGREDIENTS

2 lb pork tenderloin, cubed
2 cups chicken broth
3 tbsp olive oil

1 onion, chopped
Salt and black pepper to taste
2 garlic cloves, minced

1 cup canned diced tomatoes
1 cup bacon, chopped
1 head cauliflower, cut into florets

DIRECTIONS

Warm the olive oil in a saucepan over medium heat. Add in the bacon, pork, onion, and garlic and sauté for 3-4 minutes until the onion is tender. Pour in the chicken stock and tomatoes and simmer for 20-25 minutes. Add in the cauliflower and cook for 10 more minutes. Season with salt and pepper. Serve warm.

Pork Sausage with Spinach

Ready in about: 35 minutes | **Serves**: 6 | **Per serving**: Kcal 352, Fat 28g, Net Carbs 6.2g, Protein 29g

INGREDIENTS

1 onion, chopped
2 tbsp olive oil
2 lb Italian pork sausage, sliced

1 red bell pepper, chopped
Salt and black pepper to taste
4 lb spinach, chopped

1 garlic, minced
¼ cup green chili peppers, chopped
1 cup water

DIRECTIONS

Warm the olive oil in a pan over medium heat. Add in the sausage and cook for 10 minutes. Stir in onion, garlic, and bell pepper and sauté for 4 minutes. Place in spinach, salt, water, pepper, chili pepper, and cook for 10 minutes until the liquid has reduced by half. Transfer to a plate and serve.

Beef & Cheddar Stuffed Eggplants

Ready in about: 30 minutes | **Serves**: 4 | **Per serving**: Kcal 574, Fat 27.5g, Net Carbs 9.8g, Protein 61,8g

INGREDIENTS

2 eggplants
2 tbsp olive oil
1 ½ lb ground beef

1 medium red onion, chopped
1 roasted red pepper, chopped
Pink salt and black pepper to taste

1 cup yellow cheddar cheese, grated
2 tbsp dill, chopped

DIRECTIONS

Preheat oven to 350°F. Lay the eggplants on a flat surface, trim off the ends, and cut in half lengthwise. Scoop out the pulp from each half to make shells. Chop the pulp. Heat oil in a skillet over medium heat. Add the ground beef, red onion, pimiento, and eggplant pulp and season with salt and pepper.

Cook for 6 minutes while stirring to break up lumps until beef is no longer pink. Spoon the beef into the eggplant shells and sprinkle with cheddar cheese. Place on a greased baking sheet and cook to melt the cheese for 15 minutes until eggplant is tender. Serve warm topped with dill.

Sweet Chipotle Grilled Beef Ribs

Ready in about: 35 minutes + marinating time | **Serves**: 4 | **Per serving**: Kcal 395, Fat 33g, Net Carbs 3g, Protein 21g

INGREDIENTS

4 tbsp sugar-free BBQ sauce + extra for serving

2 tbsp erythritol	2 tbsp olive oil	1 tsp garlic powder
Pink salt and black pepper to taste	2 tsp chipotle powder	1 lb beef spare ribs

DIRECTIONS

Mix the erythritol, salt, pepper, oil, chipotle, and garlic powder. Brush on the meaty sides of the ribs and wrap in foil. Sit for 30 minutes to marinate.

Preheat oven to 400°F. Place wrapped ribs on a baking sheet and cook for 40 minutes until cooked through. Remove ribs and aluminium foil, brush with BBQ sauce, and brown under the broiler for 10 minutes on both sides. Slice and serve with extra BBQ sauce and lettuce tomato salad.

Grilled Sirloin Steak with Sauce Diane

Ready in about: 25 minutes | **Serves**: 6 | **Per serving**: Kcal 434, Fat 17g, Net Carbs 2.9g, Protein 36g

INGREDIENTS

Sirloin steak

1 ½ lb sirloin steak	Salt and black pepper to taste	1 tsp olive oil

Sauce Diane

1 tbsp olive oil	1 small onion, finely diced	2 tbsp Worcestershire sauce
1 clove garlic, minced	2 tbsp butter	¼ cup whiskey
1 cup sliced porcini mushrooms	1 tbsp Dijon mustard	2 cups heavy cream

DIRECTIONS

Put a grill pan over high heat and as it heats, brush the steak with oil, sprinkle with salt and pepper, and rub the seasoning into the meat with your hands. Cook the steak in the pan for 4 minutes on each side for medium-rare and transfer to a chopping board to rest for 4 minutes before slicing. Reserve the juice.

Heat the oil in a frying pan over medium heat and sauté the onion for 3 minutes. Add the butter, garlic, and mushrooms, and cook for 2 minutes. Add the Worcestershire sauce, the reserved juice, and mustard.

Stir and cook for 1 minute. Pour in the whiskey and cook further 1 minute until the sauce reduces by half. Swirl the pan and add the cream. Let it simmer to thicken for about 3 minutes. Adjust the taste with salt and pepper. Spoon the sauce over the steaks slices and serve with celeriac mash.

Easy Zucchini Beef Lasagna

Ready in about: 1 hour | **Serves**: 4 | **Per serving**: Kcal 344, Fat 17.8g, Net Carbs 2.9g, Protein 40.4g

INGREDIENTS

1 lb ground beef	3 tomatoes, chopped	1 tsp dried basil
2 large zucchinis, sliced lengthwise	Salt and black pepper to taste	1 cup mozzarella cheese, shredded
3 cloves garlic	2 tsp sweet paprika	1 tbsp olive oil
1 medium white onion, chopped	1 tsp dried thyme	

DIRECTIONS

Preheat the oven to 370°F. Heat the olive oil in a skillet over medium heat. Cook the beef for 4 minutes while breaking any lumps as you stir. Top with onion, garlic, tomatoes, salt, paprika, and pepper. Stir and continue cooking for 5 minutes. Lay ⅓ of the zucchini slices in the baking dish.

Top with ⅓ of the beef mixture and repeat the layering process two more times with the same quantities. Season with basil and thyme. Sprinkle the mozzarella cheese on top and tuck the baking dish in the oven. Bake for 35 minutes. Remove the lasagna and let it rest for 10 minutes before serving.

Rib Roast with Roasted Shallots & Garlic

Ready in about: 40 minutes | **Serves:** 6 | **Per serving:** Kcal 556, Fat 38.6g, Net Carbs 2.5g, Protein 58.4g

INGREDIENTS

5 lb beef rib roast, on the bone
3 heads garlic, cut in half
3 tbsp olive oil

6 shallots, peeled and halved
2 lemons, zested and juiced
3 tbsp mustard seeds

3 tbsp swerve
Salt and black pepper to taste
3 tbsp thyme leaves

DIRECTIONS

Preheat oven to 400°F. Place garlic heads and shallots in a roasting dish, toss with olive oil, and bake for 15 minutes. Pour lemon juice on them. Score shallow crisscrosses patterns on the meat and set aside.

Mix swerve, mustard seeds, thyme, salt, pepper, and lemon zest to make a rub and apply it all over the beef. Place the beef on the shallots and garlic and cook in the oven for 20 minutes. Once ready, remove the dish, and let sit covered for 15 minutes before slicing. Serve.

Habanero & Beef Balls

Ready in about: 45 minutes | **Serves:** 6 | **Per serving:** Kcal 455, Fat 31g, Net Carbs 8.3g, Protein 27g

INGREDIENTS

3 garlic cloves, minced
2 lb ground beef
1 onion, chopped
2 habanero peppers, chopped
1 tsp dried thyme
2 tsp fresh cilantro, chopped

½ tsp allspice
1 tsp cumin
½ tsp ground cloves
Salt and black pepper to taste
2 tbsp butter
3 tbsp butter, melted

6 oz cream cheese
1 tsp turmeric
¼ tsp stevia
½ tsp baking powder
1½ cups flax meal
½ cup coconut flour

DIRECTIONS

In a blender, mix the onion with garlic, habaneros, and ½ cup water. Set a pan over medium heat, add 2 tbsp butter, and cook the beef for 3 minutes. Stir in the onion mixture, and cook for 2 minutes. Stir in cilantro, cloves, salt, cumin, turmeric, thyme, allspice, and pepper and cook for 3 minutes.

In a bowl, combine the coconut flour, stevia, flax meal, and baking powder and stir well. In a separate bowl, whisk the melted butter with the cream cheese. Mix the 2 mixtures to obtain a dough.

Form 12 balls from the mixture and roll them into circles. Split the beef mix on one-half of the dough circles, cover with the other half, seal edges, and lay on a lined sheet. Bake for 25 minutes in the oven at 350°F.

Warm Rump Steak Salad

Ready in about: 40 minutes | **Serves:** 4 | **Per serving:** Kcal 325, Fat 19g, Net Carbs 4g, Protein 28g

INGREDIENTS

1 lb rump steak, excess fat trimmed
3 green onions, sliced
3 tomatoes, sliced

1 cup cooked green beans, sliced
2 kohlrabi, peeled and chopped
1 tbsp butter, softened

2 cups mixed salad greens
Salt and black pepper to taste

Salad dressing

2 tsp Dijon mustard
1 tbsp erythritol

Salt and black pepper to taste
3 tbsp olive oil

1 tbsp red wine vinegar

DIRECTIONS

Preheat oven to 400°F. Place the kohlrabi on a baking sheet, drizzle with olive oil and bake in the oven for 25 minutes. Let it cool. In a bowl, mix the mustard, erythritol, salt, pepper, vinegar, and oil; reserve.

Melt the butter in a pan over high heat. Season the meat with salt and pepper. Place the steak in the pan and brown on both sides for 4 minutes each. Remove and let it rest for 4 more minutes before slicing.

In a salad bowl, add green onions, tomatoes, green beans, kohlrabi, salad greens, and steak slices. Drizzle the dressing over and toss with two spoons. Serve the steak salad warm with chunks of low carb bread.

Mustard-Lemon Beef

Ready in about: 25 minutes | Serves: 4 | Per serving: Kcal 435, Fat 30g, Net Carbs 5g, Protein 32g

INGREDIENTS

2 tbsp olive oil
1 tbsp fresh rosemary, chopped
2 garlic cloves, minced
1 ½ lb beef rump steak, thinly sliced
Salt and black pepper to taste

1 shallot, chopped
½ cup heavy cream
½ cup beef stock
1 tbsp mustard
2 tsp Worcestershire sauce

2 tsp lemon juice
1 tsp erythritol
2 tbsp butter
1 tbsp fresh rosemary, chopped
1 tbsp fresh thyme, chopped

DIRECTIONS

In a bowl, combine 1 tbsp of oil with black pepper, garlic, rosemary, and salt. Toss in the beef to coat and set aside for some minutes. Heat a pan with the rest of the oil over medium heat, place in the beef steak, cook for 6 minutes, flipping halfway through. Set aside and keep warm.

Melt the butter in the pan. Add in the shallot and cook for 3 minutes. Stir in the stock, Worcestershire sauce, erythritol, thyme, cream, mustard, and rosemary and cook for 8 minutes. Mix in the lemon juice, pepper, and salt. Arrange the beef slices on serving plates, sprinkle over the sauce, and enjoy!

Ribeye Steak with Shitake Mushrooms

Ready in about: 25 minutes | Serves: 4 | Per serving: Kcal 478, Fat: 31g, Net Carbs: 3g, Protein: 33g

INGREDIENTS

1 lb ribeye steaks
1 tbsp butter

2 tbsp olive oil
1 cup shitake mushrooms, sliced

Salt and black pepper to taste
2 tbsp fresh parsley, chopped

DIRECTIONS

Heat the olive oil in a pan over medium heat. Rub the steaks with salt and black pepper and cook about 4 minutes per side; reserve. Melt the butter in the pan and cook the shitakes for 4 minutes. Scatter the parsley over and pour the mixture over the steaks to serve.

Parsley Beef Burgers

Ready in about: 25 minutes | Serves: 6 | Per serving: Kcal 354, Fat: 28g, Net Carbs: 2.5g, Protein: 27g

INGREDIENTS

2 lb ground beef
1 tbsp onion flakes

¾ cup almond flour
¼ cup beef broth

2 tbsp fresh parsley, chopped
1 tbsp Worcestershire sauce

DIRECTIONS

Combine all ingredients in a bowl. Mix well with your hands and make 6 patties out of the mixture. Arrange on a lined baking sheet. Bake at 370°F for about 18 minutes, until nice and crispy. Serve.

Beef Cauliflower Curry

Ready in about: 26 minutes | Serves: 6 | Per serving: Kcal 374, Fat 33g, Net Carbs 2g, Protein 22g

INGREDIENTS

1 tbsp olive oil
1 ½ lb ground beef
1 tbsp ginger paste

1 tsp garam masala
1 (7 oz) can whole tomatoes
1 head cauliflower, cut into florets

Salt to taste
2 garlic cloves, minced
½ tsp hot paprika

DIRECTIONS

Heat oil in a saucepan over medium heat. Add the beef, ginger, garlic, garam masala, paprika, and salt and cook for 5 minutes while breaking any lumps. Stir in the tomatoes and cauliflower. Cook covered for 6 minutes. Add ½ cup water and bring to a boil. Simmer for 10 minutes or until the water has reduced by half. Spoon the curry into serving bowls and serve with shirataki rice.

Italian Beef Ragout

Ready in about: 1 hour 55 minutes | **Serves**: 4 | **Per serving**: Kcal 328, Fat 21.6g, Net Carbs 4.2g, Protein 36.6g

INGREDIENTS

1 lb chuck steak, cubed	1 onion, diced	4 oz tomato puree
2 tbsp olive oil	½ cup dry white wine	3 tsp smoked paprika
Salt and black pepper to taste	1 red bell pepper, seeded and diced	1 cup beef broth
2 tbsp almond flour	2 tsp Worcestershire sauce	2 tbsp fresh thyme, chopped

DIRECTIONS

Lightly dredge the meat in the almond flour. Place a large skillet over medium heat, add the olive oil to heat and then sauté the onion and bell pepper for 3 minutes. Stir in paprika. Add the beef and cook for 10 minutes in total while turning them halfway. Stir in white wine and let it reduce by half, about 3 minutes.

Add in Worcestershire sauce, tomato puree, beef broth, salt, and pepper. Let the mixture boil for 2 minutes, reduce the heat, and let simmer for 1 ½ hours, stirring often. Serve garnished with thyme.

Beef Meatballs

Ready in about: 35 minutes | **Serves**: 4 | **Per serving**: Kcal 332, Fat 18g, Net Carbs 7g, Protein 25g

INGREDIENTS

½ cup pork rinds, crushed	1 ½ lb ground beef	¼ cup free-sugar ketchup
1 egg	10 oz canned onion soup	3 tsp Worcestershire sauce
Salt and black pepper to taste	1 tbsp almond flour	½ tsp dry mustard

DIRECTIONS

In a bowl, combine ⅓ cup of the onion soup with the beef, pepper, pork rinds, egg, and salt. Shape the mixture into 12 meatballs. Heat a greased pan over medium heat. Brown the meatballs for 12 minutes.

In a separate bowl, combine the rest of the soup with the almond flour, dry mustard, ketchup, Worcestershire sauce, and ¼ cup water. Pour this over the beef meatballs, cover the pan, and cook for 10 minutes as you stir occasionally. Split among bowls and serve.

Beef & Ale Pot Roast

Ready in about: 2 hours 20 minutes | **Serves**: 6 | **Per serving**: Kcal 513, Fat 34g, Net Carbs 6g, Protein 26g

INGREDIENTS

1 ½ lb brisket	2 medium red onions, quartered	2 bay leaves
2 tbsp olive oil	1 celery stalk, cut into chunks	1 ½ cups low carb beer (ale)
8 baby carrots, peeled	Salt and black pepper to taste	

DIRECTIONS

Preheat oven to 370°F. Heat the olive oil in a large skillet over medium heat. Season the brisket with salt and pepper. Brown the meat on both sides for 8 minutes. After, transfer to a deep casserole dish. In the dish, arrange the carrots, onions, celery, and bay leaves around the brisket and pour the beer all over it.

Cover the pot and cook in the oven for 2 hours. When ready, remove the casserole. Transfer the beef to a chopping board and cut it into thick slices. Serve the beef and vegetables with a drizzle of the sauce.

Beef Tripe Pot

Ready in about: 1 hour 30 minutes + cooling time | **Serves**: 6 | **Per serving**: Kcal 248, Fat 12.8g, Net Carbs 4g, Protein 8g

INGREDIENTS

1 ½ lb beef tripe, cleaned	3 tbsp olive oil	3 tomatoes, diced
4 cups buttermilk	2 onions, sliced	1 tsp paprika
Salt and black pepper to taste	4 garlic cloves, minced	2 chili peppers, minced

DIRECTIONS

Put the tripe in a bowl and cover with buttermilk. Refrigerate for 3 hours to extract bitterness and gamey taste. Remove from buttermilk, drain and rinse well under cold running water. Place in a pot over medium heat and cover with water. Bring to a boil and cook about for 1 hour until tender. Remove the tripe with a perforated spoon and let cool. Strain the broth and reserve. Chop the cooled tripe.

Heat the oil in a skillet over medium heat. Sauté the onions, garlic, and chili peppers for 3 minutes until soft. Stir in the paprika and add in the tripe. Cook for 5-6 minutes. Include the tomatoes and 4 cups of the reserved tripe broth and cook for 10 minutes. Adjust the seasoning with salt and pepper. Serve.

Beef Stovies

Ready in about: 45 minutes | **Serves**: 4 | **Per serving**: Kcal 316, Fat 18g, Net Carbs 3g, Protein 14g

INGREDIENTS

1 lb ground beef	2 tbsp olive oil	¼ tsp allspice
1 large onion, chopped	2 garlic cloves, minced	2 tsp fresh rosemary, chopped
2 parsnips, peeled and chopped	Salt and black pepper to taste	1 tbsp Worcestershire sauce
1 large carrot, chopped	1 cup chicken broth	½ small cabbage, shredded

DIRECTIONS

Heat the olive oil in a skillet over medium heat and cook the beef for 4 minutes. Season with salt and pepper, stirring occasionally while breaking the lumps in it. Add in onion, garlic, carrot, rosemary, and parsnips. Stir and cook for a minute, and pour in the chicken broth, allspice, and Worcestershire sauce.

Reduce the heat to low and cook for 20 minutes. Stir in the cabbage, season with salt and black pepper, and cook further for 15 minutes. Turn the heat off, plate the stovies, and serve warm.

Beef Sausage Casserole

Ready in about: 60 minutes | **Serves**: 4 | **Per serving**: Kcal 456, Fat 35g, Net Carbs 4g, Protein 32g

INGREDIENTS

¼ cup almond flour	¼ tsp red pepper flakes	¼ tsp dried oregano
1 egg	¼ cup Parmesan cheese, grated	½ cup ricotta cheese, crumbled
1 lb beef sausages, chopped	¼ tsp onion powder	½ cup sugar-free marinara sauce
Salt and black pepper to taste	½ tsp garlic powder	½ cups cheddar cheese, shredded

DIRECTIONS

In a bowl, combine the sausages, black pepper, pepper flakes, oregano, egg, Parmesan cheese, onion powder, almond flour, salt, and garlic powder and mix well. Form balls and lay them on a greased baking sheet. Place in the oven and bake for 15 minutes at 370°F. Remove the balls from the oven.

Cover the meatballs with half of the marinara sauce. Pour ricotta cheese all over, followed by the rest of the marinara sauce, and scatter with the cheddar cheese. Bake for 10 minutes. Allow to cool and serve.

Homemade Classic Beef Burgers

Ready in about: 15 minutes | **Serves**: 4 | **Per serving**: Kcal 664, Fat: 55g, Net Carbs: 7.9g, Protein: 39g

INGREDIENTS

1 lb ground beef	1 tsp Dijon mustard	1 tsp sriracha sauce
½ tsp onion powder	4 zero carb buns, halved	4 tbsp cabbage slaw
2 tbsp ghee	¼ cup mayonnaise	Salt and black pepper to taste

DIRECTIONS

Mix well the beef, onion powder, mustard, salt, and pepper in a bowl. Create 4 burgers. Melt the ghee in a skillet over medium heat and cook the burgers for about 3 minutes per side. Place in buns, top with mayonnaise, sriracha sauce, and cabbage slaw. Serve.

Spicy Spinach Pinwheel Steaks

Ready in about: 40 minutes | **Serves:** 6 | **Per serving:** Kcal 490, Fat 41g, Net Carbs 2g, Protein 28g

INGREDIENTS

1 ½ lb beef flank steak
Salt and black pepper to taste

1 cup feta cheese, crumbled
½ loose cup baby spinach

1 jalapeño pepper, chopped
¼ cup chopped basil leaves

DIRECTIONS

Preheat oven to 400°F. Wrap the steak in plastic wrap, place on a flat surface, and gently run a rolling pin over to flatten. Take off the wraps. Sprinkle with half of the feta cheese, top with spinach, jalapeno, basil leaves, and the remaining cheese. Roll the steak over on the stuffing and secure with toothpicks.

Place in the baking sheet and cook for 30 minutes, flipping once until nicely browned on the outside and the cheese melted within. Cool for 3 minutes, slice into pinwheels, and serve with sautéed veggies.

Classic Italian Bolognese Sauce

Ready in about: 35 minutes | **Serves:** 4 | **Per serving:** Kcal 318, Fat: 20g, Net Carbs: 5.9g, Protein: 26g

INGREDIENTS

1 lb ground beef
2 garlic cloves, minced
1 onion, chopped

½ tsp dried oregano
½ tsp dried sage
½ tsp dried rosemary

14 oz canned diced tomatoes
2 tbsp olive oil

DIRECTIONS

Heat olive oil in a saucepan. Add onion and garlic and cook for 3 minutes. Add beef and cook until browned, about 4-5 minutes. Stir in the herbs and tomatoes. Cook for 15 minutes. Serve with zoodles.

Beef Cheeseburger Casserole

Ready in about: 30 minutes | **Serves:** 6 | **Per serving:** Kcal 385, Fat 25g, Net Carbs 5g, Protein 20g

INGREDIENTS

3 tbsp olive oil
2 lb ground beef

1 cup cauli rice
2 cups cabbage, chopped

14 oz can diced tomatoes
1 cup Colby jack cheese, shredded

DIRECTIONS

Preheat oven to 370°F. Warm the olive oil in a pan over medium heat. Add in the ground beef and cook for 6 minutes until no longer pink. Stir in the cauli rice, cabbage, tomatoes, and ¼ cup water. Bring to boil and cook covered for 5 minutes until the sauce thickens.

Spoon the beef mixture into a baking dish and spread evenly. Sprinkle with cheese and bake for 15 minutes until the cheese has melted. Remove and cool for 4 minutes. Serve with zero carb crusted bread.

Herby Beef & Veggie Stew

Ready in about: 50 minutes | **Serves:** 4 | **Per serving:** Kcal 253, Fat 13g, Net Carbs 5.2g, Protein 30g

INGREDIENTS

1 lb stewed beef, cubed
2 tbsp olive oil
1 onion, chopped
2 garlic cloves, minced

14 oz canned diced tomatoes
¼ tsp dried oregano
¼ tsp dried basil
¼ tsp dried marjoram

Salt and black pepper to taste
2 carrots, sliced
2 celery stalks, chopped
1 cup vegetable broth

DIRECTIONS

Warm the olive oil in a pan over medium heat. Add in the onion, celery, and garlic and sauté for 5 minutes. Place in the ground beef and stir-fry for 6 minutes. Mix in the tomatoes, carrots, vegetable broth, black pepper, oregano, marjoram, basil, and salt and simmer for 35 minutes. Serve and enjoy!

Beef with Grilled Vegetables

Ready in about: 30 minutes | Serves: 4 | Per serving: Kcal 515, Fat 32.1g, Net Carbs 5.6g, Protein 66g

INGREDIENTS

4 sirloin steaks

Vegetables

½ lb asparagus, trimmed

1 cup green beans

2 tbsp olive oil

1 cup snow peas

1 red bell peppers, cut into strips

3 tbsp balsamic vinegar

1 orange bell peppers, cut into strips

1 medium red onion, quartered

DIRECTIONS

Set a grill pan over high heat. Grab 2 separate bowls and put the beef in one and the vegetables in another. Mix salt, pepper, olive oil, and balsamic vinegar in a small bowl and pour half of the mixture over the beef and the other half over the vegetables. Coat the ingredients in both bowls with the sauce.

Place the steaks in the grill pan and sear both sides for 2-3 minutes each. When done, remove the beef onto a plate; set aside. Pour the vegetables and marinade in the pan and cook for 5 minutes, turning once. Share the vegetables into plates. Top with beef, drizzle the sauce from the pan all over, and serve.

Beef with Dilled Yogurt

Ready in about: 25 minutes | Serves: 6 | Per serving: Kcal 408, Fat 22.4g, Net Carbs 8.3g, Protein 27g

INGREDIENTS

¼ cup almond milk

2 lb ground beef

1 onion, grated

5 zero carb bread slices, torn

1 egg, whisked

Salt and black pepper to taste

2 garlic cloves, minced

¼ cup fresh mint, chopped

½ tsp dried oregano

¼ cup olive oil

1 cup cherry tomatoes, halved

1 cucumber, sliced

1 cup baby spinach

1 ½ tbsp lemon juice

1 cup dilled Greek yogurt

DIRECTIONS

Place the torn zero carb bread in a bowl, add in the milk, and let it soak for 3 minutes. Squeeze the bread and place it into a bowl. Stir in the beef, salt, mint, onion, parsley, pepper, egg, oregano, and garlic. Form balls out of this mixture and place them on a working surface.

Set a pan over medium heat and warm half of the oil. Fry the meatballs for 8 minutes on all sides. Remove to a tray. On a salad plate, combine the spinach with the cherry tomatoes and cucumber. Mix in the remaining oil, lemon juice, pepper, and salt. Spread dilled yogurt over. Top with meatballs to serve.

Beef Zucchini Boats

Ready in about: 45 minutes | Serves: 4 | Per serving: Kcal 422, Fat 33g, Net Carbs 7.8g, Protein 39g

INGREDIENTS

2 garlic cloves, minced

1 tsp cumin

2 tbsp olive oil

1 lb ground beef

½ cup onions, chopped

1 tsp smoked paprika

Salt and black pepper to taste

4 zucchinis

¼ cup fresh cilantro, chopped

½ cup Monterey Jack cheese, grated

1 ½ cups enchilada sauce

1 avocado, chopped, for serving

Green onions, chopped, for serving

Tomatoes, chopped, for serving

DIRECTIONS

Set a pan over high heat and warm the oil. Add the onions, and cook for 2 minutes. Stir in the beef and brown for 4-5 minutes. Stir in the paprika, pepper, garlic, cumin, and salt; cook for 2 minutes.

Slice the zucchini in half lengthwise and scoop out the seeds. Set the zucchini in a greased baking pan, stuff each with the beef, scatter enchilada sauce on top, and spread with the Monterey cheese.

Bake in the oven at 350°F for 20 minutes while covered. Uncover, spread with cilantro, and bake for 5 minutes. Top with tomatoes, green onions, and avocado and place on serving plates. Enjoy!

Soy-Glazed Meatloaf

Ready in about: 60 minutes | **Serves**: 6 | **Per serving**: Kcal 474, Fat 21.4g, Net Carbs 7.5g, Protein 46g

INGREDIENTS

1 cup white mushrooms, chopped
2 lb ground beef
2 tbsp fresh parsley, chopped
2 garlic cloves, minced
1 onion, chopped

1 red bell pepper, chopped
½ cup almond flour
⅓ cup Parmesan cheese, grated
2 eggs
Salt and black pepper to taste

½ tbsp swerve sugar
1 tbsp soy sauce
2 tbsp sugar-free ketchup
2 cups balsamic vinegar

DIRECTIONS

Preheat oven to 370°F. In a bowl, mix the beef, salt, mushrooms, bell pepper, Parmesan cheese, parsley, garlic, pepper, onion, almond flour, salt, and eggs. Shape into a loaf pan and bake for 30 minutes.

Meanwhile, heat a small pan over medium heat, add in the balsamic vinegar, swerve, soy sauce, and ketchup and cook for 20 minutes. Remove the meatloaf from the oven, spread the glaze over the meatloaf, and bake in the oven for 5 more minutes. Allow the meatloaf to cool, slice, and enjoy.

Beef Stuffed Roasted Squash

Ready in about: 1 hour 15 minutes | **Serves**: 4 | **Per serving**: Kcal 406, Fat 14.7g, Net Carbs 12.4g, Protein 34g

INGREDIENTS

2 lb butternut squash, pricked with a fork
Salt and black pepper to taste
2 garlic cloves, minced
1 onion, chopped

1 cup button mushrooms, sliced
28 oz canned diced tomatoes
1 tsp dried oregano

¼ tsp cayenne pepper
1 lb ground beef
1 green bell pepper, chopped

DIRECTIONS

Lay the butternut squash on a lined baking sheet, set in the oven at 400°F, and bake for 40 minutes. After, cut in half and set aside to cool. Deseed, scoop out most of the flesh, and let sit. Heat a greased pan over medium heat. Add in the garlic, mushrooms, onion, and beef and cook until the meat browns.

Stir in the green pepper, salt, tomatoes, oregano, pepper, butternut flesh, and cayenne and cook for 10 minutes. Stuff the squash halves with the beef mixture and bake in the oven for 10 minutes. Serve.

Broccoli & Beef Slow Cooker Casserole

Ready in about: 4 hours 15 minutes | **Serves**: 6 | **Per serving**: Kcal 434, Fat 21g, Net Carbs 5.6g, Protein 51g

INGREDIENTS

2 tbsp olive oil
2 lb ground beef
1 head broccoli, cut into florets
Salt and black pepper to taste

1 tsp mustard
2 tsp Worcestershire sauce
28 oz canned diced tomatoes
2 cups mozzarella cheese, grated

16 oz tomato sauce
2 tbsp fresh parsley, chopped
1 tsp dried oregano

DIRECTIONS

Season the broccoli florets with pepper and salt to and drizzle over the olive oil. Toss to coat. In a separate bowl, combine the beef with Worcestershire sauce, salt, mustard, and black pepper, and stir well. Press on the slow cooker's bottom. Scatter with the broccoli and stir in the tomatoes, parsley, mozzarella, oregano, and tomato sauce. Cook for 4 hours on High. Split the casserole among bowls and serve hot.

Beef & Cauliflower Rice Bowls

Ready in about: 25 minutes | **Serves**: 4 | **Per serving**: Kcal 320, Fat 26g, Net Carbs 4g, Protein 15g

INGREDIENTS

2 cups cauli rice
3 cups frozen mixed vegetables

3 tbsp ghee
1 lb skirt steaks

Salt and black pepper to taste
4 eggs

DIRECTIONS

Mix the cauli rice and vegetables in a bowl. Sprinkle with a little water and steam them in the microwave for 1 minute until tender. Share into 4 serving bowls. Melt the ghee in a skillet over medium heat. Season the beef with salt and pepper and brown for 5 minutes on each side. Remove onto the vegetables.

Wipe out the skillet and return to medium heat. Crack in an egg, season with salt and pepper, and cook until the egg white has set, but the yolk is still runny 3 minutes. Remove egg onto the vegetable bowl and fry the remaining 3 eggs. Add to the other bowls and serve.

Mexican Beef Chili

Ready in about: 40 minutes | **Serves**: 4 | **Per serving**: Kcal 437, Fat 26g, Net Carbs 5g, Protein 17g

INGREDIENTS

15 oz canned tomatoes with green chilies, chopped

1 onion, chopped	½ cup pickled jalapeños, chopped	Salt and black pepper to taste
2 tbsp olive oil	1 tsp chipotle chili paste	½ tsp cayenne pepper
1 ½ lb ground beef	2 garlic cloves, minced	1 tsp cumin
1 cup beef broth	3 celery stalks, chopped	1 bay leaf
1 tbsp tomato paste	2 tbsp coconut aminos	1 tbsp fresh cilantro, chopped

DIRECTIONS

Heat the olive oil in a pan over medium heat. Add in the onion, celery, garlic, ground beef, black pepper, and salt and cook until the meat browns, about 6-8 minutes. Stir in jalapeños, tomato paste, canned tomatoes with green chilies, salt, bay leaf, cayenne pepper, coconut aminos, chipotle chili paste, beef broth, and cumin. Cook for 30 minutes. Remove and discard the bay leaf. Serve in bowls sprinkled with cilantro.

Beef Meatballs with Onion Sauce

Ready in about: 35 minutes | **Serves**: 4 | **Per serving**: Kcal 435, Fat 23g, Net Carbs 6g, Protein 32g

INGREDIENTS

1 lb ground beef	1 cup beef stock	1 onion, sliced
Salt and black pepper to taste	¾ cup almond flour	2 tbsp butter
½ tsp garlic powder	1 tbsp fresh parsley, chopped	¼ cup sour cream
1 ¼ tbsp coconut aminos	1 tbsp dried onion flakes	

DIRECTIONS

In a bowl, mix the beef, salt, garlic powder, almond flour, onion flakes, parsley, 1 tbsp coconut aminos, and pepper. Form balls. Place them on a greased baking sheet. Bake in the oven for 20 minutes at 370°F.

Warm the butter in a pan over medium heat. Stir in the onion and cook for 3 minutes. Pour in the beef stock, sour cream, and remaining coconut aminos and bring to a simmer. Season with salt and pepper and cook for 3-4 minutes until the sauce thickens. Pour the sauce over the meatballs and serve.

Beef Provençal

Ready in about: 50 minutes | **Serves**: 4 | **Per serving**: Kcal 230, Fat 11.3g, Net Carbs 5.2g, Protein 19g

INGREDIENTS

12 oz beef steak racks	Salt and black pepper to taste	½ cup apple cider vinegar
1 fennel bulb, sliced	3 tbsp olive oil	1 tsp herbs de Provence

DIRECTIONS

In a bowl, mix the fennel with 2 tbsp of the olive oil and vinegar. Toss to coat and transfer to a baking dish. Season with herbs de Provence, pepper, and salt and cook in the oven at 400°F for 15 minutes.

Sprinkle the beef with pepper and salt. Place into an oiled pan over medium heat and cook for 2 minutes. Place the beef to the baking dish with the fennel and bake for 20 minutes. Split among plates and serve.

Beef Stew with Bacon

Ready in about: 1 hour 15 minutes | **Serves**: 6 | **Per serving**: Kcal 592, Fat 36g, Net Carbs 5.7g, Protein 63g

INGREDIENTS

4 oz bacon, chopped
4 lb beef meat for stew, cubed
2 garlic cloves, minced
1 onion, chopped
2 tbsp olive oil

2 tbsp red vinegar
2 cups beef stock
2 tbsp tomato puree
1 cinnamon stick
3 lemon peel strips

½ cup fresh parsley, chopped
4 thyme sprigs
2 tbsp butter
Salt and black pepper to taste

DIRECTIONS

Set a saucepan over medium heat and warm oil. Add in the garlic, bacon, and onion and cook for 5 minutes. Stir in the beef and cook until slightly brown, about 4-5 minutes. Pour in the vinegar, black pepper, butter, lemon peel strips, stock, salt, tomato puree, cinnamon, and thyme and stir for 3 minutes. Cook for 1 hour while covered. Get rid of the thyme, lemon peel, and cinnamon. Top with parsley to serve.

Chuck Roast Beef

Ready in about: 3 hours 15 minutes | **Serves**: 6 | **Per serving**: Kcal 325, Fat 18g, Net Carbs 7g, Protein 28g

INGREDIENTS

2 lb beef chuck roast, cubed
2 tbsp olive oil
14.5 oz canned diced tomatoes
2 carrots, chopped

Salt and black pepper to taste
½ lb mushrooms, sliced
1 celery stalk, chopped
1 onion, chopped

2 cups beef stock
1 tbsp fresh thyme, chopped
½ tsp dry mustard
1 tbsp almond flour

DIRECTIONS

Set an ovenproof pot over medium heat, warm olive oil, and brown the beef on all sides for 5-6 minutes; set aside. Add onions, carrots, mushrooms, and celery to the pot and sauté for 5 minutes. Pour in the stock and tomatoes and return the beef. Bring to a boil and simmer for 30 minutes.

In a bowl, combine 1 cup of the cooking liquid with almond flour and dry mustard. Pour in the pot, sprinkle with thyme, salt, and black pepper, and cook for 3-4 minutes. Serve warm.

Caribbean Beef

Ready in about: 1 hour 10 minutes | **Serves**: 4 | **Per serving**: Kcal 305, Fat 14g, Net Carbs 8g, Protein 25g

INGREDIENTS

1 onion, chopped
2 tbsp avocado oil
2 lb beef stew meat, cubed
1 red bell pepper, chopped
1 habanero pepper, chopped

2 green chilies, chopped
14.5 oz canned diced tomatoes
2 tbsp fresh cilantro, chopped
2 garlic cloves, minced
1 ½ cups vegetable broth

Salt and black pepper to taste
½ tsp cumin
½ cup black olives, chopped
½tsp dried oregano

DIRECTIONS

Set a pan over medium heat and warm the avocado oil. Brown the beef on all sides for 5-6 minutes. Set aside. Stir-fry the bell pepper, green chilies, oregano, garlic, habanero pepper, onions, and cumin in the pan for about 5-6 minutes. Pour in the tomatoes and vegetable broth and return the beef. Cook for 1 hour. Stir in the olives, adjust the seasonings, and serve in bowls sprinkled with fresh cilantro.

Jalapeno Beef Pot Roast

Ready in about: 1 hour 25 minutes | **Serves**: 4 | **Per serving**: Kcal 745, Fat 46g, Net Carbs 3.2g, Protein 87g

INGREDIENTS

1 ½ lb beef roast
4 oz mushrooms, sliced

12 oz beef stock
1 oz onion soup mix

½ cup Italian dressing
2 jalapeño peppers, shredded

DIRECTIONS

In a bowl, combine the stock with the Italian dressing and onion soup mixture. Place the beef roast in a baking pan, add in the stock mixture, mushrooms, and jalapeños, and cover with aluminum foil.

Set in the oven and bake for 1 hour at 360°F. Take out the foil and continue baking for 15 minutes. Allow the roast to cool slightly. Slice and serve alongside a topping of the gravy.

Beef Bourguignon

Ready in about: 60 minutes + marinated time | **Serves**: 4 | **Per serving**: Kcal 435, Fat 26g, Net Carbs 7g, Protein 45g

INGREDIENTS

3 tbsp coconut oil
1 tbsp dried parsley flakes
1 cup red wine
1 tsp dried thyme

Salt and black pepper to taste
1 bay leaf
⅓ cup coconut flour
2 lb beef, cubed

12 small white onions
4 pancetta slices, chopped
2 garlic cloves, minced
½ lb mushrooms, chopped

DIRECTIONS

In a bowl, combine the wine with bay leaf, olive oil, thyme, pepper, parsley, salt, and the beef cubes and toss to coat. Marinate for 3 hours. Drain the meat and reserve the marinade. Coat the meat with the flour.

Heat a pan over medium heat, stir in the pancetta, and cook until slightly browned. Place in the onions and garlic, and cook for 3 minutes. Stir-fry in the meat and mushrooms for 4-5 minutes. Pour in the marinade and 1 cup of water; cover and cook for 50 minutes. Season to taste and serve.

Beef & Feta Salad

Ready in about: 20 minutes | **Serves**: 4 | **Per serving**: Kcal 434, Fat 43g, Net Carbs 3.5g, Protein 17g

INGREDIENTS

3 tbsp olive oil
½ lb beef rump steak, cut into strips
Salt and black pepper to taste
1 tsp cumin

½ tsp dried thyme
2 garlic cloves, minced
4 oz feta cheese, crumbled
½ cup pecans

2 cups spinach
1 ½ tbsp lemon juice
¼ cup fresh mint, chopped

DIRECTIONS

Season the beef with salt, some olive oil, garlic, thyme, pepper, and cumin. Place on a preheated to medium heat grill and cook for 10 minutes, flipping once. Remove to a cutting board, leave to cool, and slice into strips. Toast the pecans in a dry pan over medium heat for 2 minutes, shaking often.

In a salad bowl, combine the spinach with the remaining olive oil, mint, salt, black pepper, and lemon juice and toss well to coat. Sprinkle with feta cheese and pecans. Top with the beef slices and serve.

Italian Sausage Stew

Ready in about: 35 minutes | **Serves**: 6 | **Per serving**: Kcal 314, Fat 25g, Net Carbs 7g, Protein 16g

INGREDIENTS

1 lb Italian sausage, sliced
1 red bell pepper, chopped
2 onions, chopped
Salt and black pepper to taste
1 cup fresh parsley, chopped

6 green onions, chopped
¼ cup avocado oil
1 cup beef stock
4 garlic cloves
24 oz canned diced tomatoes

16 oz okra, trimmed and sliced
6 oz tomato sauce
2 tbsp coconut aminos
1 tbsp hot sauce

DIRECTIONS

Set a pot over medium heat and warm oil, place in the sausages, and cook for 2 minutes. Stir in the onions, green onions, garlic, black pepper, bell pepper, and salt and cook for 5 minutes.

Add in the hot sauce, beef stock, tomatoes, coconut aminos, okra, and tomato sauce, bring to a simmer. Cook for 15 minutes. Share into serving bowls and sprinkle with fresh parsley to serve.

Russian-Style Beef Gratin

Ready in about: 45 minutes | **Serves**: 4 | **Per serving**: Kcal 584, Fat 48g, Net Carbs 5g, Protein 41g

INGREDIENTS

1 onion, chopped
1 ½ lb ground beef
2 garlic cloves, minced

Salt and black pepper to taste
1 cup mozzarella cheese, shredded
2 cups fontina cheese, shredded

1 cup crème fraîche
20 dill pickle slices
1 iceberg lettuce head, torn

DIRECTIONS

Set a pan over medium heat, place in beef, garlic, salt, onion, and pepper and cook for 5 minutes. Remove to a baking dish, stir in crème fraîche, mozzarella cheese, and spread 1 cup of the fontina cheese.

Lay the pickle slices on top and spread over the remaining fontina cheese. Place in the oven at 350°F and bake for 20 minutes. Arrange the lettuce on a serving platter and top with the gratin.

Roasted Spicy Beef

Ready in about: 70 minutes | **Serves**: 4 | **Per serving**: Kcal 480, Fat 23.5g, Net Carbs 3.5g, Protein 55g

INGREDIENTS

2 lb beef brisket
½ tsp celery salt
1 tsp chili powder

2 tbsp avocado oil
½ tsp cayenne pepper
½ tsp garlic powder

½ cup beef stock
1 tbsp garlic, minced
¼ tsp dry mustard

DIRECTIONS

Preheat oven to 340°F. In a bowl, combine the dry mustard, chili powder, salt, garlic powder, cayenne pepper, and celery salt and mix well. Rub the meat with the mixture. Set a pan over medium heat.

Warm the avocado oil in the pan. Place in the beef and sear until brown. Remove to a baking dish. Pour in the stock, add garlic, and bake for 60 minutes. Set the beef to a cutting board, leaving to cool before slicing. Take the juices from the baking dish and strain. Sprinkle over the meat and serve.

Adobo Beef Fajitas

Ready in about: 35 minutes + marinating time | **Serves**: 4 | **Per serving**: Kcal 348, Fat 25g, Net Carbs 5g, Protein 18g

INGREDIENTS

1 ½ lb skirt steak
2 tbsp adobo seasoning

2 tbsp olive oil
2 large white onion, chopped

1 cup mixed bell peppers, chopped
8 zero carb tortillas

DIRECTIONS

Brush the steak with adobo seasoning and put in the fridge for 1 hour. Preheat grill to high heat. Cook the steak for 12 minutes, flipping once until lightly browned. Remove, wrap in foil, and let sit for 10 minutes.

Heat olive oil in a skillet over medium heat and sauté onion and bell peppers for 5 minutes until soft. Cut steak against the grain into strips and share on the tortillas. Top with the veggies and serve.

Beef Skewers with Ranch Dressing

Ready in about: 25 minutes | **Serves**: 4 | **Per serving**: Kcal 230, Fat 14g, Net Carbs 3g, Protein 21g

INGREDIENTS

1 lb sirloin steak, boneless, cubed

¼ cup ranch dressing

Chopped scallions to garnish

DIRECTIONS

Preheat the grill to 400°F. Thread the beef cubes on skewers. Brush half of the ranch dressing on the skewers (all around) and place them on the grill grate to cook for 12 minutes, turning once.

Brush the remaining ranch dressing on the meat and cook them for 1 more minute on each side. Plate, garnish with the scallions, and serve with a mixed veggie salad and extra ranch dressing.

Beef Cotija Cheeseburger

Ready in about: 15 minutes | Serves: 4 | Per serving: Kcal 386, Fat 32g, Net Carbs 2g, Protein 21g

INGREDIENTS

1 ½ lb ground beef
1 tsp dried parsley

½ tsp Worcestershire sauce
Salt and black pepper to taste

1 cup cotija cheese, shredded
4 zero carb buns, halved

DIRECTIONS

Preheat grill to 400°F. Mix the beef, parsley, Worcestershire sauce, salt, and black pepper with your hands until evenly combined. Make medium-sized patties out of the mixture.

Cook on the grill for 5 minutes. Flip and top with cheese. Cook for 5 more minutes until the cheese melts. Remove and sandwich into two halves of a bun each. Serve with a tomato sauce and zucchini fries.

Thai Beef with Shiitake Mushrooms

Ready in about: 30 minutes | Serves: 6 | Per serving: Kcal 224, Fat 15g, Net Carbs 3g, Protein 19g

INGREDIENTS

1 cup beef stock
4 tbsp butter
¼ tsp garlic powder
¼ tsp onion powder

1 tbsp coconut aminos
1 ½ tsp lemon pepper
1 lb beef steak, cut into strips
Salt and black pepper to taste

1 cup shiitake mushrooms, sliced
3 green onions, chopped
1 tbsp Thai red curry paste

DIRECTIONS

Melt butter in a pan over medium heat. Add in the beef, garlic powder, pepper, salt, and onion powder, stir, and cook for 4 minutes. Mix in the mushrooms and stir-fry for 5 minutes. Pour in the stock, coconut aminos, lemon pepper, and Thai curry paste and cook for 15 minutes. Top with green onions and serve.

Beef & Butternut Squash Stew

Ready in about: 40 minutes | Serves: 4 | Per serving: Kcal 343, Fat 17g, Net Carbs 7.3g, Protein 32g

INGREDIENTS

2 tsp olive oil
1 ½ lb ground beef
1 cup beef stock
14 oz canned tomatoes with juice

1 tbsp stevia
1 lb butternut squash, chopped
1 tbsp Worcestershire sauce
2 bay leaves

Salt and black pepper to taste
1 onion, chopped
½ tsp dried sage
1 tbsp garlic, minced

DIRECTIONS

Set a pan over medium heat and heat olive oil. Stir in the onion, garlic, and beef and cook for 10 minutes. Add in butternut squash, Worcestershire sauce, bay leaves, stevia, stock, canned tomatoes, sage, salt, and pepper and bring to a boil. Simmer for 30 minutes. Remove and discard the bay leaves. Serve warm.

Winter Veal with Sauerkraut

Ready in about: 60 minutes | Serves: 4 | Per serving: Kcal 430, Fat 27g, Net Carbs 6g, Protein 29g

INGREDIENTS

1 lb veal, cut into cubes
18 oz sauerkraut, rinsed and drained
Salt and black pepper to taste

½ cup ham, chopped
1 keek, chopped
2 garlic cloves, minced

3 tbsp butter
1 cup canned tomatoes, chopped
1 cup beef broth

DIRECTIONS

Heat a pot with the butter over medium heat. Add in the leek and garlic cook for 3 minutes, stirring occasionally. Place in the veal and ham and cook until slightly browned, about 5-6 minutes.

Pour in the broth, tomatoes, and sauerkraut and cook until the meat becomes tender, about 30 minutes. Season with pepper and salt. Transfer to a baking dish. Bake in the oven for 10 minutes at 350°F. Serve.

Pecorino Veal Cutlets

Ready in about: 55 minutes | **Serves**: 6 | **Per serving**: Kcal 362, Fat 21g, Net Carbs 6g, Protein 26g

INGREDIENTS

6 veal cutlets
½ cup Pecorino cheese, grated
6 provolone cheese slices

Black pepper to taste
4 cups tomato sauce
A pinch of garlic salt

2 tbsp butter
2 tbsp coconut oil, melted
1 tsp Italian seasoning

DIRECTIONS

Season the veal cutlets with garlic salt and pepper. Set a pan over medium heat and warm coconut oil and butter. Add in the veal and cook until browned on all sides. Spread half of the tomato sauce on a greased baking dish. Place in the veal cutlets, then sprinkle with Italian seasoning and remaining sauce.

Set in the oven at 360° F and bake for 40 minutes. Scatter with the provolone cheese, then sprinkle with Pecorino cheese, and bake for another 5 minutes until the cheese is golden and melted. Serve warm.

Veal Stew

Ready in about: 2 hours | **Serves**: 6 | **Per serving**: Kcal 415, Fat 21g, Net Carbs 5.2g, Protein 44g

INGREDIENTS

3 tbsp olive oil
3 lb veal shoulder, cubed
1 onion, chopped
1 garlic clove, minced

Salt and black pepper to taste
1 cup water
1 ½ cups red wine
12 oz canned tomato sauce

1 carrot, chopped
1 cup mushrooms, chopped
½ cup green beans
2 tsp dried oregano

DIRECTIONS

Set a pot over medium heat and warm the olive oil. Brown the veal for 5-6 minutes. Stir in the onion and garlic and cook for 3 minutes. Place in the wine, oregano, carrot, black pepper, salt, tomato sauce, water, and mushrooms. Bring to a boil and reduce the heat to low. Cook for 1 hour and 45 minutes, then add in the green beans, and cook for 5 minutes. Adjust the seasoning and split among bowls to serve.

Venison Tenderloin with Cheese Stuffing

Ready in about: 30 minutes | **Serves**: 8 | **Per serving**: Kcal 194, Fat: 12g, Net Carbs: 1.7g, Protein: 25g

INGREDIENTS

2 lb venison tenderloin
2 garlic cloves, minced

2 tbsp almonds, chopped
½ cup gorgonzola cheese, crumbled

½ cup feta cheese, crumbled
1 tsp chopped onion

DIRECTIONS

Preheat the grill to medium heat. Slice the tenderloin lengthwise to make a pocket for the filling. Combine the rest of the ingredients in a bowl. Stuff the tenderloin with the filling. Shut the meat with skewers and grill for as long as it takes to reach your desired density. Serve warm with sautéed vegetables.

Lamb Shashlyk

Ready in about: 20 minutes | **Serves**: 4 | **Per serving**: Kcal 467, Fat: 37g, Net Carbs: 3.2g, Protein: 27g

INGREDIENTS

1 lb ground lamb
¼ tsp cinnamon

1 egg
1 grated onion

Salt and black pepper to taste

DIRECTIONS

Place all ingredients in a bowl. Mix with your hands to combine well. Divide the meat into 4 pieces. Shape all meat portions around previously-soaked skewers.

Preheat grill to medium heat and grill the kebabs for about 5 minutes per side. Serve.

Rack of Lamb in Red Bell Pepper Sauce

Ready in about: 65 minutes + marinating time | **Serves**: 4 | **Per serving**: Kcal 415, Fat 25g, Carbs 2g, Protein 46g

INGREDIENTS

1 lb rack of lamb
Salt to taste

Sauce

2 tbsp olive oil
1 large red bell pepper, seeded, diced

1 tbsp garlic powder
⅓ cup olive oil

2 cloves garlic, minced
1 cup chicken broth

⅓ cup white wine
6 sprigs fresh rosemary

2 oz butter
Salt and white pepper to taste

DIRECTIONS

Mix the olive oil with wine, salt, and garlic powder in a bowl. Brush the mixture all over the lamb. Drop the rosemary sprigs on it, cover the bowl with plastic wrap, and place in the refrigerator to marinate.

Preheat the grill to high heat. Cook the lamb for 6 minutes on both sides. Remove and let rest for 4 minutes. Heat the olive oil in a frying pan and sauté the garlic and bell pepper for 5 minutes.

Pour in the chicken broth and continue cooking the ingredients until the liquid reduces by half, about 10 minutes. Add the butter, salt, and white pepper. Stir to melt the butter and turn the heat off.

Use a stick blender to puree the ingredients until very smooth and strain the sauce through a fine-mesh into a bowl. Slice the lamb and serve drizzled with the sauce.

Lamb Stew with Veggies

Ready in about: 1 hour 50 minutes | **Serves**: 2 | **Per serving**: Kcal 584, Fat 42g, Net Carbs 8.1g, Protein 38g

INGREDIENTS

1 garlic clove, minced
1 parsnip, chopped
1 onion, chopped
1 tbsp olive oil
1 celery stalk, chopped
10 oz lamb fillet, cut into pieces

Salt and black pepper to taste
1 ¼ cups vegetable stock
1 carrot, chopped
½ tbsp fresh rosemary, chopped
1 leek, chopped
1 tbsp mint sauce

1 tsp stevia
1 tbsp tomato puree
½ head cauliflower, cut into florets
½ head celeriac, chopped
2 tbsp butter

DIRECTIONS

Set a pot over medium heat and warm the oil. Add in the celery, onion, and garlic and cook for 5 minutes. Stir in the lamb pieces and cook for 3 minutes. Add in the stevia, carrot, parsnip, rosemary, mint sauce, stock, leek, and tomato puree. Bring to a boil, reduce the heat, and cook for 1 hour and 30 minutes.

Heat a pot with water over medium heat and place in the celeriac. Cover and simmer for 10 minutes. Add in the cauliflower florets and cook for 15 minutes. Drain everything and combine with butter, pepper, and salt. Mash using a potato masher. Top with vegetable mixture and lamb and serve.

Grilled Lamb in Lemony Sauce

Ready in about: 25 minutes | **Serves**: 4 | **Per serving**: Kcal 392, Fat: 31g, Net Carbs: 1g, Protein: 29g

INGREDIENTS

1 ½ lb lamb chops

Sauce

¼ cup olive oil
1 tsp red pepper flakes
2 tbsp lemon juice

Sal and black pepper to taste

2 tbsp fresh mint
3 garlic cloves, pressed
2 tbsp lemon zest

2 tbsp olive oil

¼ cup parsley
½ tsp smoked paprika

DIRECTIONS

Rub lamb with olive oil, salt, and pepper. Preheat the grill to medium heat. Grill the lamb chops for about 3 minutes per side. Whisk together the sauce ingredients in a bowl. Serve the lamb topped with sauce.

North African Lamb

Ready in about: 25 minutes | **Serves**: 4 | **Per serving**: Kcal 445, Fat 32g, Net Carbs 4g, Protein 34g

INGREDIENTS

1 tsp paprika
2 garlic cloves, minced
½ tsp dried oregano
½ tbsp sumac
12 lamb cutlets

¼ cup sesame oil
1 tsp cumin
2 carrots, sliced
2 tbsp fresh parsley, chopped
1 tsp harissa paste

1 tbsp red wine vinegar
Salt and black pepper to taste
2 tbsp black olives, sliced
2 cucumbers, sliced

DIRECTIONS

In a bowl, combine the cutlets with paprika, oregano, pepper, 2 tbsp water, half of the sesame oil, sumac, garlic, and salt and mix well. Place the carrots in a pot over medium heat and cover with water. Bring to a boil. Cook for 2 minutes. Drain, put in a salad bowl, and let them cool. Mix in cucumbers and olives.

In another bowl, combine the harissa paste with the rest of the oil, a splash of water, parsley, vinegar, and cumin. Drizzle over the carrots mixture, season with pepper and salt, and toss to coat.

Preheat the grill to medium heat. Arrange the lamb cutlets on it, grill each side for 3 minutes, and split among separate plates. Serve alongside the carrot salad.

Rolled Lamb Shoulder with Basil & Pine Nuts

Ready in about: 1 hour | **Serves**: 4 | **Per serving**: Kcal 547, Fat 37.7g, Net Carbs 2.2g, Protein 42.7g

INGREDIENTS

½ cup green olives, pitted and chopped
1 ½ lb lamb shoulder, boneless
1 ½ cups basil leaves, chopped

2 tbsp pine nuts, chopped
2 cloves garlic, minced

Salt and black pepper to taste
1 cup chicken broth

DIRECTIONS

Preheat oven to 450°F. In a bowl, combine basil, pine nuts, olives, and garlic. Season with salt and pepper. Untie the lamb flat onto a chopping board, spread the basil mixture all over, and rub the spices onto the meat. Roll the lamb over the spice mixture and tie it together using 3 to 4 strings of butcher's twine.

Place the lamb onto a baking dish, pour in the chicken broth, and cook in the oven for 10 minutes. Reduce the heat to 350°F and continue cooking for 40 minutes. When ready, transfer the meat to a cleaned chopping board. Let it rest for 10 minutes before slicing. Serve with roasted root vegetables.

White Wine Lamb Chops

Ready in about: 1 hour 10 minutes | **Serves**: 6 | **Per serving**: Kcal 397, Fat: 30g, Net Carbs: 4.3g, Protein: 16g

INGREDIENTS

6 lamb chops
½ tsp sage
½ tsp thyme

1 onion, sliced
3 garlic cloves, minced
2 tbsp olive oil

½ cup white wine
Salt and black pepper to taste

DIRECTIONS

Heat the olive oil in a pan. Add onion and garlic and cook for 3 minutes until soft. Rub the sage and thyme over the lamb chops. Cook it in the pan for about 3 minutes per side. Set aside.

Pour the white wine and 1 cup of water into the pan and bring the mixture to a boil. Cook until the liquid is reduced by half, about 5 minutes. Add in the chops, reduce the heat, and let simmer for 1 hour. Serve.

SEAFOOD & FISH RECIPES

Trout & Fennel Parcels

Ready in about: 20 minutes | **Serves**: 4 | **Per serving**: Kcal 234, Fat 9.3g, Net Carbs 2.8g, Protein 17g

INGREDIENTS

1 lb deboned trout, butterflied
Salt and black pepper to taste
3 tbsp olive oil + extra for tossing

4 sprigs thyme
4 butter cubes
1 fennel bulb, thinly sliced

1 medium red onion, sliced
8 lemon slices
3 tsp capers

DIRECTIONS

Preheat oven to 400°F. Cut out parchment paper wide enough for each trout. In a bowl, toss the fennel and onion with a little bit of olive oil and share into the middle parts of the papers.

Place the fish on each veggie mound, top with a drizzle of olive oil each, salt, pepper, 1 sprig of thyme, and 1 cube of butter. Lay the lemon slices on the fish. Wrap and close the packets securely and place them on a baking sheet. Bake in the oven for 15 minutes. Garnish the fish with capers and serve.

Creamy Hoki with Almond Bread Crust

Ready in about: 50 minutes | **Serves**: 4 | **Per serving**: Kcal 386, Fat 27g, Net Carbs 3.5g, Protein 28.5g

INGREDIENTS

1 cup flaked smoked hoki, boneless
1 cup cubed hoki fillets, cubed
4 eggs
1 cup water

3 tbsp almond flour
1 onion, sliced
2 cups sour cream
1 tbsp chopped parsley

1 cup pork rinds, crushed
1 cup grated cheddar cheese
Salt and black pepper to taste
2 tbsp butter

DIRECTIONS

Preheat oven to 360°F. Boil the eggs in water in a pot over medium heat for 10 minutes. Run the eggs under cold water and peel the shells. After, place on a cutting board and chop them.

Melt the butter in a saucepan over medium heat and sauté the onion for 4 minutes. Turn the heat off and stir in the almond flour to form a roux. Turn the heat back on and cook the roux until golden brown and stir in the sour cream until the mixture is smooth. Season with salt and pepper and stir in the parsley.

Spread the smoked and cubed fish on a greased baking dish, sprinkle the eggs on top, and spoon the sauce over. In a bowl, mix the pork rinds with the cheddar cheese and spread it over the sauce.

Bake the casserole in the oven for 20 minutes until the top is golden and the sauce and cheese are bubbly. Remove the bake after and serve with a steamed green vegetable mix.

Tuna Steaks with Shirataki Noodles

Ready in about: 30 minutes | **Serves**: 4 | **Per serving**: Kcal 310, Fat 18.2g, Net Carbs 2g, Protein 22g

INGREDIENTS

1 pack (7 oz) miracle noodle angel hair
3 cups water
1 red bell pepper, seeded and halved

4 tuna steaks
Salt and black pepper to taste
2 tbsp olive oil

2 tbsp pickled ginger
2 tbsp chopped cilantro

DIRECTIONS

In a colander, rinse the shirataki noodles with running cold water. Bring a pot of salted water to a boil. Blanch the noodles for 2 minutes. Drain and transfer to a dry skillet over medium heat. Dry roast for a minute until opaque. Grease a grill's grate with cooking spray and preheat to medium heat.

Season the red bell pepper and tuna with salt and pepper, brush with olive oil, and grill covered for 3 minutes on each side. Transfer to a plate to cool. Assemble the noodles, tuna, and bell pepper into a serving platter. Top with pickled ginger and garnish with cilantro. Serve with roasted sesame sauce.

Blackened Fish Tacos with Slaw

Ready in about: 20 minutes | **Serves**: 4 | **Per serving**: Kcal 268, Fat: 20g, Net Carbs: 3.5g, Protein: 13.8g

INGREDIENTS

1 tbsp olive oil
1 tsp chili powder

2 tilapia fillets
1 tsp paprika

4 low carb tortillas

Slaw

½ cup red cabbage, shredded
1 tbsp lemon juice

1 tsp apple cider vinegar
1 tbsp olive oil

Salt and black pepper to taste

DIRECTIONS

Season the tilapia with chili powder and paprika. Heat the olive oil in a skillet over medium heat.

Add tilapia and cook until blackened, about 3 minutes per side. Cut into strips. Divide the tilapia between the tortillas. Combine all slaw ingredients in a bowl and top the fish to serve.

Spicy Sea Bass with Hazelnuts

Ready in about: 20 minutes | **Serves**: 2 | **Per serving**: Kcal 467, Fat: 31g, Net Carbs: 2.8g, Protein: 40g

INGREDIENTS

2 sea bass fillets
2 tbsp butter, melted

⅓ cup roasted hazelnuts
A pinch of cayenne pepper

DIRECTIONS

Preheat oven to 425°F. Line a baking dish with waxed paper. Brush the butter over the fish. Process the cayenne pepper and hazelnuts in a food processor to achieve a smooth consistency. Coat the sea bass with the hazelnut mixture. Place in the oven and bake for about 15 minutes. Serve with mashed parsnips.

Salmon Panzanella

Ready in about: 22 minutes | **Serves**: 4 | **Per serving**: Kcal 338, Fat 21.7g, Net Carbs 3.1g, Protein 28.5g

INGREDIENTS

1 lb skinned salmon, cut into 4 steaks each
1 cucumber, peeled, seeded, cubed
Salt and black pepper to taste
8 black olives, pitted and chopped

1 tbsp capers, rinsed
2 large tomatoes, diced
3 tbsp red wine vinegar

¼ cup red onion, thinly sliced
3 tbsp olive oil
2 slices zero carb bread, cubed

DIRECTIONS

Preheat a grill to 350°F. In a bowl, mix the cucumber, olives, pepper, capers, tomatoes, wine vinegar, onion, olive oil, and bread. Let sit for a few minutes to incorporate the flavors. Season the salmon with salt and pepper. Grill them on both sides for 8 minutes in total. Serve the salmon with the veggies' salad.

Red Cabbage Tilapia Bowl

Ready in about: 20 minutes | **Serves**: 4 | **Per serving**: Kcal 269, Fat 23.4g, Net Carbs 4g, Protein 16.5g

INGREDIENTS

2 cups cauli rice
2 tsp ghee

4 tilapia fillets, cut into cubes
Salt and chili pepper to taste

¼ head red cabbage, shredded
1 ripe avocado, pitted and chopped

DIRECTIONS

Sprinkle cauli rice in a bowl with a little water and microwave for 3 minutes. Fluff after with a fork and set aside. Melt ghee in a skillet over medium heat, rub the tilapia with the taco seasoning, salt, and chili pepper and fry until brown on all sides, about 8 minutes. Transfer to a plate and set aside. Share the cauli rice, cabbage, fish, and avocado in 4 serving bowls. Serve with chipotle lime sour cream dressing.

Sicilian-Style Sardines with Zoodles

Ready in about: 10 minutes | **Serves:** 2 | **Per serving:** Kcal 355, Fat: 31g, Net Carbs: 6g, Protein: 20g

INGREDIENTS

4 cups zoodles (zucchini spirals)
2 oz cubed bacon

4 oz canned sardines, chopped
½ cup canned tomatoes, chopped

1 tbsp capers
1 garlic clove, minced

DIRECTIONS

Pour some of the sardine oil in a pan over medium heat. Add the garlic and sauté for 1 minute. Stir in bacon and cook for 2 more minutes. Pour in the tomatoes and simmer for 5 minutes. Add zoodles and sardines and cook for 3 minutes. Transfer to a serving plate and top with capers. Serve.

Sour Cream Salmon with Parmesan

Ready in about: 25 minutes | **Serves:** 4 | **Per serving:** Kcal 288, Fat 23.4g, Net Carbs 1.2g, Protein 16.2g

INGREDIENTS

1 cup sour cream
1 tbsp fresh dill, chopped

½ lemon, zested and juiced
Pink Salt and black pepper to taste

4 salmon steaks
½ cup Parmesan cheese, grated

DIRECTIONS

Preheat oven to 400°F. In a bowl, mix the sour cream, dill, lemon zest, juice, salt, and pepper. Season the fish with salt and black pepper, drizzle lemon juice on both sides of the fish, and arrange them on a lined baking sheet. Spread the sour cream mixture on each fish and sprinkle with Parmesan cheese.

Bake the fish for 15 minutes and after broil the top for 2 minutes with a close watch for a nice brown color. Plate the fish and serve with buttery green beans.

Tilapia with Olives & Tomato Sauce

Ready in about: 30 minutes | **Serves:** 4 | **Per serving:** Kcal 282, Fat: 15g, Net Carbs: 6g, Protein: 23g

INGREDIENTS

4 tilapia fillets
2 garlic cloves, minced
½ tsp dried oregano

14 oz canned tomatoes, diced
2 tbsp olive oil
½ red onion, chopped

2 tbsp fresh parsley, chopped
¼ cup Kalamata olives

DIRECTIONS

Heat olive oil in a skillet over medium heat and cook the onion for 3 minutes. Add garlic and oregano and cook for 30 seconds. Stir in tomatoes and bring the mixture to a boil. Reduce the heat and simmer for 5 minutes. Add olives and tilapia and cook for about 8 minutes. Serve the tilapia with tomato sauce.

Seared Scallops with Chorizo and Asiago Cheese

Ready in about: 15 minutes | **Serves:** 4 | **Per serving:** Kcal 491, Fat 32g, Net Carbs 5g, Protein 36g

INGREDIENTS

2 tbsp ghee
16 fresh scallops
8 oz chorizo, chopped

1 red bell pepper, seeds removed, sliced
1 cup red onions, finely chopped

1 cup asiago cheese, grated
Salt and black pepper to taste

DIRECTIONS

Melt half of the ghee in a skillet over medium heat, and cook the onion and bell pepper for 5 minutes until tender. Add the chorizo and stir-fry for another 3 minutes. Remove and set aside.

Pat dry the scallops with paper towels and season with salt and pepper. Add the remaining ghee to the skillet and sear the scallops for 2 minutes on each side to have a golden brown color. Add the chorizo mixture back and warm through. Transfer to serving platter and top with asiago cheese.

Pistachio-Crusted Salmon

Ready in about: 25 minutes | **Serves**: 4 | **Per serving**: Kcal 563, Fat: 47g, Net Carbs: 6g, Protein: 34g

INGREDIENTS

4 salmon fillets
Salt and black pepper to taste
¼ cup mayonnaise

½ cup chopped pistachios
1 shallot, chopped
2 tsp lemon zest

2 tbsp olive oil
1 cup heavy cream

DIRECTIONS

Preheat oven to 370°F. Brush the salmon with mayonnaise and season with salt and pepper. Coat with pistachios, place in a lined baking dish, and bake for 15 minutes. Heat olive oil in a saucepan and sauté the shallot for 3 minutes. Stir in the rest of the ingredients. Cook until thickened, 10 minutes. Serve.

Cod in Garlic Butter Sauce

Ready in about: 20 minutes | **Serves**: 6 | **Per serving**: Kcal 264, Fat 17.3g, Net Carbs 2.3g, Protein 20g

INGREDIENTS

2 tsp olive oil
6 Alaska cod fillets
Salt and black pepper to taste

4 tbsp butter
3 cloves garlic, minced
⅓ cup lemon juice

3 tbsp white wine
2 tbsp chopped chives

DIRECTIONS

Heat the oil in a skillet over medium heat. Season the cod with salt and black pepper. Fry the fillets in the oil for 4 minutes on one side, flip, and cook for 1 minute. Take out, plate, and set aside.

In the same skillet over, melt the butter and sauté the garlic for 3 minutes. Add the lemon juice, white wine, and chives. Season with salt and black pepper and cook for 3 minutes until the wine slightly reduces. Put the fish in a platter, spoon the sauce over, and serve with buttered green beans.

Herby Salmon in Creamy Sauce

Ready in about: 15 minutes | **Serves**: 2 | **Per serving**: Kcal 468, Fat: 40g, Net Carbs: 1.5g, Protein: 22g

INGREDIENTS

2 salmon fillets
1 tsp dried tarragon

1 tsp dried dill
3 tbsp butter

¼ cup heavy cream
Salt and black pepper to taste

DIRECTIONS

Season the salmon with some dill and tarragon. Warm butter in a pan over medium heat. Add salmon and cook for 4 minutes on both sides. Set aside. In the same pan, add the remaining dill and tarragon.

Cook for 30 seconds to infuse the flavors. Whisk in the heavy cream, season with salt and black pepper, and cook for 2-3 minutes. Serve the salmon topped with the sauce.

Parmesan Fish Bake

Ready in about: 30 minutes | **Serves**: 4 | **Per serving**: Kcal 354, Fat 17g, Net Carbs 4g, Protein 28g

INGREDIENTS

2 salmon fillets, cubed
1 lb white fish, cubed
1 head broccoli, cut into florets

1 tbsp butter, melted
Salt and black pepper to taste
1 cup crème fraiche

¼ cup grated Parmesan cheese
Grated Parmesan cheese for topping

DIRECTIONS

Preheat oven to 400°F. Toss the fish cubes and broccoli in butter and season with salt and pepper. Spread in a greased dish. Mix the crème fraiche with Parmesan cheese, pour, and smear the cream on the fish. Sprinkle with some more Parmesan cheese. Bake for 15-20 minutes until golden brown on top. Serve.

Grilled Shrimp with Chimichurri Sauce

Ready in about: 10 minutes + marinating time | **Serves**: 4 | **Per serving**: Kcal 283, Fat: 20.3g, Net Carbs: 3.5g, Protein: 16g

INGREDIENTS

1 lb shrimp, peeled and deveined

Chimichurri

½ tsp salt
¼ cup olive oil
2 garlic cloves

2 tbsp olive oil

¼ cup red onions, chopped
¼ cup red wine vinegar
½ tsp pepper

Juice of 1 lime

2 cups parsley
¼ tsp red pepper flakes

DIRECTIONS

Process the chimichurri ingredients in a blender until smooth; set aside. Combine the shrimp, olive oil, and lime juice in a bowl. Let marinate in the fridge for 30 minutes. Preheat the grill to medium heat. Add shrimp and cook for about 2 minutes per side. Serve shrimp drizzled with the chimichurri sauce.

Sushi Shrimp Rolls

Ready in about: 10 minutes | **Serves**: 4 | **Per serving**: Kcal 216, Fat: 10g, Net Carbs: 1g, Protein: 18.7g

INGREDIENTS

2 cups cooked and chopped shrimp
1 tbsp sriracha sauce

1 cucumber, julienned
4 hand roll nori sheets

¼ cup mayonnaise
¼ cup sugar-free soy sauce

DIRECTIONS

Combine shrimp, mayonnaise, cucumber, and sriracha sauce in a bowl. Lay out a single nori sheet on a flat surface and spread about 1/4 of the shrimp mixture. Roll the nori sheet as desired. Repeat with the other ingredients. Serve with sugar-free soy sauce.

Coconut Crab Patties

Ready in about: 15 minutes | **Serves**: 4 | **Per serving**: Kcal 215, Fat: 11.5g, Net Carbs: 3.6g, Protein: 15.3g

INGREDIENTS

2 tbsp coconut oil
1 tbsp lemon juice

1 lb lump crab meat
2 tsp Dijon mustard

1 egg, beaten
1 ½ tbsp coconut flour

DIRECTIONS

In a bowl, add all the ingredients except the oil and mix well. Make patties out of the mixture. Melt the coconut oil in a skillet over medium heat. Add the crab patties and cook for about 2-3 minutes per side.

Shrimp in Curry Sauce

Ready in about: 15 minutes | **Serves**: 2 | **Per serving**: Kcal 560, Fat: 41g, Net Carbs: 4.3g, Protein: 24.4g

INGREDIENTS

½ oz Parmesan cheese, grated
1 egg, beaten

Sauce

2 tbsp curry leaves
2 tbsp butter

¼ tsp curry powder
2 tsp almond flour

½ onion, diced
½ cup heavy cream

½ lb shrimp, shelled
3 tbsp coconut oil

½ oz cheddar cheese, shredded

DIRECTIONS

Combine all dry ingredients for the batter. Melt the coconut oil in a skillet over medium heat. Dip the shrimp in the egg first, and then coat with the dry mixture. Fry until golden and crispy, about 5-6 minutes.

Melt the butter in the skillet. Add onion and cook for 3 minutes. Stir in curry leaves for 30 seconds. Mix in heavy cream and cheddar cheese and cook until thickened, 2 minutes. Add shrimp. Stir to coat. Serve.

Lemon Garlic Shrimp

Ready in about: 22 minutes | **Serves:** 6 | **Per serving:** Kcal 258, Fat 22g, Net Carbs 2g, Protein 13g

INGREDIENTS

½ cup butter, divided
2 lb shrimp, peeled and deveined

Salt and black pepper to taste
¼ tsp sweet paprika

3 garlic cloves, minced
1 lemon, zested and juiced

DIRECTIONS

Melt the butter in a skillet over medium heat. Season the shrimp with salt, pepper, and paprika and add to the butter. Cook for 4 minutes on both sides until pink. Set aside. Include the lemon zest, juice, garlic, and 3 tbsp water to the skillet. Return the shrimp and cook for 2 minutes. Serve warm.

Coconut Curry Mussels

Ready in about: 25 minutes | **Serves:** 6 | **Per serving:** Kcal 356, Fat 20.6g, Net Carbs 0.3g, Protein 21.1g

INGREDIENTS

3 lb mussels, cleaned, de-bearded
1 cup minced shallots
3 tbsp minced garlic

1 ½ cups coconut milk
2 cups dry white wine
2 tsp red curry powder

⅓ cup coconut oil
⅓ cup chopped green onions
⅓ cup chopped parsley

DIRECTIONS

Pour the wine into a saucepan and cook the shallots and garlic over medium heat, 5 minutes. Stir in the coconut milk and red curry powder and cook for 3 minutes. Add the mussels and steam for 7 minutes or until their shells are opened. Then, use a slotted spoon to remove to a bowl leaving the sauce in the pan.

Discard any closed mussels at this point. Stir the coconut oil into the sauce, turn the heat off, and stir in the parsley and green onions. Serve the mussels immediately with a butternut squash mash.

Shrimp Stuffed Zucchini

Ready in about: 50 minutes | **Serves:** 4 | **Per serving:** Kcal 135, Fat 14.4g, Net Carbs 3.2g, Protein 24.6g

INGREDIENTS

4 medium zucchinis
1 lb small shrimp, peeled, deveined
1 tbsp onion paste

2 tsp cold butter
¼ cup tomatoes, chopped
Salt and black pepper to taste

1 cup pork rinds, crushed
1 tbsp basil leaves, chopped
2 tbsp butter, melted

DIRECTIONS

Preheat oven to 350°F. Trim off the top and bottom ends of the zucchinis. Lay them flat on a chopping board and cut a ¼-inch off the top to create a boat for the stuffing. Scoop out the seeds and set aside.

Melt the cold butter in a skillet and sauté the onion, zucchini flesh, and tomato for 6 minutes. Transfer the mixture to a bowl and add the shrimp, half of the pork rinds, basil, salt, and pepper and mix well.

Stuff the zucchini boats with the mixture. Sprinkle the top of the boats with the remaining pork rinds and drizzle the melted butter over them. Place on a baking sheet and bake for 15-20 minutes. The shrimp should no longer be pink by this time. Remove the zucchinis after and serve with a tomato salad.

Tuna Caprese Salad

Ready in about: 10 minutes | **Serves:** 4 | **Per serving:** Kcal 360, Fat 31g, Net Carbs 1g, Protein 21g

INGREDIENTS

2 (10 oz) cans tuna in water, drained
2 tomatoes, sliced

8 oz fresh mozzarella cheese, sliced
6 basil leaves

2 tbsp extra virgin olive oil
½ lemon, juiced

DIRECTIONS

Place the tuna in the center of a serving platter. Arrange the cheese and tomato slices around the tuna. Alternate a slice of tomato, cheese, and a basil leaf. Drizzle with olive oil and lemon juice and serve.

MEATLESS MEALS

Vegetable Greek Mousaka

Ready in about: 50 minutes | **Serves**: 6 | **Per serving**: Kcal 476, Fat 35g, Net Carbs 9.6g, Protein 33g

INGREDIENTS

2 large eggplants, sliced
1 cup diced celery
1 cup diced carrots
1 small white onion, chopped

2 eggs
2 tbsp olive oil
3 cups Parmesan cheese, grated
1 cup ricotta cheese, crumbled

3 cloves garlic, minced
2 tsp Italian seasoning blend
Salt to taste

Sauce

1 ½ cups heavy cream
¼ cup butter, melted

1 cup mozzarella cheese, grated
2 tsp Italian seasoning

¾ cup almond flour

DIRECTIONS

Preheat the oven to 350°F. Heat olive oil in a skillet over medium heat and sauté the onion, celery, and carrots for 5 minutes. Stir in the garlic and cook further for 30 seconds; set aside to cool. Mix the eggs, 1 cup of Parmesan cheese, ricotta cheese, and salt in a bowl.

Pour the heavy cream in a pot and bring to heat over a medium fire while continually stirring. Stir in the remaining Parmesan cheese and 1 teaspoon of Italian seasoning. Turn the heat off and set aside.

To lay the mousaka, spread a small amount of the sauce at the bottom of the baking dish. Make a single layer of the eggplant slices on the sauce. Spread a layer of ricotta cheese on the eggplants, sprinkle some veggies on it, and repeat the layering process until all the ingredients are exhausted.

Evenly mix the melted butter, almond flour, and 1 teaspoon of Italian seasoning in a small bowl. Spread the top of the mousaka layers with it and sprinkle the top with mozzarella cheese. Cover the dish with foil and place it in the oven to bake for 25 minutes. Remove the foil and bake for 5 minutes until the cheese is slightly burned. Slice the mousaka and serve warm.

Tofu Sandwich with Cabbage Slaw

Ready in about: 10 minutes + marinating time | **Serves**: 4 | **Per serving**: Kcal 386, Fat 33g, Net Carbs 7.8g, Protein 14g

INGREDIENTS

½ lb firm tofu, sliced

4 zero carb buns

1 tbsp olive oil

Marinade

Salt and black pepper to taste
2 tsp allspice
1 tbsp erythritol

2 tsp chopped thyme
1 habanero pepper, seeded and minced

3 green onions, thinly sliced
2 cloves garlic
¼ cup olive oil

Slaw

½ small cabbage, shredded
1 carrot, grated
½ red onion, grated

½ tsp swerve sugar
2 tbsp white vinegar
1 tsp Italian seasoning

¼ cup olive oil
1 tsp Dijon mustard
Salt and black pepper to taste

DIRECTIONS

In a food processor, make the marinade by blending the allspice, salt, black pepper, erythritol, thyme, habanero, green onions, garlic, and olive oil, for a minute. Pour the mixture in a bowl and put in the tofu. Toss to coat. Place in the fridge to marinate for 4 hours.

In a large bowl, combine the white vinegar, swerve sugar, olive oil, mustard, Italian seasoning, salt, and pepper. Stir in the cabbage, carrot, and onion and place it in the refrigerator to chill.

Heat 1 teaspoon of oil in a skillet over medium heat, remove the tofu from the marinade, and cook it in the oil to brown on both sides for 6 minutes in total. Remove onto a plate after and toast the buns in the skillet. In the buns, add the tofu and top with the slaw. Close the bread and serve with a sweet chili sauce.

Zucchini Lasagna with Ricotta & Spinach

Ready in about: 50 minutes | **Serves**: 4 | **Per serving**: Kcal 390, Fat 39g, Net Carbs 2g, Protein 7g

INGREDIENTS

2 zucchinis, sliced
Salt and black pepper to taste

2 cups ricotta cheese
2 cups shredded mozzarella cheese

3 cups tomato sauce
1 cup baby spinach

DIRECTIONS

Preheat oven to 370°F. Put the zucchini slices in a colander and sprinkle with salt. Let sit and drain liquid for 5 minutes and pat dry with paper towels. Mix the ricotta cheese, mozzarella cheese, salt, and black pepper to evenly combine and spread ¼ cup of the mixture in the bottom of the baking dish.

Layer ⅓ of the zucchini slices on top, spread 1 cup of tomato sauce over, and scatter a ⅓ cup of spinach on top. Repeat the layering process two more times to exhaust the ingredients while finally making sure to layer with the last ¼ cup of cheese mixture.

Grease one end of foil with cooking spray and cover the baking dish with the foil. Bake for 35 minutes, remove foil, and bake further for 5 to 10 minutes or until the cheese has a nice golden brown color. Remove the dish, sit for 5 minutes, make slices of the lasagna, and serve warm.

Asparagus & Tarragon Flan

Ready in about: 65 minutes | **Serves**: 4 | **Per serving**: Kcal 264, Fat 11.6g, Net Carbs 2.5g, Protein 12.5g

INGREDIENTS

16 asparagus, stems trimmed
½ cup whipping cream
1 cup almond milk

2 eggs + 2 egg yolks, beaten in a bowl
2 tbsp fresh tarragon, chopped
Salt and black pepper to taste

2 tbsp Parmesan cheese, grated
2 tbsp butter, melted
1 tbsp butter, softened

DIRECTIONS

Cover the asparagus with salted water and bring them to boil over medium heat for 6 minutes. Drain the asparagus, cut their tips, and reserve for garnishing. Chop the remaining asparagus into small pieces.

In a blender, add chopped asparagus, whipping cream, almond milk, tarragon, salt, pepper, and Parmesan cheese. Process until smooth. Pour the mixture through a sieve into a bowl and whisk in the eggs.

Preheat oven to 350°F. Grease 4 ramekins with softened butter and share the asparagus mixture among the ramekins. Pour the melted butter over each mixture and top with 2-3 asparagus tips. Pour 3 cups water into a baking dish, place in the ramekins, and insert in the oven.

Bake for 45 minutes until their middle parts are no longer watery. Remove the ramekins and let cool. Garnish the flan with the asparagus tips and serve with chilled white wine.

Briam with Tomato Sauce

Ready in about: 40 minutes | **Serves**: 4 | **Per serving**: Kcal 365, Fat 12g, Net Carbs 12.5g, Protein 11.3g

INGREDIENTS

3 tbsp olive oil
1 large eggplant, halved and sliced
1 large onion, thinly sliced
3 cloves garlic, sliced

2 tomatoes, diced
1 rutabaga, diced
1 cup sugar-free tomato sauce
4 zucchinis, sliced

¼ cup water
Salt and black pepper to taste
¼ tsp dried oregano
2 tbsp fresh parsley, chopped

DIRECTIONS

Preheat oven to 400°F. Heat the olive oil in a skillet over medium heat and fry the eggplant and zucchini slices for 6 minutes until golden. Remove to a baking casserole and arrange them in a single layer.

Sauté onion and garlic in the oil for 3 minutes. Remove to a bowl. Add in the tomatoes, rutabaga, tomato sauce, and water and mix well. Stir with salt, pepper, oregano, and parsley. Pour the mixture over the eggplant and zucchini. Place the dish in the oven and bake for 25-30 minutes. Serve the briam warm.

Tofu Sesame Skewers with Warm Kale Salad

Ready in about: 30 minutes + marinating time | **Serves**: 4 | **Per serving**: Kcal 263, Fat 12.9g, Net Carbs 6.1g, Protein 5.6g

INGREDIENTS

14 oz firm tofu, cut into strips
4 tsp sesame oil

Kale salad

4 cups kale, chopped
2 tbsp olive oil
1 white onion, thinly sliced

1 lemon, juiced
5 tbsp sugar-free soy sauce

2 cloves garlic, minced
1 cup sliced white mushrooms
1 tsp fresh rosemary, chopped

4 tbsp coconut flour
⅓ cup sesame seeds

Salt and black pepper to taste
1 tbsp balsamic vinegar

DIRECTIONS

In a bowl, mix sesame oil, lemon juice, soy sauce, and coconut flour. Stick the tofu on skewers, height-wise. Place onto a plate, pour the soy sauce mixture over, and turn in the sauce to coat. Cover the dish with cling film and marinate in the fridge for 2 hours.

Heat a griddle pan over high heat. Roll the tofu skewers in the sesame seeds for a generous coat. Grill the tofu in the griddle pan until golden brown on both sides, about 12 minutes in total.

Heat the olive oil in a skillet over medium heat and sauté onion to begin browning for 5 minutes with continuous stirring. Add in the mushrooms, garlic, rosemary, salt, pepper, and balsamic vinegar.

Continue cooking for 5 minutes. Put the kale in a salad bowl. Pour the onion mixture over and toss well. Serve the tofu skewers with the warm kale salad and a peanut butter dipping sauce.

Vegetable Tempeh Kabobs

Ready in about: 30 minutes + chilling time | **Serves**: 4 | **Per serving**: Kcal 228, Fat 15g, Net Carbs 3.6g, Protein 13.2g

INGREDIENTS

10 oz tempeh, cut into chunks
1 red onion, cut into chunks

1 red bell pepper, cut chunks
1 yellow bell pepper, cut into chunks

2 tbsp olive oil
1 cup sugar-free barbecue sauce

DIRECTIONS

Bring the 1 ½ cups water to boil in a pot over medium heat, and once it has cooked, turn the heat off, and add the tempeh. Cover the pot and let the tempeh steam for 5 minutes to remove its bitterness. Drain. Pour the barbecue sauce in a bowl, add in the tempeh, and coat with the sauce. Refrigerate for 2 hours.

Preheat grill to 350°F. Thread the tempeh, yellow bell pepper, red bell pepper, and onion onto skewers. Brush the grate of the grill with olive oil, place the skewers on it, and brush with barbecue sauce. Cook the kabobs for 3 minutes on each side while rotating and brushing with more barbecue sauce. Serve.

Cauliflower & Gouda Cheese Casserole

Ready in about: 25 minutes | **Serves**: 4 | **Per serving**: Kcal 215, Fat 15g, Net Carbs 4g, Protein 12g

INGREDIENTS

2 heads cauliflower, cut into florets
2 tbsp olive oil
2 tbsp butter, melted

1 white onion, chopped
Salt and black pepper to taste
¼ almond milk

½ cup almond flour
1 ½ cups gouda cheese, grated

DIRECTIONS

Preheat oven to 350°F. Put the cauli florets in a large microwave-safe bowl. Sprinkle with a bit of water, and steam in the microwave for 4 to 5 minutes. Warm the olive oil in a saucepan over medium heat and sauté the onion for 3 minutes. Add the cauliflower, season with salt and pepper, and mix in almond milk.

Simmer for 3 minutes. Mix the melted butter with almond flour. Stir into the cauliflower as well as half of the cheese. Sprinkle the top with the remaining cheese and bake for 10 minutes until the cheese has melted and golden brown on the top. Plate the bake and serve with salad.

Creamy Vegetable Stew

Ready in about: 25 minutes | **Serves**: 4 | **Per serving**: Kcal 310, Fat 26.4g, Net Carbs 6g, Protein 8g

INGREDIENTS

2 tbsp ghee
1 tbsp onion-garlic puree
2 medium carrots, chopped

1 head cauliflower, cut into florets
2 cups green beans, halved
Salt and black pepper to taste

1 cup water
1 ½ cups heavy cream

DIRECTIONS

Melt the ghee in a saucepan over medium heat and sauté onion-garlic puree to be fragrant, 2 minutes. Stir in carrots, cauliflower, and green beans for 5 minutes. Season with salt and black pepper.

Pour in the water, stir again, and cook on low heat for 15 minutes. Mix in the heavy cream to be incorporated and turn the heat off. Serve the stew with almond flour bread.

Creamy Cucumber Avocado Soup

Ready in about: 15 minutes | **Serves**: 4 | **Per serving**: Kcal 170, Fat 7.4g, Net Carbs 4.1g, Protein 3.7g

INGREDIENTS

4 large cucumbers, seeded, chopped
1 large avocado, peeled and halved
Salt and black pepper to taste

1 tbsp fresh cilantro, chopped
3 tbsp olive oil
2 limes, juiced

2 tsp minced garlic
2 tomatoes, chopped
1 avocado, chopped for garnish

DIRECTIONS

Pour the cucumbers, avocado halves, salt, black pepper, olive oil, lime juice, cilantro, 2 cups water, and garlic in the food processor. Puree the ingredients for 2 minutes or until smooth. Pour the mixture in a bowl and top with chopped avocado and tomatoes. Serve chilled with zero-carb bread.

Lemon Cauliflower "Couscous" with Halloumi

Ready in about: 5 minutes | **Serves**: 4 | **Per serving**: Kcal 185, Fat 15.6g, Net Carbs 2.1g, Protein 12g

INGREDIENTS

4 oz halloumi, sliced
2 tbsp olive oil
1 cauliflower head, cut into florets

¼ cup chopped cilantro
¼ cup chopped parsley
¼ cup chopped mint

½ lemon juiced
Salt and black pepper to taste
1 avocado, sliced to garnish

DIRECTIONS

Warm the olive oil in a skillet over medium heat. Add the halloumi and fry for 2 minutes on each side until golden brown; set aside. Pour the cauli florets in a food processor and pulse until it crumbles and resembles couscous. Transfer to a bowl and steam in the microwave for 2 minutes.

Remove the bowl from the microwave and let the cauli cool. Stir in cilantro, parsley, mint, lemon juice, salt, and pepper. Top couscous with avocado slices and serve with grilled halloumi and vegetable sauce.

Avocado & Tomato Burritos

Ready in about: 10 minutes | **Serves**: 4 | **Per serving**: Kcal 303, Fat 25g, Net Carbs 6g, Protein 8g

INGREDIENTS

2 cups cauli rice
6 low carb tortillas

2 cups sour cream sauce
1 ½ cups tomato herb salsa

2 avocados, peeled, pitted, sliced

DIRECTIONS

Pour the cauli rice in a bowl, sprinkle with a bit of water, and soften in the microwave for 2 minutes. On the tortillas, spread the sour cream all over and distribute the salsa on top. Top with cauli rice and scatter the avocado evenly on top. Fold and tuck the burritos and cut into two. Serve.

Roasted Asparagus with Spicy Eggplant Dip

Ready in about: 35 minutes | **Serves**: 6 | **Per serving**: Kcal 149; Fat: 12.1g, Net Carbs: 9g, Protein: 3.6g

INGREDIENTS

1 ½ lb asparagus spears, trimmed

¼ cup + 2 tbsp olive oil

½ tsp paprika

Eggplant dip

1 lb eggplants
½ cup scallions, chopped
2 cloves garlic, minced

1 tbsp fresh lemon juice
½ tsp chili pepper
Salt and black pepper to taste

¼ cup fresh cilantro, chopped

DIRECTIONS

Preheat oven to 390°F. Line a parchment paper to a baking sheet. Add in the asparagus. Toss with 2 tbsp of the olive oil, paprika, black pepper, and salt. Roast until cooked through for 9 minutes. Remove.

Place the eggplants on a lined cookie sheet. Bake in the oven for about 20 minutes. Let the eggplants cool. Peel them and discard the stems. Warm the remaining olive oil in a frying pan over medium heat and add in the garlic and scallions. Sauté for 3 minutes until tender.

In a food processor, pulse together black pepper, roasted eggplants, salt, lemon juice, scallion mixture, and chili pepper. Add in cilantro and serve alongside roasted asparagus spears.

Portobello Mushroom Burgers

Ready in about: 15 minutes | **Serves**: 4 | **Per serving**: Kcal 190, Fat 8g, Net Carbs 3g, Protein 16g

INGREDIENTS

4 zero carb buns
4 portobello mushroom caps
1 clove garlic, minced
½ tsp salt

2 tbsp olive oil
½ cup roasted red peppers, sliced
2 medium tomatoes, chopped
¼ cup feta cheese, crumbled

1 tbsp red wine vinegar
2 tbsp Kalamata olives, chopped
½ tsp dried oregano
2 cups baby salad greens

DIRECTIONS

Heat a grill pan over medium heat. Crush the garlic with salt in a bowl using the back of a spoon. Stir in 1 tbsp of the oil and brush the mushrooms and each inner side of the buns with the mixture.

Place the mushrooms in the heated pan and grill them on both sides for 8 minutes until tender. Also, toast the buns in the pan until they are crisp, about 2 minutes. Set aside.

In a bowl, mix the red peppers, tomatoes, olives, feta cheese, vinegar, oregano, baby salad greens, and remaining oil; toss to coat. In a bun slice, add a mushroom cap, a scoop of vegetables, and another slice of bread. Serve with cheese dip.

Sriracha Tofu with Yogurt Sauce

Ready in about: 40 minutes | **Serves**: 4 | **Per serving**: Kcal 351; Fat: 25.9g, Net Carbs: 8.1g, Protein: 17.5g

INGREDIENTS

12 oz tofu, pressed and sliced
1 cup green onions, chopped

1 garlic clove, minced
2 tbsp vinegar

1 tbsp sriracha sauce
2 tbsp olive oil

Yogurt sauce

2 cloves garlic, pressed
2 tbsp fresh lemon juice

Salt and black pepper to taste
1 tsp fresh dill weed

1 cup Greek yogurt
1 cucumber, shredded

DIRECTIONS

Put tofu slices, garlic, sriracha sauce, vinegar, and green onions in a bowl. Allow to settle for 30 minutes. Set a nonstick skillet to medium heat and add oil to warm. Cook tofu for 5 minutes until golden brown.

For the preparation of the sauce: in a bowl, mix garlic, salt, yogurt, black pepper, lemon juice, and dill. Add in shredded cucumber as you stir to combine. Serve the tofu with a dollop of yogurt sauce.

Keto Pizza Margherita

Ready in about: 25 minutes | **Serves:** 2 | **Per serving:** Kcal 510, Fat: 39g, Net Carbs: 3.7g, Protein: 31g

INGREDIENTS

Crust

6 oz mozzarella cheese, grated
2 tbsp cream cheese, softened

2 tbsp Parmesan cheese, grated
1 tsp dried oregano

½ cup almond flour
2 tbsp psyllium husk

Topping

4 oz cheddar cheese, grated
¼ cup marinara sauce

1 bell pepper, sliced
1 tomato, sliced

2 tbsp fresh basil, chopped

DIRECTIONS

Preheat oven to 400°F. Melt the mozzarella cheese in a microwave. Combine the remaining crust ingredients in a large bowl and add the mozzarella cheese. Mix with your hands to combine. Divide the dough in two. Roll out the two crusts in circles and place on a lined baking sheet. Bake for 10 minutes.

Remove and spread the marinara sauce evenly. Top with cheddar cheese, bell pepper, and tomato slices. Return to the oven and bake for 10 more minutes. Serve sliced sprinkled with basil.

Wild Mushroom & Asparagus Stew

Ready in about: 25 minutes | **Serves:** 4 | **Per serving:** Kcal 114; Fat: 7.3g, Net Carbs: 9.5g, Protein: 2.1g

INGREDIENTS

2 tbsp olive oil
1 onion, chopped
2 garlic cloves, pressed
1 celery stalk, chopped
2 carrots, chopped

1 cup wild mushrooms, sliced
2 tbsp dry white wine
2 rosemary sprigs, chopped
1 thyme sprig, chopped
2 cups vegetable stock

½ tsp chili pepper
1 tsp smoked paprika
2 tomatoes, chopped
1 tbsp flaxseed meal

DIRECTIONS

Warm the olive oil in a pot over medium heat. Add in onions and cook until tender, about 3 minutes. Place in carrots, celery, and garlic and cook until soft for 4 more minutes. Add in mushrooms and cook until the liquid evaporates; set aside. Stir in wine to deglaze the pot's bottom. Place in thyme and rosemary.

Pour in tomatoes, vegetable stock, paprika, and chili pepper, add in reserved vegetables, and bring to a boil. Reduce the heat to low and let the mixture to simmer for 15 minutes. Stir in flaxseed meal to thicken the stew, about 2-3 minutes. Spoon into individual bowls and serve warm.

Sautéed Celeriac with Tomato Sauce

Ready in about: 20 minutes | **Serves:** 4 | **Per serving:** Kcal 135; Fat: 13.6g, Net Carbs: 3g, Protein: 0.9g

INGREDIENTS

2 tbsp olive oil
1 garlic clove, crushed

1 celeriac, sliced
¼ cup vegetable stock

Salt and black pepper to taste

For the sauce

2 tomatoes, halved
2 tbsp olive oil
½ cup onions, chopped

2 cloves garlic, minced
1 chili, minced
1 bunch fresh basil, chopped

1 tbsp fresh cilantro, chopped
Salt and black pepper to taste

DIRECTIONS

Set a pan over medium heat and warm olive oil. Add in garlic and sauté for 1 minute. Stir in celeriac slices, stock and cook until softened. Sprinkle with pepper and salt. Brush the tomatoes with olive oil.

Microwave for 5 minutes. Get rid of any excess liquid. Remove the tomatoes to a food processor. Add the rest of the ingredients for the sauce and puree to obtain the desired consistency. Serve the celeriac topped with tomato sauce.

Grilled Cheese the Keto Way

Ready in about: 15 minutes | **Serves**: 1 | **Per serving**: Kcal 623, Fat: 51g, Net Carbs: 6.1g, Protein: 25g

INGREDIENTS

2 eggs
½ tsp baking powder

2 tbsp butter
2 tbsp almond flour

1 ½ tbsp psyllium husk powder
2 oz cheddar cheese, shredded

DIRECTIONS

Whisk together all ingredients, except 1 tbsp butter and cheddar cheese. Place in a square oven-proof bowl and microwave for 90 seconds. Flip the bun over and cut in half.

Place the cheddar cheese on one half of the bun and top with the other. Melt the remaining butter in a skillet. Add the sandwich and grill until the cheese is melted and the bun is crispy.

Walnut Tofu Sauté

Ready in about: 15 minutes | **Serves**: 4 | **Per serving**: Kcal 320, Fat 24g, Net Carbs 4g, Protein 18g

INGREDIENTS

1 tbsp olive oil
1 (8 oz) block firm tofu, cubed
1 tbsp tomato paste

1 garlic clove, minced
1 onion, chopped
1 tbsp balsamic vinegar

Salt and black pepper to taste
½ tsp mixed dried herbs
1 cup chopped raw walnuts

DIRECTIONS

Heat the oil in a skillet over medium heat and cook the tofu for 3 minutes until brown. Stir in the garlic, onion, tomato paste, and vinegar and cook for 4 minutes. Season with salt and pepper. Add in the herbs and walnuts. Stir and cook on low heat for 3 minutes. Spoon on plates and serve warm.

Jalapeño & Veggie Stew

Ready in about: 40 minutes | **Serves**: 4 | **Per serving**: Kcal 65; Fat: 2.7g, Net Carbs: 9g, Protein: 2.7g

INGREDIENTS

2 tbsp butter
1 cup leeks, chopped
1 garlic clove, minced
½ cup celery stalks, chopped
½ cup carrots, chopped

1 green bell pepper, chopped
1 jalapeño pepper, chopped
1 zucchini, chopped
1 cup mushrooms, sliced
1 ½ cups vegetable stock

2 tomatoes, chopped
2 tbsp fresh parsley, chopped
2 bay leaves
Salt and black pepper to taste
1 tsp vinegar

DIRECTIONS

Melt the butter in a pot over medium heat. Add in garlic and leeks and sauté for 3 minutes until soft and translucent. Add in the celery, mushrooms, zucchini, and carrots and sauté for 5 more minutes.

Stir in the rest of the ingredients. Season with salt and pepper. Bring to a boil and allow to simmer for 15-20 minutes or until cooked through. Divide between individual bowls and serve warm.

Vegetarian Burgers

Ready in about: 20 minutes | **Serves**: 2 | **Per serving**: Kcal 637, Fat: 55g, Net Carbs: 8.5g, Protein: 23g

INGREDIENTS

1 garlic clove, minced
2 portobello mushrooms, sliced
1 tbsp coconut oil, melted

1 tbsp fresh basil, chopped
2 eggs, fried
2 low carb buns

2 tbsp mayonnaise
2 lettuce leaves
Salt to taste

DIRECTIONS

Combine the melted coconut oil, garlic, basil, and salt in a bowl. Add in the mushrooms and toss to coat. Form into burger patties. Preheat the grill to medium heat. Grill the patties for 2 minutes per side. Cut the buns in half. Add the lettuce, mushrooms, eggs, and mayonnaise. Top with the other bun half. Serve.

Pizza Bianca

Ready in about: 20 minutes | **Serves:** 1 | **Per serving:** Kcal 591, Fat: 55g, Net Carbs: 2g, Protein: 22g

INGREDIENTS

2 large eggs
1 tbsp water
½ jalapeño pepper, diced

1 oz Monterey Jack cheese, grated
1 chopped green onion
1 cup egg Alfredo sauce

¼ tsp cumin
2 tbsp olive oil

DIRECTIONS

Preheat the oven to 350°F. Heat the olive oil in a skillet over medium heat. Whisk the eggs along with water and cumin. Pour the eggs into the skillet. Cook until set. Top with the alfredo sauce and jalapeño pepper. Sprinkle the green onion and cheese over. Place in the oven and bake for 5 minutes. Serve.

Pumpkin Bake

Ready in about: 45 minutes | **Serves:** 6 | **Per serving:** Kcal 125, Fat 4.8g, Net Carbs 5.7g, Protein 2.7g

INGREDIENTS

3 large pumpkins, peeled and sliced
1 cup almond flour

1 cup grated mozzarella cheese
3 tbsp olive oil

½ cup fresh parsley, chopped

DIRECTIONS

Preheat oven to 350°F. Arrange the pumpkin slices in a baking dish and drizzle with olive oil. Bake for 35 minutes. Mix almond flour, mozzarella cheese, and parsley and pour over the pumpkin. Place back in the oven and bake for another 5 minutes until the top is golden brown. Serve warm.

Spaghetti Squash with Eggplant & Parmesan

Ready in about: 15 minutes | **Serves:** 4 | **Per serving:** Kcal 139, Fat: 8.2g, Net Carbs: 6.8g, Protein: 6.9g

INGREDIENTS

2 tbsp butter
1 cup cherry tomatoes
1 eggplant, cubed

¼ cup Parmesan cheese, shredded
3 tbsp scallions, chopped
1 cup snap peas

1 tsp lemon zest
2 cups spaghetti squash, cooked
Salt and black pepper to taste

DIRECTIONS

Melt butter in a saucepan and cook eggplant for 5 minutes until tender. Add in the tomatoes and peas and cook for 5 minutes. Stir in the zest, scallions, salt, and pepper. Remove the pan from heat. Stir in spaghetti squash and Parmesan cheese and serve.

Classic Tangy Ratatouille

Ready in about: 47 minutes | **Serves:** 6 | **Per serving:** Kcal 154, Fat 12.1g, Net Carbs 5.6g, Protein 1.7g

INGREDIENTS

2 eggplants, chopped
3 zucchinis, chopped
2 red onions, diced
1 (28 oz) can tomatoes, diced

2 red bell peppers, cut into chunks
1 yellow bell pepper, cut into chunks
3 garlic cloves, sliced
½ cup fresh basil leaves, chopped

4 sprigs thyme
1 tbsp balsamic vinegar
2 tbsp olive oil
½ lemon, zested

DIRECTIONS

In a casserole pot, heat the olive oil over medium heat and sauté the eggplants, zucchinis, and bell peppers for 5 minutes. Spoon the veggies into a large bowl. In the same pan, sauté garlic, onions, and thyme leaves for 5 minutes. Add in the canned tomatoes, balsamic vinegar, basil, salt, and black pepper.

Return the cooked veggies to the pan. Stir and cover the pot. Cook the ingredients on low heat for 30 minutes. Open the lid and stir in the remaining basil leaves, lemon zest, and adjust the seasoning. Turn the heat off. Plate the ratatouille and serve with some low carb crusted bread.

Cremini Mushroom Stroganoff

Ready in about: 25 minutes | **Serves**: 4 | **Per serving**: Kcal 284, Fat 28g, Net Carbs 1,5g, Protein 8g

INGREDIENTS

3 tbsp butter
1 white onion, chopped

4 cups cremini mushrooms, cubed
½ cup heavy cream

½ cup Parmesan cheese, grated
1 ½ tbsp dried mixed herbs

DIRECTIONS

Melt the butter in a saucepan over medium heat and sauté the onion for 3 minutes until soft. Stir in the mushrooms and cook until tender, about 5 minutes. Add 2 cups water and bring to boil.

Cook for 10-15 minutes until the water reduces slightly. Pour in the heavy cream and Parmesan cheese. Stir to melt the cheese. Mix in the dried herbs and season. Simmer for 5 minutes. Serve warm.

Blue Cheese Stuffed Mushrooms

Ready in about: 30 minutes | **Serves**: 2 | **Per serving**: Kcal 334, Fat: 29g, Net Carbs: 5.5g, Protein: 14g

INGREDIENTS

4 portobello mushrooms, stems removed
2 tbsp olive oil

2 cups lettuce

1 cup blue cheese, crumbled

DIRECTIONS

Preheat oven to 350°F. Fill the mushrooms with blue cheese and place on a lined baking sheet. Bake for 20 minutes. Serve with lettuce drizzled with olive oil.

Parmesan Roasted Cabbage

Ready in about: 25 minutes | **Serves**: 4 | **Per serving**: Kcal 268, Fat 19.3g, Net Carbs 4g, Protein 17.5g

INGREDIENTS

1 large head green cabbage
4 tbsp melted butter

1 tsp garlic powder
Salt and black pepper to taste

1 cup grated Parmesan cheese
1 tbsp fresh parsley, chopped

DIRECTIONS

Preheat oven to 400°F. Line a baking sheet with foil and grease with cooking spray. Stand the cabbage and run a knife from the top to bottom to cut the cabbage into wedges. Remove stems and wilted leaves. Place on the baking sheet. Mix the butter, garlic, salt, and black pepper until evenly combined.

Brush the mixture on all sides of the cabbage wedges and sprinkle with some Parmesan cheese. Bake for 20 minutes to soften the cabbage and melt the cheese. Remove the cabbages when golden brown, plate, and sprinkle with remaining Parmesan cheese and parsley. Serve warm with pan-glazed tofu.

Smoked Tofu with Rosemary Sauce

Ready in about: 20 minutes | **Serves**: 4 | **Per serving**: Kcal 336; Fat: 22.2g, Net Carbs: 9.3g, Protein: 27.6g

INGREDIENTS

10 oz smoked tofu, cubed
2 tbsp sesame oil
1 onion, chopped
1 tsp garlic, minced

½ cup vegetable broth
½ tsp turmeric powder
Salt and black pepper to taste
2 tbsp olive oil

1 cup tomato sauce
2 tbsp white wine
1 tsp fresh rosemary, chopped
1 tsp chili garlic sauce

DIRECTIONS

Warm the sesame oil in a pan over medium heat. Brown the tofu for about 5 minutes. Stir in turmeric powder, onion, garlic, salt, pepper for 3 minutes Pour in broth and cook until all liquid evaporates.

Warn the olive oil in another pan over medium heat. Place in tomato sauce and heat until cooked through. Place in the rest of the ingredients and simmer for 10 minutes. Pour over the tofu and serve

Cauliflower Risotto with Mushrooms

Ready in about: 15 minutes | **Serves**: 4 | **Per serving**: Kcal 264, Fat: 18g, Net Carbs: 8.4g, Protein: 11g

INGREDIENTS

2 shallots, diced
2 tbsp olive oil
¼ cup veggie broth

⅓ cup Parmesan cheese, shredded
2 tbsp butter
3 tbsp chives, chopped

1 lb mushrooms, sliced
4 cups cauliflower rice
Salt and black pepper to taste

DIRECTIONS

Heat olive oil in a saucepan over medium heat. Add the mushrooms and shallots and cook for 5 minutes until tender. Set aside. Add in the cauliflower, broth, salt, and pepper and cook until the liquid is absorbed, about 4-5 minutes. Stir in butter and Parmesan cheese until the cheese is melted. Serve warm.

Vegetable Tempura

Ready in about: 20 minutes | **Serves**: 4 | **Per serving**: Kcal 218, Fat 17g, Net Carbs 0.9g, Protein 3g

INGREDIENTS

½ cup coconut flour + extra for dredging
Salt and black pepper to taste
3 egg yolks
2 red bell peppers, cut into strips

1 squash, peeled and cut into strips
1 broccoli, cut into florets
1 cup chilled water

4 tbsp olive oil
4 lemon wedges
½ cup sugar-free soy sauce

DIRECTIONS

In a deep frying pan, heat the olive oil over medium heat. Beat the eggs lightly with ½ cup of coconut flour and water. The mixture should be lumpy. Dredge the vegetables lightly in some flour, shake off the excess flour, dip it in the batter, and then into the hot oil.

Fry in batches for 1 minute each, not more, and remove with a perforated spoon onto a wire rack. Sprinkle with salt and pepper and serve with the lemon wedges and soy sauce.

Colorful Vegan Soup

Ready in about: 25 minutes | **Serves**: 6 | **Per serving**: Kcal 142; Fat: 11.4g, Net Carbs: 9g, Protein: 2.9g

INGREDIENTS

2 tsp olive oil
1 red onion, chopped
2 cloves garlic, minced
1 celery stalk, chopped
1 head broccoli, chopped
1 carrot, sliced

1 cup spinach, torn into pieces
1 cup collard greens, chopped
Salt and black pepper to taste
2 thyme sprigs, chopped
1 rosemary sprig, chopped
2 bay leaves

6 cups vegetable stock
2 tomatoes, chopped
1 cup almond milk
1 tbsp white miso paste
½ cup arugula

DIRECTIONS

Place a large pot over medium heat and warm oil. Add in carrot, celery, onion, broccoli, garlic, and sauté until soft, about 5 minutes. Place in spinach, salt, rosemary, tomatoes, bay leaves, black pepper, collard greens, thyme, and vegetable stock. Bring to a boil and simmer the mixture for 15 minutes while the lid is slightly open. Stir in white miso paste, arugula, and almond milk and cook for 5 more minutes.

Spicy Cauliflower Steaks with Steamed Green Beans

Ready in about: 20 minutes | **Serves**: 4 | **Per serving**: Kcal 118, Fat 9g, Net Carbs 4g, Protein 2g

INGREDIENTS

2 heads cauliflower, sliced lengthwise into 'steaks'
¼ cup olive oil
¼ cup chili sauce
1 tsp erythritol

Salt and black pepper to taste
2 shallots, diced
1 bunch green beans, trimmed

2 tbsp fresh lemon juice
2 tbsp fresh parsley, chopped

DIRECTIONS

In a bowl, mix the olive oil, chili sauce, and erythritol. Brush the cauliflower with the mixture. Place them on the preheated grill. Close the lid and grill for 12 minutes, flipping once. Remove the grilled steaks to a plate and sprinkle with salt, black pepper, shallots, and parsley.

Bring salted water to boil over high heat, place the green beans in a sieve, and set over the steam from the boiling water. Cover with a clean napkin to keep the steam trapped in the sieve. Cook for 6 minutes. Remove to a bowl and toss with lemon juice. Add them to the cauliflower steaks and serve.

Mushroom & Bell Pepper Pizza

Ready in about: 35 minutes | **Serves**: 4 | **Per serving**: Kcal 295, Fat 20g, Net Carbs 8g, Protein 15g

INGREDIENTS

2 tsp olive oil
1 cup button mushrooms, chopped
½ cup mixed bell peppers, sliced

Salt and black pepper to taste
2 cauliflower pizza crusts
1 cup tomato sauce

½ cup Parmesan cheese, grated
2 tbsp sugar-free berry juice

DIRECTIONS

Warm the olive oil in a skillet over medium heat. Sauté the mushrooms and bell peppers for 10 minutes until softened. Season with salt and black pepper. Put the pizza crusts on a large pan and bake in the oven at 400°F for 10 minutes. Remove and let sit for 5 minutes. Spread the tomato sauce all over the top.

Scatter vegetables evenly on top. Season with a little more salt and sprinkle with some Parmesan cheese. Return to the oven and bake for 5-10 minutes until the vegetables are soft and the cheese has melted and is bubbly. Garnish with extra Parmesan cheese. Serve with chilled berry juice.

Cauliflower & Mushroom Stuffed Peppers

Ready in about: 40 minutes | **Serves**: 4 | **Per serving**: Kcal: 77; Fat 4.8g, Net Carbs 8.4g, Protein 1.6g,

INGREDIENTS

1 head cauliflower
4 bell peppers, cored and seeded
1 cup mushrooms, sliced

2 tbsp oil
1 onion, chopped
1 cup celery, chopped

1 garlic clove, minced
1 tsp chili powder
2 tomatoes, pureed

DIRECTIONS

Preheat oven to 360°F. To prepare cauliflower rice, grate the cauliflower into rice-size. Set in a kitchen towel to attract and remove any excess moisture. Line a baking pan with a parchment paper.

Warm the oil over medium heat. Add in garlic, celery, and onion and sauté until soft and translucent, about 3 minutes. Stir in chili powder, mushrooms, and cauliflower rice. Cook for 6 minutes until tender.

Split the cauliflower mixture among the bell peppers. Place in the baking dish. Top with tomatoes. Bake for 20-25 minutes. Plate and serve warm.

Onion & Nut Stuffed Mushrooms

Ready in about: 30 minutes | **Serves**: 4 | **Per serving**: Kcal 139; Fat: 11.2g, Net Carbs: 7.4g, Protein: 4.8g

INGREDIENTS

2 tbsp sesame oil
1 onion, chopped

1 garlic clove, minced
1 lb mushrooms, stems removed

Salt and black pepper to taste
¼ cup raw pine nuts

DIRECTIONS

Preheat oven to 360°F. Warm the sesame oil in a frying pan over medium heat. Place in garlic and onion and cook for 3 minutes. Chop mushroom stems and add to the pan. Cook for 3-4 minutes until tender.

Sprinkle with pepper and salt and add in pine nuts. Stuff the mushroom caps with the mixture. Set on a greased baking sheet. Bake the stuffed mushrooms for 30 minutes. Let cool slightly and serve.

Greek-Style Zucchini Pasta

Ready in about: 15 minutes | **Serves**: 4 | **Per serving**: Kcal 231, Fat: 19.5g, Net Carbs: 6.5g, Protein: 6.5g

INGREDIENTS

¼ cup sun-dried tomatoes
2 garlic cloves, minced
1 cup spinach, chopped

2 large zucchinis, spiralized
¼ cup feta cheese, crumbled
¼ cup halloumi cheese, shredded

10 kalamata olives, halved
2 tbsp olive oil
2 tbsp fresh parsley, chopped

DIRECTIONS

Heat the olive oil in a pan over medium heat. Add in zoodles, garlic, and spinach and cook for 5 minutes. Stir in the olives, tomatoes, feta, and parsley for 2 more minutes. Top with halloumi cheese and serve.

Garlicky Bok Choy Stir-Fry

Ready in about: 20 minutes | **Serves**: 4 | **Per serving**: Kcal 118; Fat: 7g, Net Carbs: 13.4g, Protein: 2.9g

INGREDIENTS

2 pounds bok choy, chopped
2 tbsp avocado oil

2 garlic cloves, sliced
2 tbsp pine nuts

½ tsp red pepper flakes
Salt and black pepper, to the taste

DIRECTIONS

Toast the pine nuts in a dry pan over medium heat for 2 minutes, shaking often; set aside. Warm the avocado oil in the pan and sauté the garlic for 30 seconds until soft. Stir in the bok choy for 4-5 minutes. Season with salt, black pepper, and red pepper flakes. Top with the pine nuts and serve.

Cheesy Cauliflower Falafel

Ready in about: 15 minutes | **Serves**: 4 | **Per serving**: Kcal 315, Fat 26g, Net Carbs 2g, Protein 8g

INGREDIENTS

1 head cauliflower, cut into florets
⅓ cup silvered ground almonds
2 tbsp cheddar cheese, shredded

½ tsp mixed spices
Salt and chili pepper to taste
3 tbsp coconut flour

3 fresh eggs
4 tbsp ghee

DIRECTIONS

Blend the cauli florets in a food processor until a grain meal consistency is formed. Pour the rice in a bowl, add the ground almonds, mixed spices, salt, cheddar, chili pepper, and coconut flour and mix well.

Beat the eggs in a bowl until creamy in color and mix with the cauli mixture. Shape ¼ cup each into patties. Melt the ghee in a pan over medium heat and fry the patties for 5 minutes on each side until firm and browned. Remove onto a wire rack to cool, share into serving plates, and top with tahini sauce.

Cajun Stuffed Cremini Mushrooms

Ready in about: 35 minutes | **Serves**: 4 | **Per serving**: Kcal 206; Fat: 13.4g, Net Carbs: 10g, Protein: 12.7g

INGREDIENTS

1 lb cremini mushrooms, stems removed
½ head broccoli, cut into florets
2 tbsp coconut oil
1 onion, chopped

1 garlic clove, minced
1 bell pepper, chopped
1 tsp cajun seasoning

Salt and black pepper to taste
1 cup cheddar cheese, shredded

DIRECTIONS

Preheat oven to 360°F. Bake mushroom caps until tender for 8 to 12 minutes. In a food processor, pulse broccoli florets until they become like small rice-like granules. Warm the coconut oil in a skillet over medium heat. Stir in bell pepper, garlic, and onion and sauté until fragrant, about 5 minutes.

Sprinkle with black pepper, salt, and cajun seasoning. Fold in broccoli rice. Equally, separate the filling mixture among mushroom caps. Cover with cheddar cheese and bake for 15 more minutes. Serve warm.

Zesty Frittata with Roasted Chilies

Ready in about: 20 minutes | Serves: 4 | Per serving: Kcal 153, Fat 10.3g, Net Carbs 2.3g, Protein 6.4g

INGREDIENTS

2 large green bell peppers, chopped
4 red and yellow chilies, roasted
2 tbsp red wine vinegar
1 knob butter, melted

2 tbsp fresh parsley, chopped
8 eggs, beaten
4 tbsp olive oil
½ cup Parmesan cheese, grated

¼ cup goat cheese, crumbled
2 cloves garlic, minced
1 cup arugula

DIRECTIONS

Preheat oven to 400°F. With a knife, seed the chilies, cut into long strips, and pour into a bowl. Mix in the vinegar, butter, parsley, half of the olive oil, and garlic; set aside. In another bowl, whisk the eggs with salt, pepper, bell peppers, and Parmesan cheese.

Heat the remaining oil in a pan over medium heat and pour the egg mixture along with the goat cheese. Let cook for 3 minutes. Transfer the pan to the oven. Bake the frittata for 4 more minutes, remove, and top with the chili mixture. Garnish the frittata with arugula and serve for lunch.

Vegetable Burritos

Ready in about: 10 minutes | Serves: 4 | Per serving: Kcal 373, Fat 23.2g, Net Carbs 5.4g, Protein 17.9g

INGREDIENTS

2 large low carb tortillas
2 tsp olive oil
1 small onion, sliced

1 bell pepper, seeded and sliced
1 ripe avocado, pitted and sliced
1 cup lemon cauli couscous

Salt and black pepper to taste
⅓ cup sour cream
3 tbsp Mexican salsa

DIRECTIONS

Heat the olive oil in a skillet over medium heat. Sauté the onion and bell pepper until they start to brown on the edges, about 4 minutes. Lay the tortillas on a flat surface and top each one with the bell pepper mixture, avocado, and cauli couscous. Season with salt and black pepper

Top with sour cream and Mexican salsa. Fold in each tortilla's sides and roll them in and over the filling to be completely enclosed. Wrap with foil, cut in halves, and serve.

Cauliflower Mac & Cheese

Ready in about: 20 minutes | Serves: 4 | Per serving: Kcal 160, Fat: 12g, Net Carbs: 2g, Protein: 8.6g

INGREDIENTS

1 cauliflower head, riced
1 ½ cups mozzarella cheese, grated

2 tsp paprika
¾ tsp rosemary

1 tsp turmeric
Salt and black pepper to taste

DIRECTIONS

Microwave the cauliflower for 5 minutes. Place it in cheesecloth and squeeze the extra juices out. Place the cauli in a pot over medium heat. Add paprika, turmeric, salt, pepper, and rosemary. Stir in mozzarella cheese and cook until the cheese is melted, about 10 minutes. Serve topped with rosemary.

Roasted Brussels Sprouts with Sunflower Seeds

Ready in about: 45 minutes | Serves: 6 | Per serving: Kcal: 186; Fat 17g, Net Carbs 8g, Protein 2.1g

INGREDIENTS

¼ cup olive oil
3 lb brussels sprouts, halved

Salt and black pepper to taste
1 tsp sunflower seeds

2 tbsp fresh chives, chopped

DIRECTIONS

Preheat oven to 390°F. Arrange sprout halves on a greased baking sheet. Shake in pepper, salt, sunflower seeds, and olive oil. Roast for 40 minutes until the cabbage becomes soft. Top with chives and serve.

Baked Tomatoes with Pepita Seed Topping

Ready in about: 15 minutes | **Serves**: 6 | **Per serving**: Kcal 161; Fat: 14g, Net Carbs: 7.2g, Protein: 4.6g

INGREDIENTS

5 tomatoes, sliced
¼ cup olive oil
1 tbsp chili seasoning mix

½ cup pepitas seeds
1 tbsp nutritional yeast
Salt and black pepper to taste

½ tsp nutmeg
½ tsp ginger powder
1 tsp garlic puree

DIRECTIONS

Set oven to 400°F. Over the sliced tomatoes, drizzle olive oil. In a food processor, add pepita seeds, nutritional yeast, garlic puree, nutmeg, ginger powder, salt, and pepper and pulse until the desired consistency is attained. Transfer to a bowl and stir in the chili seasoning mix. Arrange the tomato slices on a baking pan and top them with the pepita seed mixture. Bake for 10 minutes. Remove and serve.

Greek Salad with Poppy Seed Dressing

Ready in about: 3 hours 15 minutes | **Serves**: 4 | **Per serving**: Kcal 208; Fat: 15.6g, Net Carbs: 6.7g, Protein: 7.6g

INGREDIENTS

Dressing

1 cup poppy seeds
2 cups water
2 tbsp green onions, chopped

1 garlic clove, minced
1 lime, freshly squeezed
Salt and black pepper to taste

¼ tsp dill, minced
2 tbsp almond milk

Salad

1 head lettuce, separated into leaves
3 tomatoes, diced

3 cucumbers, sliced
2 tbsp kalamata olives, pitted

DIRECTIONS

Put all dressing ingredients, except for the poppy seeds, in a food processor and pulse until well incorporated. Add in poppy seeds and mix well with a fork. Mix and divide the salad ingredients between 4 plates. Add the dressing to each and shake to coat. Serve.

Cream of Zucchini with Avocado

Ready in about: 35 minutes | **Serves**: 4 | **Per serving**: Kcal 165 Fat: 13.4g, Net Carbs: 9g, Protein: 2.2g

INGREDIENTS

3 tsp vegetable oil
1 onion, chopped
1 carrot, sliced

1 turnip, sliced
3 cups zucchinis, chopped
1 avocado, peeled and diced

Salt and black pepper to taste
4 cups vegetable broth
1 tomato, pureed

DIRECTIONS

In a pot, warm the oil and sauté onion until translucent, about 3 minutes. Add in turnip, zucchini, and carrot and cook for 7 minutes until tender. Season with salt and black pepper.

Mix in pureed tomato and vegetable broth. Bring to a boil. Simmer for 20 minutes. Lift from the heat. Add the soup and avocado to a blender. Puree until creamy and smooth. Serve warm.

Spicy Green Cabbage with Tofu

Ready in about: 25 minutes | **Serves**: 4 | **Per serving**: Kcal 182; Fat: 10.3g, Net Carbs: 8.3g, Protein: 8.1g

INGREDIENTS

2 tbsp olive oil
14 oz block tofu, pressed and cubed
1 celery stalk, chopped
1 bunch of scallions, chopped

1 tsp cayenne pepper
1 tsp garlic powder
2 tbsp Worcestershire sauce
Salt and black pepper to taste

1 lb green cabbage, shredded
½ tsp turmeric
¼ tsp dried basil

DIRECTIONS

Warm the olive oil a large skillet over medium heat. Stir in tofu cubes and cook for 8 minutes. Set aside. Add scallions, celery, and garlic in the same pan and sauté for 5 minutes until soft. Stir in cayenne pepper, Worcestershire sauce, garlic powder, turmeric, basil, salt, and pepper for 2 more minutes. Add in the green cabbage and cook for 8-10 minutes, stirring often. Serve topped with the tofu.

Carrot Noodles with Cashew Sauce

Ready in about: 15 minutes | **Serves**: 4 | **Per serving**: Kcal 145; Fat: 10.6g, Net Carbs: 7,9g, Protein: 5.5g

INGREDIENTS

4 carrots, cut into long strips	2 tbsp olive oil	Salt and black pepper to taste

Cashew sauce

½ cup raw cashews	Salt and black pepper to taste	½ tsp garlic powder
3 tbsp nutritional yeast	¼ tsp onion powder	¼ cup olive oil

DIRECTIONS

Set a pan over medium heat and warm the olive oil. Cook the carrots for 1 minute as you stir. Add in ½ cup water and cook for an additional 6 minutes. Sprinkle with salt and pepper.

Place all the sauce ingredients in a food processor and pulse until you attain the required "cheese" consistency. Serve cooked noodles with a topping of cashew sauce.

Buffalo Salad with Baked Cauliflower

Ready in about: 50 minutes | **Serves**: 4 | **Per serving**: Kcal 255; Fat: 23.2g, Net Carbs: 5.5g, Protein: 4.1g

INGREDIENTS

1 Iceberg lettuce, chopped	3/4 cup almond flour	¼ fennel bulb, sliced
½ cup Tabasco hot sauce	2 tsp garlic powder	1 cup cherry tomatoes, halved
1 tbsp avocado oil	2 tsp onion powder	1 large avocado, sliced
1 head cauliflower, cut into florets	1 tsp paprika	1 carrot, shredded
½ cup almond milk	Salt and black pepper to taste	½ cup Ranch dressing

DIRECTIONS

Preheat the oven to 425°F. In a bowl, combine the almond flour, almond milk, garlic powder, onion powder, paprika, ½ cup water, salt, and pepper. Add in the cauliflower and toss to coat. Spread the cauliflower on a baking sheet in a single layer and bake for 20 minutes.

In a bowl, whisk the Tabasco sauce with avocado oil. Shake and sprinkle the cauliflower with the hot sauce. Return in the oven and bake for 20 more minutes. In a salad bowl, combine the lettuce, fennel, cherry tomatoes, and carrot and drizzle with the Ranch dressing. Top with roasted cauliflower and serve.

Crispy-Topped Baked Vegetables

Ready in about: 40 minutes | **Serves**: 4 | **Per serving**: Kcal 242; Fat: 16.3g, Net Carbs: 8.6g, Protein: 16.3g

INGREDIENTS

2 tbsp olive oil	½ lb turnips, sliced	½ tsp liquid smoke
1 onion, chopped	1 cup vegetable broth	1 cup Parmesan cheese, shredded
1 celery stalk, chopped	1 tsp turmeric	2 tbsp fresh chives, chopped
2 carrots, grated	Salt and black pepper to taste	

DIRECTIONS

Preheat oven to 360°F. Set a skillet over medium heat and warm olive oil. Sweat the onion until soft. Place in the turnips, carrots, and celery and cook for 4 minutes. Remove to a greased baking dish.

Combine vegetable broth with turmeric, pepper, liquid smoke, and salt. Spread this mixture over the vegetables. Sprinkle with Parmesan cheese and bake for about 30 minutes. Garnish with chives to serve.

Chili Stuffed Zucchini

Ready in about: 50 minutes | **Serves**: 4 | **Per serving**: Kcal 148; Fat: 10g, Net Carbs: 9.8g, Protein: 7.5g

INGREDIENTS

2 zucchinis, cut into halves, scoop out the insides

2 tbsp olive oil

12 oz firm tofu, crumbled

2 garlic cloves, pressed

½ cup onions, chopped

2 cups tomato sauce

¼ tsp turmeric

Sea salt and chili pepper to taste

1 tbsp nutritional yeast

¼ cup almonds, chopped

DIRECTIONS

Set pan over medium heat and warm the olive oil. Add in onion, garlic, and tofu and cook for 5 minutes. Place in scooped zucchini flesh, turmeric, and 1 cup of tomato sauce and cook for 6 more minutes.

Preheat oven to 360°F. Divide the tofu mixture among the zucchini shells. Arrange the stuffed zucchini shells in a greased baking dish. Pour in the remaining 1 cup of tomato sauce. Bake for about 30 minutes. Sprinkle with almonds and nutritional yeast and continue baking for 5 to 6 more minutes. Serve.

Easy Cauliflower & Kale Soup

Ready in about: 35 minutes | **Serves**: 4 | **Per serving**: Kcal 172; Fat: 10.3g, Net Carbs: 11.8g, Protein: 8.1g

INGREDIENTS

2 tbsp olive oil

1 onion, finely chopped

2 garlic cloves, minced

1 head cauliflower, cut into florets

1 cup kale, chopped

4 cups vegetable broth

½ cup almond milk

½ tsp salt

½ tsp red pepper flakes

1 tbsp fresh parsley, chopped

½ cup cheddar cheese, grated

DIRECTIONS

Set a pot over medium heat and warm the oil. Add garlic and onion and sauté until softened. Place in vegetable broth, kale, and cauliflower and cook for 10 minutes until the mixture boils.

Stir in the pepper flakes, salt, and almond milk; reduce the heat and simmer the soup for 10-15 minutes. Remove from the heat and stir in the cheddar cheese. Blitz the soup with an immersion blender to achieve the desired consistency. Top with parsley and serve immediately.

Cauliflower & Hazelnut Salad

Ready in about: 15 minutes + chilling time | **Serves**: 4 | **Per serving**: Kcal 221; Fat: 18g, Net Carbs: 6.6g, Protein: 4.2g

INGREDIENTS

1 head cauliflower, cut into florets

1 cup green onions, chopped

4 oz roasted peppers, chopped

¼ cup extra-virgin olive oil

1 tbsp red wine vinegar

1 tsp yellow mustard

Salt and black pepper to taste

½ cup black olives, pitted and chopped

½ cup hazelnuts, chopped

DIRECTIONS

Place the cauliflower florets in a steamer basket over boiling water. Cover and steam for 5 minutes. Remove to a bowl and let cool. Add in the roasted peppers and green onions and stir.

In a small dish, combine salt, olive oil, mustard, pepper, and vinegar. Sprinkle the mixture over the veggies. Top with hazelnuts and black olives and serve.

Fried Tofu with Mushrooms

Ready in about: 40 minutes | **Serves**: 2 | **Per serving**: Kcal 223; Fat: 15.9g, Net Carbs: 8.1g, Protein: 15.6g

INGREDIENTS

12 oz extra-firm tofu, cubed

1 ½ tbsp flaxseed meal

Salt and black pepper to taste

1 tsp garlic clove, minced

½ tsp paprika

1 tsp onion powder

2 tbsp olive oil

1 cup mushrooms, sliced

1 jalapeño pepper, deveined, sliced

In a bowl, add onion powder, tofu, salt, paprika, black pepper, jalapeño pepper, flaxseed, and garlic. Toss the mixture to coat and allow to marinate for 30 minutes. Warm the olive oil in a pan over medium heat.

Cook mushrooms for 5 minutes until tender, stirring continuously. Add in the tofu mixture and stir. Cook for 4-5 more minutes. Divide between plates and serve warm.

Parsnip Chips with Avocado Dip

Ready in about: 20 minutes | **Serves**: 6 | **Per serving**: Kcal 269; Fat: 26.7g, Net Carbs: 9.4g, Protein: 2.3g

INGREDIENTS

2 avocados, mashed
2 tsp lime juice

Salt and black pepper to taste
2 garlic cloves, minced

3 tbsp olive oil
3 cups parsnips, thinly sliced

DIRECTIONS

Preheat oven to 370°F. Set parsnip slices on a baking sheet. Season with salt and pepper and drizzle with some olive oil. Bake for 15 minutes until slices become dry. In a bowl, stir avocado with lime juice, remaining olive oil, garlic, salt, and pepper until combined. Serve the chips with the chilled avocado dip.

Tomato Stuffed Avocado

Ready in about: 10 minutes | **Serves**: 4 | **Per serving**: Kcal 263; Fat: 24.8g, Net Carbs: 5.5g, Protein: 3.5g

INGREDIENTS

2 avocados
1 tomato, chopped
¼ cup walnuts, ground

2 carrots, chopped
1 garlic clove
1 tsp lemon juice

1 tbsp soy sauce
Salt and black pepper to taste

DIRECTIONS

Halve and pit the avocados. Spoon out some of the pulp of each avocado. In a bowl, mix soy sauce, carrots, avocado pulp, tomato, lemon juice, and garlic. Add black pepper and salt. Fill the avocado halves with the mixture and scatter walnuts over to serve.

Zoodles with Avocado & Olives

Ready in about: 15 minutes | **Serves**: 4 | **Per serving**: Kcal 449, Fat: 42g, Net Carbs: 8.4g, Protein: 6.3g

INGREDIENTS

4 zucchinis, spiralized
½ cup pesto
2 avocados, sliced

1 cup Kalamata olives, chopped
¼ cup fresh basil, chopped
2 tbsp olive oil

¼ cup sun-dried tomatoes, chopped
Salt and black pepper to taste

DIRECTIONS

Heat olive oil in a pan over medium heat. Cook the zoodles for 4 minutes. Transfer to a plate. In a bowl, stir pesto, basil, salt, pepper, tomatoes, and olives. Pour over the zoodles and top with avocado slices.

Morning Coconut Smoothie

Ready in about: 5 minutes | **Serves**: 4 | **Per serving**: Kcal 247; Fat: 21.7g, Net Carbs: 6.9g, Protein: 2.6g

INGREDIENTS

½ cup water
1 ½ cups coconut milk

1 cup frozen strawberries
2 cups fresh blueberries

¼ tsp vanilla extract
1 tbsp protein powder

DIRECTIONS

In a blender, combine all the ingredients and pulse until you attain a uniform and creamy consistency. Divide between glasses and serve chilled.

Morning Granola

Ready in about: 1 hour | **Serves**: 6 | **Per serving**: Kcal 262; Fat: 24.3g, Net Carbs: 9.2g, Protein: 5.1g

INGREDIENTS

1 tbsp coconut oil
⅓ cup almond flakes
½ cup almond milk
½ tbsp liquid stevia

1/8 tsp salt
1 tsp lime zest
½ tsp ground cinnamon
½ cup pecans, chopped

½ cup almonds, slivered
2 tbsp pepitas
3 tbsp sunflower seeds
¼ cup flax seeds

DIRECTIONS

Preheat the oven to 300°F. Set a deep pan over medium heat and warm the coconut oil. Add almond flakes and toast for about 2 minutes. Stir in the remaining ingredients.

Lay the mixture in an even layer onto a baking sheet lined with a parchment paper. Bake for 1 hour, making sure that you shake gently in intervals of 15 minutes. Serve alongside additional almond milk.

Brussels Sprouts with Tofu

Ready in about: 20 minutes | **Serves**: 4 | **Per serving**: Kcal 179; Fat: 11.7g, Net Carbs: 9.1g, Protein: 10.5g

INGREDIENTS

2 tbsp olive oil
2 garlic cloves, minced
½ cup onions, chopped

10 oz tofu, crumbled
2 tbsp water
2 tbsp soy sauce

1 tbsp tomato puree
½ lb Brussels sprouts, quartered
Salt and black pepper to taste

DIRECTIONS

Set a saucepan over medium heat and warm the olive oil. Add onion and garlic and cook until tender, 3 minutes. Place in the soy sauce, water, and tofu. Cook for 5 minutes until the tofu starts to brown. Add in Brussels sprouts; adjust the seasonings. Cook for 13 minutes while stirring frequently. Serve warm.

Chard Swiss Dip

Ready in about: 25 minutes | **Serves**: 6 | **Per serving**: Kcal 105; Fat: 7.3g, Net Carbs: 7.9g, Protein: 2.9g

INGREDIENTS

2 lb Swiss chard
1 cup tofu, pressed, crumbled
½ cup almond milk

2 tsp nutritional yeast
2 garlic cloves, minced
2 tbsp olive oil

Salt and black pepper to taste
½ tsp paprika
½ tsp fresh mint leaves, chopped

DIRECTIONS

Place a large pot of salted water over medium heat. Bring to a boil and add in the chard. Cook for 5 minutes until wilted. Drain and let cool. Transfer to a blender and add in the remaining ingredients. Puree until you get a homogeneous mixture. Serve alongside baked vegetables.

Tofu Stir Fry with Asparagus

Ready in about: 30 minutes | **Serves**: 4 | **Per serving**: Kcal 138; Fat: 8.9g, Net Carbs: 5.9g, Protein: 6.4g

INGREDIENTS

1 lb asparagus, cut off stems
2 tbsp olive oil
2 blocks tofu, pressed and cubed

2 garlic cloves, minced
1 tsp cajun spice mix
1 tsp Dijon mustard

1 bell pepper, chopped
¼ cup vegetable broth
Salt and black pepper to taste

DIRECTIONS

In a large saucepan, warm the olive oil. Place in the asparagus and cook until tender for 10 minutes; set aside. Add the tofu cubes in the saucepan and cook for 6 minutes, stirring often.

Place in garlic and cook for 30 seconds until soft. Stir in the rest of the ingredients, including reserved asparagus, and cook for an additional 4 minutes. Divide among plates and serve.

Kale Cheese Waffles

Ready in about: 45 minutes | Serves: 4 | Per serving: Kcal 283, Fat: 20.2g, Net Carbs: 3.6g, Protein: 16g

INGREDIENTS

2 green onions, chopped
1 tbsp olive oil
2 eggs

⅓ cup Parmesan cheese, grated
1 cup kale, chopped
1 cup mozzarella cheese, grated

½ cauliflower head, chopped
1 tbsp sesame seeds
2 tsp chopped thyme

DIRECTIONS

Place the chopped cauliflower in the food processor and process until rice is formed. Add in kale, spring onions, and thyme. Pulse until smooth. Transfer to a bowl. Stir in the rest of the ingredients and mix well.

Heat waffle iron and spread in ¼ cup of the mixture, evenly. Cook following the manufacturer's instructions until golden, about 10 minutes in total. Repeat with the remaining batter. Serve warm.

Artichoke & Cauliflower Bake

Ready in about: 30 minutes | Serves: 4 | Per serving: Kcal 113; Fat: 6.7g, Net Carbs: 11.6g, Protein: 5g

INGREDIENTS

1 head cauliflower, cut into florets
8 oz artichoke hearts, halved
2 garlic cloves, smashed

2 tomatoes, pureed
¼ cup coconut oil, melted
1 tsp chili paprika paste

¼ tsp marjoram
½ tsp curry powder
Salt and black pepper to taste

DIRECTIONS

Preheat oven to 390°F. Apply a cooking spray to a baking dish. Lay artichokes and cauliflower on the baking dish. Around the vegetables, scatter smashed garlic. Place in the pureed tomatoes. Sprinkle over melted coconut oil and stir in chili paprika paste, curry, black pepper, salt, and marjoram. Roast for 25 minutes, shaking often. Place on a serving plate and serve with green salad.

Coconut Cauliflower & Parsnip Soup

Ready in about: 25 minutes | Serves: 4 | Per serving: Kcal 94; Fat: 7.2g, Net Carbs: 7g, Protein: 2.7g

INGREDIENTS

4 cups vegetable broth
2 heads cauliflower, cut into florets
1 cup parsnips, chopped

1 onion, finely chopped
2 garlic cloves, finely chopped
2 tbsp coconut oil

2 tbsp lime juice
1 cup coconut milk
½ tsp red pepper flakes

DIRECTIONS

Warm the coconut oil in a pot over medium heat. Sauté the onion, parsnips, and garlic for 3 minutes. Add in the vegetable broth and cauliflower and bring to a boil. Cook for about 15 minutes. Puree the mixture with an immersion blender. After, stir in the coconut milk and red pepper flakes. Serve warm.

Easy Vanilla Granola

Ready in about: 1 hour | Serves: 6 | Per serving: Kcal 449; Fat: 44.9g, Net Carbs: 5.1g, Protein: 9.3g

INGREDIENTS

½ cup hazelnuts, chopped
1 cup walnuts, chopped
⅓ cup flax meal
⅓ cup coconut milk

⅓ cup poppy seeds
⅓ cup pumpkin seeds
8 drops stevia
⅓ cup coconut oil, melted

1 ½ tsp vanilla paste
1 tsp ground cloves
1 tsp grated nutmeg
1 tsp lemon zest

DIRECTIONS

Preheat oven to 300°F. Line a parchment paper to a baking sheet. In a bowl, combine all ingredients and mix well. Stir in ⅓ cup water. Spread the mixture onto the baking sheet in an even layer. Bake for 55 minutes as you stir at intervals of 15 minutes. Let cool at room temperature. Serve.

Butternut Squash Risotto with Almonds

Ready in about: 25 minutes | **Serves**: 4 | **Per serving**: Kcal 492; Fat: 39g, Net Carbs: 9.4g, Protein: 7.2g

INGREDIENTS

1 leek, chopped
2 lb butternut squash, peeled, cubed
¼ cup almonds, chopped
2 tbsp olive oil

2 garlic cloves, minced
Salt and black pepper to taste
2 cups almond milk
1 lime, juiced

1 celery stalk, chopped
2 cups baby spinach
2 tbsp fresh cilantro, chopped

DIRECTIONS

In a food processor, pulse butternut squash until it becomes like small rice-like granules. Place in a bowl. Warm the olive oil in a large saucepan over medium heat. Add the leek, garlic, and celery and cook for 3 minutes until tender. Stir in the butternut rice for 2-3 minutes. Sprinkle with salt and pepper.

Pour in the almond milk and cook for 5-7 minutes. Stir in the spinach for 2-3 more minutes until it is wilted. Drizzle with the lime juice, scatter almonds all over, and top with cilantro. Serve warm.

Fall Baked Vegetables

Ready in about: 45 minutes | **Serves**: 4 | **Per serving**: Kcal 165; Fat: 14.3g, Net Carbs: 8.2g, Protein: 2.1g

INGREDIENTS

3 mixed bell peppers, sliced
½ head broccoli, cut into florets
2 zucchinis, sliced
2 leeks, chopped

4 garlic cloves, halved
2 thyme sprigs, chopped
1 tsp dried sage, crushed
2 tbsp olive oil

2 tbsp vinegar
Salt and black pepper to taste
Salt to taste
1 tsp cayenne pepper

DIRECTIONS

Preheat oven to 425°F. Apply nonstick cooking spray to a rimmed baking sheet. Mix in all the vegetables with olive oil, seasonings, and vinegar. Roast for 40 minutes, stirring every 10 minutes. Serve immediately.

Tasty Cauliflower Dip

Ready in about: 10 minutes | **Serves**: 4 | **Per serving**: Kcal 100; Fat: 8.2g, Net Carbs: 4.7g, Protein: 3.7g

INGREDIENTS

1 head cauliflower, cut into florets
¼ cup olive oil

Salt and black pepper to taste
1 garlic clove, smashed

1 tbsp sesame paste
½ tsp garam masala

DIRECTIONS

Boil cauliflower until tender for 7 minutes in salted water in a large pot. Transfer to a blender and pulse until you attain a rice-like consistency. Place in garam masala, olive oil, black paper, garlic, salt, and sesame paste. Blend the mixture until well combined. Drizzle with some olive oil and serve.

Walnut-Crusted Tofu

Ready in about: 35 minutes | **Serves**: 4 | **Per serving**: Kcal 232; Fat: 21.6g, Net Carbs: 5.3g, Protein: 8.3g

INGREDIENTS

3 tsp olive oil
1 block extra-firm tofu, sliced
1 cup walnuts

2 tbsp tamari sauce
3 tbsp vegetable broth
½ tsp smashed garlic

Salt and black pepper to taste
2 tsp sunflower seeds

DIRECTIONS

Preheat oven to 425°F. Brush the tofu with tamari sauce. In a food processor, mix walnuts, vegetable broth, olive oil, garlic, sunflower seeds, salt, and pepper and blend until uniform. Coat the tofu with the walnut mixture and arrange on a lined baking dish. Bake for 25-30 minutes, flipping once until golden.

Creamy Almond & Turnip Soup

Ready in about: 25 minutes | **Serves**: 4 | **Per serving**: Kcal 114, Fat: 6.5g, Net Carbs: 9.2g, Protein: 3.8g

INGREDIENTS

2 tbsp olive oil
1 onion, chopped
1 celery stalk, chopped

2 turnips, peeled and chopped
4 cups vegetable broth
Salt and white pepper to taste

¼ cup ground almonds
1 cup almond milk
1 tbsp fresh cilantro, chopped

DIRECTIONS

Set a pot over medium heat and warm the olive oil. Add in celery and onion and sauté for 6 minutes. Stir in white pepper, vegetable broth, salt, and almonds. Boil the mixture. Simmer for 17 minutes. Blend the soup with an immersion blender. Stir in the almond milk and decorate with cilantro before serving.

Bell Pepper & Pumpkin with Avocado Sauce

Ready in about: 15 minutes | **Serves**: 4 | **Per serving**: Kcal 233; Fat: 20.2g, Net Carbs: 11g, Protein: 1.9g

INGREDIENTS

1 lb pumpkin, peeled
½ lb bell peppers
1 avocado, peeled and pitted

1 lemon, juiced and zested
2 tbsp sesame oil
2 tbsp fresh cilantro, chopped

1 onion, chopped
1 jalapeño pepper, minced
2 tbsp olive oil

DIRECTIONS

Use a spiralizer to spiralize bell peppers and pumpkin. Warm the olive oil in a large skillet. Add in bell peppers and pumpkin and sauté for 8 minutes. In a blender, combine the remaining ingredients and pulse until you obtain a creamy mixture. Top the vegetable noodles with the avocado sauce and serve.

Spiced Cauliflower with Garlic & Peppers

Ready in about: 35 minutes | **Serves**: 4 | **Per serving**: Kcal 166; Fat: 13.9g, Net Carbs: 7.4g, Protein: 3g

INGREDIENTS

1 head cauliflower, cut into florets
2 red bell peppers, cut into squares

¼ cup olive oil
Salt and black pepper to taste

½ tsp cayenne pepper
2 garlic cloves, sliced

DIRECTIONS

Preheat oven to 425°F. Line a parchment paper to a baking sheet. Set the cauliflower, bell peppers, and garlic on the sheet. Sprinkle with cayenne pepper, salt, and black pepper and drizzle with olive oil; stir. Roast for 30 minutes as you toss in intervals until they start to brown. Serve with tomato dip.

Bell Pepper Stuffed Avocado

Ready in about: 10 minutes | **Serves**: 4 | **Per serving**: Kcal 255; Fat: 23.2g, Net Carbs: 7.4g, Protein: 2.4g

INGREDIENTS

2 avocados, pitted and halved
2 tbsp olive oil
3 cups green bell peppers, chopped

1 onion, chopped
1 tsp garlic puree
Salt and black pepper to taste

1 tsp deli mustard
1 tomato, chopped

DIRECTIONS

From each half of the avocados, scoop out 2 teaspoons of flesh; set aside. Warm the olive oil in a pan over medium heat. Cook the garlic, onion, and bell peppers until tender, about 5 minutes.

Mix in the reserved avocado. Add in the tomato, salt, mustard, and black pepper. Separate the mixture and mix equally among the avocado halves. Serve.

SOUPS, STEW & SALADS

Homemade Cold Gazpacho Soup

Ready in about: 15 minutes + chilling time | **Serves**: 6 | **Per serving**: Kcal 528, Fat: 45.8g, Net Carbs: 6.5g, Protein: 7.5g

INGREDIENTS

2 small green peppers, roasted
2 large red peppers, roasted
2 avocados, flesh scoped out
2 garlic cloves
2 spring onions, chopped

1 cucumber, chopped
1 cup olive oil
2 tbsp lemon juice
4 tomatoes, chopped
7 oz goat cheese, crumbled

1 small red onion, chopped
2 tbsp apple cider vinegar
1 tsp xylitol
Salt to taste

DIRECTIONS

Place the peppers, tomatoes, avocados, red onion, garlic, lemon juice, olive oil, vinegar, xylitol, and salt in a food processor. Pulse until your desired consistency is reached. Taste and adjust the seasoning.

Transfer the mixture to a pot. Stir in cucumber and spring onions. Cover and chill in the fridge at least 2 hours. Divide the soup between 6 bowls. Serve topped with goat cheese and an extra drizzle of olive oil.

Tip: For more protein, add cooked and chopped shrimp to this refreshing delight.

Cream of Thyme Tomato Soup

Ready in about: 20 minutes | **Serves**: 4 | **Per serving**: Kcal 310, Fat 27g, Net Carbs 3g, Protein 11g

INGREDIENTS

2 tbsp ghee
2 large red onions, diced
½ cup raw cashew nuts, diced

2 (28 oz) cans tomatoes
2 tsp fresh thyme leaves
1 ½ cups water

Salt and black pepper to taste
1 cup heavy cream

DIRECTIONS

Melt ghee in a pot over medium heat and sauté the onions for 4 minutes until softened. Stir in the tomatoes, thyme, water, and cashews and season with salt and black pepper. Cover and bring to a boil.

Simmer for 10 minutes until thoroughly cooked. Open, turn the heat off, and puree the ingredients with an immersion blender. Adjust the taste and stir in the heavy cream. Spoon into soup bowls and serve.

Thyme & Wild Mushroom Soup

Ready in about: 25 minutes | **Serves**: 4 | **Per serving**: Kcal 281, Fat: 25g, Net Carbs: 5.8g, Protein: 6.1g

INGREDIENTS

¼ cup butter
½ cup crème fraiche

12 oz wild mushrooms, chopped
2 tsp thyme leaves

2 garlic cloves, minced
4 cups chicken broth

DIRECTIONS

Melt the butter in a large pot over medium heat. Add garlic and cook for 1 minute until tender. Add mushrooms and cook for 10 minutes. Pour in the broth over and bring to a boil. Simmer for 10 minutes. Puree the soup with a hand blender until smooth. Stir in crème fraiche. Garnish with thyme to serve.

Power Green Soup

Ready in about: 30 minutes | **Serves**: 6 | **Per serving**: Kcal 392, Fat: 37.6g, Net Carbs: 5.8g, Protein: 4.9g

INGREDIENTS

1 broccoli head, chopped
1 cup spinach
1 onion, chopped

2 garlic cloves, minced
½ cup watercress
5 cups vegetable stock

1 cup coconut milk
1 tbsp ghee
Salt and black pepper to taste

Melt the ghee in a large pot over medium heat. Add onion and garlic and cook for 3 minutes. Add broccoli and cook for an additional 5 minutes. Pour the vegetable stock over and close the lid. Bring to a boil.

Reduce the heat. Simmer for 3 minutes. Add spinach and watercress and cook for 3 more minutes. Stir in the coconut cream, salt, and black pepper. Blend the soup with a hand blender. Serve warm.

Creamy Cauliflower Soup with Bacon Chips

Ready in about: 25 minutes | **Serves**: 4 | **Per serving**: Kcal 402, Fat 37g, Net Carbs 6g, Protein 8g

INGREDIENTS

2 tbsp ghee
1 onion, chopped
2 head cauliflower, cut into florets

2 cups water
Salt and black pepper to taste
3 cups almond milk

1 cup white cheddar cheese, grated
3 bacon strips

DIRECTIONS

Melt the ghee in a saucepan over medium heat and sauté the onion for 3 minutes until fragrant. Include the cauli florets and sauté for 3 minutes until slightly softened. Add the water and season with salt and black pepper. Bring to a boil and then reduce the heat. Cover and simme for 10 minutes.

Puree the soup with an immersion blender until the ingredients are evenly combined. Stir in the almond milk and cheese until the cheese melts. In a non-stick skillet over high heat, fry the bacon for 5 minutes until crispy. Divide soup between serving bowls, top with crispy bacon, and serve hot.

Buffalo Chicken Soup

Ready in about: 40 minutes | **Serves**: 4 | **Per serving**: Kcal 215, Fat: 11.3g, Net Carbs: 2.4g, Protein: 7.5g

INGREDIENTS

2 chicken legs
2 tbsp butter, melted
1 onion, chopped

2 garlic cloves, minced
1 carrot, chopped
1 bay leaf

2 tbsp fresh cilantro, chopped
⅓ cup buffalo sauce
Salt and black pepper to taste

DIRECTIONS

Add the chicken in a pot over medium heat and cover with water. Add in salt, pepper, and bay leaf. Boil for 15 minutes. Remove to a plate and let it cool slightly. Strain and reserve the broth.

Melt the butter in a large saucepan over medium heat. Sauté the onion, garlic, and carrot for 5 minutes until tender, stirring occasionally. Remove skin and bones from chicken and discard.

Chop the chicken and add it to the saucepan. Stir in the buffalo sauce for 1 minute and pour in the broth. Bring to a boil. Cook for 15 minutes. Adjust the taste with salt and pepper and top with cilantro. Serve.

Green Minestrone Soup

Ready in about: 25 minutes | **Serves**: 4 | **Per serving**: Kcal 227, Fat 20.3g, Net Carbs 2g, Protein 8g

INGREDIENTS

2 tbsp ghee
2 tbsp onion-garlic puree
2 heads broccoli, cut into florets

2 celery stalks, chopped
4 cups vegetable broth
1 cup baby spinach

Salt and black pepper to taste
2 tbsp Gruyere cheese, grated

DIRECTIONS

Melt the ghee in a saucepan over medium heat and sauté the onion-garlic puree for 3 minutes until softened. Mix in the broccoli and celery, and cook for 4 minutes until slightly tender.

Pour in the broth, bring to a boil, then reduce the heat to medium-low and simmer covered for about 5 minutes. Drop in the spinach to wilt, adjust the seasonings, and cook for 4 minutes. Ladle soup into serving bowls. Serve with a sprinkle of grated Gruyere cheese.

Beef Reuben Soup

Ready in about: 20 minutes | **Serves**: 6 | **Per serving**: Kcal 450, Fat: 37g, Net Carbs: 8g, Protein: 23g

INGREDIENTS

1 onion, diced
6 cups beef stock
1 tsp caraway seeds
2 celery stalks, diced

2 garlic cloves, minced
2 cups heavy cream
1 cup sauerkraut, shredded
1 lb corned beef, chopped

3 tbsp butter
1 ½ cup swiss cheese, shredded
Salt and black pepper to taste

DIRECTIONS

Melt the butter in a large pot. Add onion, garlic, and celery and fry for 3 minutes until tender. Pour the beef stock over and stir in sauerkraut, salt, caraway seeds, and add a pinch of black pepper.

Bring to a boil. Reduce the heat to low, and add the corned beef. Cook for about 15 minutes, adjust the seasoning. Stir in heavy cream and cheese and cook for 1 minute.

Slow Cooker Beer Soup with Cheddar & Sausage

Ready in about: 8 hr | **Serves**: 6 | **Per serving**: Kcal 244, Fat: 17g, Net Carbs: 4g, Protein: 5g

INGREDIENTS

1 cup heavy cream
10 oz sausages, sliced
1 celery stalk, chopped
1 carrot, chopped

2 garlic cloves, minced
4 oz cream cheese, softened
1 tsp red pepper flakes
6 oz low carb beer

2 cups beef stock
1 onion, chopped
1 cup cheddar cheese, grated
Salt and black pepper to taste

DIRECTIONS

Turn on the slow cooker. Add in beef stock, beer, sausages, carrot, onion, garlic, celery, salt, red pepper flakes, and pepper and stir well. Pour in enough water to cover all the ingredients by roughly 2 inches.

Close the lid and cook for 6 hours on Low. Open the lid and stir in the heavy cream, cheddar, and cream cheese and cook for 2 more hours. Ladle the soup into bowls and serve. Yummy!

Coconut Green Bean & Shrimp Curry Soup

Ready in about: 20 minutes | **Serves**: 4 | **Per serving**: Kcal 375, Fat 35.4g, Net Carbs 2g, Protein 9g

INGREDIENTS

1 lb jumbo shrimp, peeled and deveined
2 tbsp ghee
2 tsp ginger-garlic puree

2 tbsp red curry paste
6 oz coconut milk

Salt and chili pepper to taste
1 lb green beans, trimmed, chopped

DIRECTIONS

Melt the ghee in a medium saucepan over medium heat. Add the shrimp, season with salt and black pepper, and cook until opaque, about 2-3 minutes. Remove the shrimp to a plate. Add the ginger-garlic puree and red curry paste to the ghee and sauté for 2 more minutes until fragrant.

Stir in the coconut milk. Add in the shrimp, salt, chili pepper, and green beans. Cook for 4 minutes. Reduce the heat to a simmer and cook for an additional 5-7 minutes, occasionally stirring. Adjust the taste with salt and fetch soup into serving bowls. Serve with cauli rice.

Broccoli Cheese Soup

Ready in about: 20 minutes | **Serves**: 4 | **Per serving**: Kcal 561, Fat: 52.3g, Net Carbs: 7g, Protein: 23.8g

INGREDIENTS

¾ cup heavy cream
1 onion, diced
1 garlic clove, minced

4 cups chopped broccoli
4 cups veggie broth
2 tbsp butter

1 ½ cups cheddar cheese, grated
Salt and black pepper to taste
2 tbsp fresh mint, chopped

DIRECTIONS

Melt the butter in a large pot over medium heat. Sauté onion and garlic for 3 minutes or until tender, stirring occasionally. Season with salt and black pepper. Add the broth and broccoli and bring to a boil.

Reduce the heat and simmer for 10 minutes. Puree the soup with a hand blender until smooth. Add in 1 cup of the cheddar cheese and cook about 1 minute. Taste and adjust the seasoning. Stir in the heavy cream. Serve in bowls topped with the remaining cheddar cheese and sprinkled with fresh mint.

Salsa Verde Chicken Soup

Ready in about: 15 minutes | **Serves**: 4 | **Per serving**: Kcal 346, Fat: 23g, Net Carbs: 3g, Protein: 25g

INGREDIENTS

½ cup salsa verde
2 cups cooked and shredded chicken
2 cups chicken broth

1 cup cheddar cheese, shredded
4 oz cream cheese, softened
½ tsp chili powder

½ tsp cumin
2 tsp fresh cilantro, chopped
Salt and black pepper to taste

DIRECTIONS

Combine the cream cheese, salsa verde, and broth in a food processor; pulse until smooth. Transfer the mixture to a pot and place over medium heat. Cook until hot, but do not bring to a boil. Add chicken, chili powder, and cumin and cook for about 3-5 minutes or until it is heated through.

Stir in cheddar cheese and season with salt and pepper. If it is very thick, add a few tablespoons of water and boil for 1-3 more minutes. Serve hot in bowls sprinkled with fresh cilantro.

Creamy Cauliflower Soup with Chorizo Sausage

Ready in about: 40 minutes | **Serves**: 4 | **Per serving**: Kcal 251, Fat: 19.1g, Net Carbs: 5.7g, Protein: 10g

INGREDIENTS

1 cauliflower head, chopped
1 turnip, chopped
3 tbsp butter

1 chorizo sausage, sliced
2 cups chicken broth
1 small onion, chopped

2 cups water
Salt and black pepper to taste

DIRECTIONS

Melt 2 tbsp of the butter in a large pot over medium heat. Stir in the onion and cook until soft, 3-4 minutes. Add cauliflower and turnip and cook for another 5 minutes. Pour the broth and water over. Bring to a boil. Simmer covered for about 20 minutes until the vegetables are tender. Remove from heat.

Melt the remaining butter in a skillet. Cook the chorizo for 5 minutes until crispy. Puree the soup with a hand blender until smooth. Adjust the seasonings. Serve the soup topped with the chorizo sausage.

Pumpkin & Meat Peanut Stew

Ready in about: 45 minutes | **Serves**: 6 | **Per serving**: Kcal 451, Fat: 33g, Net Carbs: 4g, Protein: 27.5g

INGREDIENTS

1 cup pumpkin puree
2 lb chopped pork stew meat
1 tbsp peanut butter
4 tbsp peanuts, chopped
1 garlic clove, minced

1 onion, chopped
½ cup white wine
1 tbsp olive oil
1 tsp lemon juice
¼ cup granulated sweetener

¼ tsp cardamom powder
¼ tsp allspice
2 cups water
2 cups chicken stock

DIRECTIONS

Heat the olive oil in a large pot and sauté onion and garlic for 3 minutes until translucent. Add the pork and brown for about 5-6 minutes, stirring occasionally. Pour in the wine and cook for 1 minute.

Add in the remaining ingredients, except for the lemon juice and peanuts. Bring the mixture to a boil and cook for 5 minutes. Reduce the heat to low, cover the pot, and let cook for about 30 minutes. Adjust seasonings and stir in the lemon juice before serving. Ladle into bowls and serve topped with peanuts.

Brazilian Moqueca (Shrimp Stew)

Ready in about: 25 minutes | **Serves**: 6 | **Per serving**: Kcal 324, Fat: 21g, Net Carbs: 5g, Protein: 23.1g

INGREDIENTS

1 cup coconut milk
2 tbsp lime juice
¼ cup diced roasted peppers
1 ½ lb shrimp, peeled and deveined

¼ cup olive oil
1 garlic clove, minced
14 oz diced tomatoes
2 tbsp sriracha sauce

1 onion, chopped
¼ cup chopped cilantro
2 tbsp fresh dill, chopped to garnish
Salt and black pepper to taste

DIRECTIONS

Heat the olive oil in a pot over medium heat. Add onion and garlic and cook for 3 minutes until translucent. Stir in tomatoes, shrimp, and cilantro. Cook until the shrimp becomes opaque, about 3-4 minutes.

Pour in sriracha sauce and coconut milk, and cook for 2 minutes. Do not bring to a boil. Stir in the lime juice and season with salt and pepper. Spoon the stew in bowls, garnish with fresh dill, and serve.

Mediterranean Salad

Ready in about: 10 minutes | **Serves**: 4 | **Per serving**: Kcal 290, Fat: 25g, Net Carbs: 4.3g, Protein: 9g

INGREDIENTS

3 tomatoes, sliced
1 large avocado, sliced

8 kalamata olives
¼ lb buffalo mozzarella, sliced

2 tbsp pesto sauce
1 tbsp olive oil

DIRECTIONS

Arrange the tomato slices on a serving platter and place the avocado slices in the middle. Arrange the olives around the avocado slices and drop pieces of the mozzarella cheese on the platter. Drizzle the pesto sauce and olive oil all over and serve.

Tuna Salad with Lettuce & Olives

Ready in about: 5 minutes | **Serves**: 2 | **Per serving**: Kcal 248, Fat: 20g, Net Carbs: 2g, Protein: 18.5g

INGREDIENTS

1 cup canned tuna, drained
1 tsp onion flakes

3 tbsp mayonnaise
1 cup romaine lettuce, shredded

1 tbsp lime juice
6 black olives, pitted and sliced

DIRECTIONS

Combine the tuna, mayonnaise, and lime juice in a small bowl. Mix to combine. In a salad platter, arrange the shredded lettuce and onion flakes. Spread the tuna mixture over. Top with black olives and serve.

Cobb Egg Salad in Lettuce Cups

Ready in about: 25 minutes | **Serves**: 4 | **Per serving**: Kcal 325, Fat 24.5g, Net Carbs 4g, Protein 21g

INGREDIENTS

1 head green lettuce, firm leaves removed for cups
2 chicken breasts, cut into pieces
1 tbsp olive oil

Salt and black pepper to taste
6 large eggs

2 tomatoes, seeded, chopped
6 tbsp Greek yogurt

DIRECTIONS

Preheat oven to 400°F. Put the chicken in a bowl, drizzle with olive oil, and sprinkle with salt and black pepper. Toss to coat. Put the chicken on a baking sheet and spread out evenly. Slide the baking sheet in the oven and bake the chicken until cooked through and golden brown for 8 minutes, stirring once.

Boil the eggs in salted water for 10 minutes. Let them cool, peel, and chop into pieces. Transfer to a salad bowl. Remove the chicken from the oven and add to the salad bowl. Include the tomatoes and Greek yogurt and mix them. Layer 2 lettuce leaves each as cups and fill with 2 tbsp of egg salad each. Serve.

Blue Cheese Chicken Salad

Ready in about: 15 minutes | Serves: 4 | Per serving: Kcal 280, Fat 23g, Net Carbs 4g, Protein 14g

INGREDIENTS

1 chicken breast, flattened
Salt and black pepper to taste

4 tbsp olive oil
1 lb spinach and spring mix

1 tbsp red wine vinegar
1 cup blue cheese, crumbled

DIRECTIONS

Season the chicken with salt and black pepper. Heat half of the olive oil in a pan over medium heat and fry the chicken for 4 minutes on both sides until golden brown. Remove and let cool before slicing.

In a salad bowl, combine the spinach and spring mix with the remaining olive oil, red wine vinegar, and salt and mix well. Top the salad with the chicken slices and sprinkle with blue cheese. Serve.

Arugula Prawn Salad with Mayo Dressing

Ready in about: 15 minutes | Serves: 4 | Per serving: Kcal 215, Fat 20.3g, Net Carbs 2g, Protein 8g

INGREDIENTS

4 cups baby arugula
½ cup mayonnaise
3 tbsp olive oil

1 lb prawns, peeled and deveined
1 tsp Dijon mustard
Salt to taste

½ tsp chili pepper
2 tbsp lemon juice
½ tsp garlic powder

DIRECTIONS

Mix the mayonnaise, lemon juice, garlic, powder, and mustard in a small bowl until smooth and creamy. Set aside until ready to use. Heat 2 tbsp of olive oil in a skillet over medium heat. Add the prawns, season with salt and chili pepper, and fry for 3 minutes on each side until prawns are pink. Set aside to a plate.

Place the arugula in a serving bowl and pour the mayo dressing over the salad. Toss with 2 spoons until mixed. Divide the salad between 4 plates and top with prawns. Serve immediately.

Lobster Salad with Salsa Rosa

Ready in about: 10 minutes | Serves: 4 | Per serving: Kcal 256, Fat: 15g, Net Carbs: 4.3g, Protein: 17.9g

INGREDIENTS

2 hard-boiled eggs, sliced
1 cucumber, peeled and chopped
½ cup black olives
2 cups cooked lobster meat, diced

1 head Iceberg lettuce, shredded
½ cup mayonnaise
¼ tsp celery seeds
Salt to taste

2 tbsp lemon juice
½ tsp sugar-free ketchup
¼ tsp dark rum

DIRECTIONS

Combine the lettuce, cucumber, and lobster meat in a large bowl. Whisk together the mayonnaise, celery seeds, ketchup, rum, salt, and lemon juice in another bowl. Pour the dressing over the salad and gently toss to combine. Top with olives and sliced eggs and serve.

Italian-Style Green Salad

Ready in about: 15 minutes | Serves: 4 | Per serving: Kcal 205, Fat 20g, Net Carbs 2g, Protein 4g

INGREDIENTS

2 (8 oz) pack mixed salad greens
8 pancetta strips

1 cup gorgonzola cheese, crumbled
1 tbsp white wine vinegar

3 tbsp extra virgin olive oil
Salt and black pepper to taste

DIRECTIONS

Fry the pancetta strips in a skillet over medium heat for 6 minutes, until browned and crispy. Remove to paper-towel lined plate to drain. Chop it when it is cooled. Pour the salad greens in a serving bowl.

In a small bowl, whisk the white wine vinegar, olive oil, salt, and pepper. Drizzle the dressing over the salad and toss to coat. Top with gorgonzola cheese and pancetta. Divide salad into plates and serve.

Green Mackerel Salad

Ready in about: 25 minutes | **Serves**: 4 | **Per serving**: Kcal 356, Fat: 31.9g, Net Carbs: 0.8g, Protein: 1.3g

INGREDIENTS

4 oz smoked mackerel, flaked
2 eggs
1 tbsp coconut oil

1 cup green beans, chopped
1 avocado, sliced
4 cups mixed salad greens

2 tbsp olive oil
1 tbsp lemon juice
Salt and black pepper to taste

DIRECTIONS

In a bowl, whisk together the lemon juice, olive oil, salt, and pepper. Set aside. Cook the green beans in boiling salted water over medium heat for about 3 minutes. Remove with a slotted spoon and let to cool.

Add the eggs to the pot and cook for 8-10 minutes. Transfer the eggs to an ice water bath, peel the shells, and slice them. Place the mixed salad green in a serving bowl and add in the green beans and smoked mackerel. Pour the dressing over and toss to coat. Top with sliced eggs and avocado and serve.

Caesar Salad with Smoked Salmon & Poached Eggs

Ready in about: 15 minutes | **Serves**: 4 | **Per serving**: Kcal 260, Fat 21g, Net Carbs 5g, Protein 8g

INGREDIENTS

3 cups water
8 eggs

2 cups torn romaine lettuce
½ cup smoked salmon, chopped

6 slices bacon
2 tbsp low carb Caesar dressing

DIRECTIONS

Boil the water in a pot over medium heat for 5 minutes and bring to simmer. Crack each egg into a small bowl and gently slide into the water. Poach for 2 to 3 minutes, remove with a perforated spoon, transfer to a paper towel to dry, and plate. Poach the remaining 7 eggs.

Put the bacon in a skillet and fry over medium heat until browned and crispy, about 6 minutes, turning once. Remove, allow cooling, and chop into small pieces. Toss the lettuce, smoked salmon, bacon, and Caesar dressing in a salad bowl. Top with two eggs each and serve immediately or chilled.

Bacon & Spinach Salad

Ready in about: 20 minutes | **Serves**: 4 | **Per serving**: Kcal 350, Fat: 33g, Net Carbs: 3.4g, Protein: 7g

INGREDIENTS

1 avocado, chopped
1 avocado, sliced
1 spring onion, sliced
4 bacon slices, chopped

2 cups spinach
2 small lettuce heads, chopped
2 eggs
3 tbsp olive oil

1 tsp Dijon mustard
1 tbsp apple cider vinegar
Salt to taste

DIRECTIONS

Place a skillet over medium heat and cook the bacon for 5 minutes until crispy. Remove to paper-towel lined plate to drain. Boil the eggs in boiling salted water for 10 minutes. Let them cool, peel, and chop.

Combine the spinach, lettuce, eggs, chopped avocado, and spring onion in a large bowl. Whisk together the olive oil, mustard, apple cider vinegar, and salt in another bowl. Pour the dressing over the salad and toss to combine. Top with the sliced avocado and bacon and serve.

Traditional Greek Salad

Ready in about: 10 minutes | **Serves**: 4 | **Per serving**: Kcal 323, Fat: 28g, Net Carbs: 8g, Protein: 9.3g

INGREDIENTS

5 tomatoes, chopped
1 large cucumber, chopped
1 green bell pepper, chopped

1 small red onion, chopped
10 Kalamata olives, chopped
4 tbsp capers

1 cup feta cheese, cubed
2 tbsp olive oil
Salt to taste

DIRECTIONS

Place tomatoes, bell pepper, cucumber, onion, feta cheese, salt, capers, and olive oil olives in a bowl. Mix to combine well. Divide the salad between plates, top with the Kalamata olives, and serve.

Brussels Sprouts Salad with Pecorino Cheese

Ready in about: 35 minutes | **Serves**: 6 | **Per serving**: Kcal 210, Fat 18g, Net Carbs 6g, Protein 4g

INGREDIENTS

2 lb Brussels sprouts, halved	Salt and black pepper to taste	¼ head red cabbage, shredded
3 tbsp olive oil	2 tbsp balsamic vinegar	1 cup Pecorino cheese, shaved

DIRECTIONS

Preheat oven to 400°F. Toss the brussels sprouts with olive oil, salt, black pepper, and balsamic vinegar in a bowl. Spread on a baking sheet in an even layer. Bake until tender on the inside and crispy on the outside, about 20-25 minutes. Transfer to a salad bowl and add the red cabbage. Mix until well combined. Sprinkle with the cheese, share the salad onto serving plates, and serve.

Strawberry Salad with Cheese & Almonds

Ready in about: 20 minutes | **Serves**: 2 | **Per serving**: Kcal 445, Fat: 34.2g, Net Carbs: 5.3g, Protein: 33g

INGREDIENTS

4 cups kale, chopped	½ cup almonds, flaked	4 tbsp raspberry vinaigrette
4 strawberries, sliced	1 ½ cups hard goat cheese, grated	Salt and black pepper to taste

DIRECTIONS

Preheat oven to 400°F. Arrange the grated goat cheese in two circles on two pieces of parchment paper. Place in the oven and bake for 10 minutes. Find two same bowls, place them upside down, and carefully put the parchment paper on top to give the cheese a bowl-like shape. Let cool that way for 15 minutes.

Divide the kale among the bowls, sprinkle with salt and pepper and drizzle with vinaigrette. Toss to coat. Top with almonds and strawberries. Serve immediately.

Mozzarella & Tomato Salad with Anchovies & Olives

Ready in about: 10 minutes | **Serves**: 2 | **Per serving**: Kcal 430, Fat: 26.8g, Net Carbs: 2.4g, Protein:38.8g

INGREDIENTS

1 large tomato, sliced	2 tsp olive oil	4 black olives, pitted and sliced
4 basil leaves	2 canned anchovies, chopped	Salt to taste
8 mozzarella cheese slices	1 tsp balsamic vinegar	

DIRECTIONS

Arrange the tomato slices on a serving plate. Place the mozzarella slices over and top with the basil. Add the anchovies and olives on top. Drizzle with olive oil and vinegar. Sprinkle with salt and serve.

Sriracha Egg Salad with Mustard Dressing

Ready in about: 15 minutes | **Serves**: 4 | **Per serving**: Kcal 174; Fat 13g, Net Carbs 7.7g, Protein 7.4g

INGREDIENTS

5 eggs	¼ tsp mustard	½ tsp fresh lemon juice
¾ cup mayonnaise	½ cup scallions, chopped	Salt and black pepper to taste
1 tsp sriracha sauce	½ stalk celery, minced	1 head romaine lettuce, torn

DIRECTIONS

Boil the eggs in salted water for 10 minutes. Allow them to cool, peel, and chop. Place them in a salad bowl. Stir in the remaining ingredients until everything is well combined. Refrigerate before serving.

Spring Salad with Cheese Balls

Ready in about: 20 minutes | **Serves**: 6 | **Per serving**: Kcal: 234; Fat 16.7g, Net Carbs 7.9g, Protein 12.4g

INGREDIENTS

Cheese balls

3 eggs
1 cup feta cheese, crumbled

½ cup Pecorino cheese, shredded
1 cup almond flour

1 tbsp flax meal
Salt and black pepper to taste

Salad

1 head Iceberg lettuce, leaves separated
½ cup cucumber, thinly sliced
2 tomatoes, seeded and chopped
½ cup red onion, thinly sliced

½ cup radishes, thinly sliced
⅓ cup mayonnaise
1 tsp mustard

1 tsp paprika
1 tsp oregano
Salt to taste

DIRECTIONS

Preheat oven to 390°F. In a mixing dish, mix all ingredients for the cheese balls. Form balls out of the mixture. Set the balls on a lined baking sheet. Bake for 10 minutes until crisp.

Arrange lettuce leaves on a large salad platter. Add in radishes, tomatoes, cucumbers, and red onion. In a small mixing bowl, mix the mayonnaise, paprika, salt, oregano, and mustard. Sprinkle the mixture over the vegetables. Add cheese balls on top and serve.

Shrimp & Avocado Cauliflower Salad

Ready in about: 30 minutes | **Serves**: 6 | **Per serving**: Kcal 214, Fat: 17g, Net Carbs: 5g, Protein: 15g

INGREDIENTS

1 cauliflower head, florets only
1 lb medium shrimp, peeled
¼ cup + 1 tbsp olive oil

1 avocado, chopped
2 tbsp fresh dill, chopped
¼ cup lemon juice

2 tbsp lemon zest
Salt and black pepper to taste

DIRECTIONS

Heat 1 tbsp olive oil in a skillet and cook shrimp for 8 minutes. Microwave cauliflower for 5 minutes. Place shrimp, cauliflower, and avocado in a bowl. Whisk the remaining olive oil, lemon zest, juice, dill, and salt, and pepper in another bowl. Pour the dressing over, toss to combine, and serve immediately.

Broccoli Slaw Salad with Mustard Vinaigrette

Ready in about: 10 minutes | **Serves**: 6 | **Per serving**: Kcal 110, Fat: 10g, Net Carbs: 2g, Protein: 3g

INGREDIENTS

½ tsp granulated swerve sugar
1 tbsp Dijon mustard
2 tbsp olive oil

4 cups broccoli slaw
⅓ cup mayonnaise
1 tsp celery seeds

2 tbsp slivered almonds
1 ½ tbsp apple cider vinegar
Salt to taste

DIRECTIONS

In a bowl, place the mayonnaise, Dijon mustard, swerve sugar, olive oil, celery seeds, vinegar, and salt and whisk until well combined. Place broccoli slaw in a large salad bowl. Pour the vinaigrette over. Toss to coat. Sprinkle with the slivered almonds and serve immediately.

Pork Burger Salad with Yellow Cheddar

Ready in about: 25 minutes | **Serves**: 4 | **Per serving**: Kcal 310, Fat 23g, Net Carbs 2g, Protein 22g

INGREDIENTS

½ lb ground pork
Salt and black pepper to taste
2 tbsp olive oil

2 hearts romaine lettuce, torn
2 firm tomatoes, sliced
¼ red onion, sliced

3 oz yellow cheddar cheese, grated
2 tbsp butter

DIRECTIONS

Season the pork with salt and black pepper, mix, and make medium-sized patties out of them. Heat the butter in a skillet over medium heat and fry the patties on both sides for 10 minutes until browned and cook within. Transfer to a wire rack to drain oil. When cooled, cut into quarters.

Mix the lettuce, tomatoes, and red onion in a salad bowl, season with olive oil and salt. Toss and add the pork on top. Top with the cheese and serve.

Warm Baby Artichoke Salad

Ready in about: 30 minutes | **Serves**: 4 | **Per serving**: Kcal 170, Fat: 13g, Net Carbs: 5g, Protein: 1g

INGREDIENTS

6 baby artichokes	¼ cup pitted olives, sliced	1 tbsp chopped dill
6 cups water	¼ cup olive oil	Salt and black pepper to taste
1 tbsp lemon juice	¼ tsp lemon zest	1 tbsp capers
¼ cup cherry peppers, halved	2 tsp balsamic vinegar, sugar-free	¼ tsp caper brine

DIRECTIONS

Combine the water and salt in a pot over medium heat. Trim and halve the artichokes. Add them to the pot and bring to a boil. Lower the heat and let simmer for 20 minutes until tender.

Combine the rest of the ingredients, except for the olives in a bowl. Drain and place the artichokes on a serving plate. Pour the prepared mixture over; toss to combine well. Serve topped with the olives.

Spinach & Turnip Salad with Bacon

Ready in about: 40 minutes | **Serves**: 4 | **Per serving**: Kcal 193, Fat 18.3g, Net Carbs 3.1g, Protein 9.5g

INGREDIENTS

2 turnips, cut into wedges	3 turkey bacon slices	1 tbsp red wine vinegar
1 tsp olive oil	4 tbsp sour cream	Salt and black pepper to taste
1 cup baby spinach, chopped	2 tsp mustard seeds	1 tbsp chopped chives
3 radishes, sliced	1 tsp Dijon mustard	

DIRECTIONS

Preheat oven to 400°F. Line a baking sheet with parchment paper, toss the turnips with salt and black pepper, drizzle with the olive oil, and bake for 25 minutes, turning halfway. Let cool.

Spread the baby spinach in the bottom of a salad bowl and top with the radishes. Remove the turnips to the salad bowl. Fry the bacon in a skillet over medium heat until crispy, about 5 minutes.

Mix sour cream, mustard seeds, mustard, vinegar, and salt with the bacon. Add a little water to deglaze the bottom of the skillet. Pour the bacon mixture over the vegetables, scatter the chives over it. Serve.

Chicken Salad with Grapefruit & Cashews

Ready in about: 30 minutes + marinating time| **Serves**: 4 | **Per serving**: Kcal 178, Fat: 13.5g, Net Carbs: 3.2g, Protein: 9.1g

INGREDIENTS

1 grapefruit, peeled and segmented	10 oz baby spinach	1 lemon, juiced
1 chicken breast	2 tbsp cashews	3 tbsp olive oil
4 green onions, sliced	1 red chili pepper, thinly sliced	Salt and black pepper to taste

DIRECTIONS

Toast the cashews in a dry pan over high heat for 2 minutes, shaking often. Set aside to cool, then chop. Preheat the grill to medium heat. Season the chicken with salt and pepper and brush with some olive oil. Grill for 4 minutes per side. Remove to a plate and let it sit for a few minutes before slicing.

Place the baby spinach and green onions on a serving platter. Season with salt, remaining olive oil, and lemon juice. Toss to coat. Top with chicken, chili pepper, and chicken. Sprinkle with cashews and serve.

Grilled Steak Salad with Pickled Peppers

Ready in about: 15 minutes | **Serves**: 4 | **Per serving**: Kcal 315, Fat 26g, Net Carbs 2g, Protein 18g

INGREDIENTS

½ lb skirt steak, sliced
Salt and black pepper to taste
3 tsp olive oil

1 head Romaine lettuce, torn
3 chopped pickled peppers
2 tbsp red wine vinegar

½ cup queso fresco, crumbled
1 tbsp green olives, pitted, sliced

DIRECTIONS

Brush the steak slices with some olive oil and season with salt and black pepper on both sides. Heat a grill pan over high heat and cook the steaks on each side for about 5-6 minutes. Remove to a bow.

Mix the lettuce, pickled peppers, remaining olive oil, and vinegar in a salad bowl. Add the beef and sprinkle with queso fresco and green olives. Serve.

Cobb Salad with Blue Cheese Dressing

Ready in about: 30 minutes | **Serves**: 6 | **Per serving**: Kcal 122, Fat 14g, Net Carbs 2g, Protein 23g

INGREDIENTS

Dressing

½ cup buttermilk
1 cup mayonnaise

2 tbsp Worcestershire sauce
½ cup sour cream

1 cup blue cheese, crumbled
2 tbsp chives, chopped

Salad

6 eggs
2 chicken breasts
5 strips bacon
1 iceberg lettuce, cut into chunks

Salt and black pepper to taste
1 romaine lettuce, chopped
1 bibb lettuce, cored, leaves removed
2 avocado, pitted and diced

2 large tomatoes, chopped
½ cup blue cheese, crumbled
2 scallions, chopped

DIRECTIONS

In a bowl, whisk the buttermilk, mayonnaise, Worcestershire sauce, and sour cream. Stir in the blue cheese and chives. Place in the refrigerator to chill until ready to use. Bring the eggs to boil in salted water over medium heat for 10 minutes. Transfer to an ice bath to cool. Peel and chop. Set aside.

Preheat a grill pan over high heat. Season the chicken with salt and pepper. Grill for 3 minutes on each side. Remove to a plate to cool for 3 minutes and cut into bite-size chunks. Fry the bacon in the same pan until crispy, about 6 minutes. Remove, let cool for 2 minutes, and chop.

Arrange the lettuce leaves in a salad bowl, and in single piles, add the avocado, tomatoes, eggs, bacon, and chicken. Sprinkle the blue cheese over the salad as well as the scallions and black pepper. Drizzle the blue cheese dressing on the salad and serve with low carb bread.

Squid Salad with Cucumber & Chili Dressing

Ready in about: 30 minutes | **Serves**: 4 | **Per serving**: Kcal 318, Fat 22.5g, Net Carbs 2.1g, Protein 24.6g

INGREDIENTS

4 squid tubes, cut into strips
½ cup mint leaves
2 cucumbers, halved, cut into strips
½ cup cilantro, stems reserved

½ red onion, finely sliced
Salt and black pepper to taste
1 tsp fish sauce
1 red chili, roughly chopped

1 clove garlic
2 limes, juiced
1 tbsp fresh parsley, chopped
1 tsp olive oil

DIRECTIONS

In a salad bowl, mix mint leaves, cucumber strips, coriander leaves, and red onion. Season with salt, black pepper, and some olive oil; set aside. In the mortar, pound the cilantro stems and red chili to form a paste using the pestle. Add in the fish sauce and lime juice and mix with the pestle.

Heat a skillet over medium heat. Sear the squid on both sides until lightly brown, about 5 minutes. Pour the squid on the salad and drizzle with the chili dressing. Toss to coat, garnish with parsley, and serve.

SIDE DISHES & SNACKS

Cheesy Chicken Fritters with Dill Dip

Ready in about: 40 minutes + cooling time | **Serves**: 4 | **Per serving**: Kcal 151, Fat 7g, Net Carbs 0.8g, Protein 12g

INGREDIENTS

1 lb chicken breasts, thinly sliced
1 ¼ cups mayonnaise
¼ cup coconut flour
2 eggs

Salt and black pepper to taste
1 cup mozzarella cheese, grated
2 tbsp dill, chopped
2 tbsp olive oil

1 cup sour cream
½ tsp garlic powder
1 tbsp parsley, chopped
1 onion, finely chopped

DIRECTIONS

In a bowl, mix 1 cup of the mayonnaise, dill, sour cream, garlic powder, onion, and salt. Keep in the fridge. Mix the remaining mayonnaise, coconut flour, eggs, salt, pepper, and mozzarella cheese in a bowl. Add in the chicken and toss to coat. Cover the bowl with plastic wrap and refrigerate it for 2 hours.

Place a skillet over medium fire and heat the olive oil. Fetch 2 tablespoons of chicken mixture into the skillet, use the back of a spatula to flatten the top. Cook for 4 minutes, flip, and fry for 4 more.

Remove onto a wire rack and repeat the cooking process until the chicken ingredients are finished, adding more oil as needed. Garnish the fritters with parsley and serve with the dill dip.

Cheesy Mashed Cauliflower with Bacon

Ready in about: 40 minutes | **Serves**: 6 | **Per serving**: Kcal 312, Fat 25g, Net Carbs 6g, Protein 14g

INGREDIENTS

6 slices bacon
2 heads cauliflower, chopped
2 cups water

2 tbsp butter, melted
½ cup buttermilk
Salt and black pepper to taste

¼ cup yellow cheddar cheese, grated
2 tbsp chopped chives

DIRECTIONS

Preheat oven to 350°F. Fry bacon in a heated skillet over medium heat for 5 minutes until crispy. Remove to a paper towel-lined plate, allow to cool, and crumble. Set aside and keep bacon fat.

Boil the cauliflower in water in a pot over high heat for 7 minutes until tender. Drain and put in a bowl. Include butter, buttermilk, salt, and pepper and puree using a hand blender until smooth and creamy.

Lightly grease a casserole dish with the bacon fat and spread the mash on it. Sprinkle with cheddar cheese and place under the broiler for 4 minutes on high until the cheese melts. Remove and top with bacon and chopped chives. Serve with pan-seared scallops.

Layered Zucchini & Bell Pepper Bake

Ready in about: 65 minutes | **Serves**: 6 | **Per serving**: Kcal 264, Fat 21g, Net Carbs 4g, Protein 14g

INGREDIENTS

2 lb zucchinis, sliced
2 red bell peppers, seeded and sliced
Salt and black pepper to taste

1 ½ cups feta cheese, crumbled
2 tbsp butter, melted
¼ tsp xanthan gum

½ cup heavy whipping cream
2 tbsp fresh dill, chopped

DIRECTIONS

Preheat oven to 370°F. Place the sliced zucchinis in a colander over the sink, sprinkle with salt and let sit for 20 minutes. Transfer to paper towels to drain the excess liquid.

Grease a baking dish with cooking spray and make a layer of zucchini and bell peppers overlapping. Season with pepper, and sprinkle with feta cheese. Repeat the layering process a second time.

Combine the butter, xanthan gum, salt, and whipping cream in a bowl. Stir to mix completely and pour over the vegetables. Bake for 30-40 minutes or until golden brown on top. Serve sprinkled with dill

Roasted Cauliflower with Serrano Ham & Pine Nuts

Ready in about: 30 minutes | **Serves:** 6 | **Per serving:** Kcal 141, Fat 10g, Net Carbs 2.5g, Protein 10g

INGREDIENTS

2 heads cauliflower, cut into slices
2 tbsp olive oil
Salt to taste

½ tsp chili pepper
1 tsp garlic powder
10 slices Serrano ham, chopped

¼ cup pine nuts
1 tbsp capers
1 tbsp fresh parsley, chopped

DIRECTIONS

Preheat oven to 450°F. Line a baking sheet with foil. Brush the cauli steaks with olive oil and season with chili pepper, garlic, and salt. Spread the cauli slices on the baking sheet.

Roast in the oven for 10 minutes until tender and lightly browned. Remove the sheet and sprinkle the ham and pine nuts all over the cauli. Bake for another 10 minutes until the ham is crispy and a nutty aroma is perceived. Take out, sprinkle with capers and parsley and serve.

Balsamic Brussels Sprouts with Prosciutto

Ready in about: 40 minutes | **Serves:** 4 | **Per serving:** Kcal 166, Fat 14g, Net Carbs 0g, Protein 8g

INGREDIENTS

3 tbsp balsamic vinegar
1 tbsp erythritol

2 tbsp olive oil
Salt and black pepper to taste

1 lb Brussels sprouts, halved
5 slices prosciutto, chopped

DIRECTIONS

Preheat oven to 400°F. Line a baking sheet with parchment paper. Mix balsamic vinegar, erythritol, olive oil, salt, and black pepper and combine with the brussels sprouts in a bowl. Spread the mixture on the baking sheet and roast for 30 minutes until tender on the inside and crispy on the outside. Toss with prosciutto, share among 4 plates, and serve with chicken breasts.

Parmesan Crackers with Guacamole

Ready in about: 10 minutes | **Serves:** 4 | **Per serving:** Kcal 229, Fat 20g, Net Carbs 2g, Protein 10g

INGREDIENTS

1 cup Parmesan cheese, grated
¼ tsp sweet paprika

¼ tsp garlic powder
2 soft avocados, pitted and scooped

1 tomato, chopped
Salt to taste

DIRECTIONS

Preheat oven to 350°F. Line a baking sheet with parchment paper. Mix Parmesan cheese, paprika, and garlic powder. Spoon 8 teaspoons on the baking sheet, creating spaces between each mound. Flatten mounds. Bake for 5 minutes, cool, and remove to a plate.

o make the guacamole, mash the avocado with a fork in a bowl, add in tomato, and mash until it is mostly smooth. Season with salt. Serve crackers with guacamole.

Lemony Fried Artichokes

Ready in about: 20 minutes | **Serves:** 4 | **Per serving:** Kcal 35, Fat: 2.4g, Net Carbs: 2.9g, Protein: 2g

INGREDIENTS

12 fresh baby artichokes
2 tbsp lemon juice

2 tbsp olive oil
Salt to taste

DIRECTIONS

Slice the artichokes vertically into narrow wedges. Drain on paper towels before frying. Heat olive oil in a skillet over medium heat. Fry the artichokes until browned and crispy. Drain excess oil on paper towels. Sprinkle with salt and lemon juice.

Devilled Eggs with Sriracha Mayo

Ready in about: 15 minutes | Serves: 4 | Per serving: Kcal 195, Fat 19g, Net Carbs 1g, Protein 4g

INGREDIENTS

8 large eggs
Ice water bath

3 tbsp sriracha sauce
4 tbsp mayonnaise

Salt to taste
¼ tsp smoked paprika

DIRECTIONS

Boil the eggs in salted water in a pot over high heat, then reduce the heat to simmer for 10 minutes. Transfer eggs to an ice water bath, let cool completely, and peel the shells.

Slice the eggs in half height wise and empty the yolks into a bowl. Smash with a fork and mix in sriracha sauce, mayonnaise, and half of the paprika until smooth. Spoon filling into a piping bag with a round nozzle and fill the egg whites to be slightly above the brim. Garnish with remaining paprika and serve.

Crunchy Pork Rind Zucchini Sticks

Ready in about: 20 minutes | Serves: 4 | Per serving: Kcal 180, Fat 14g, Net Carbs 2g, Protein 6g

INGREDIENTS

¼ cup pork rind crumbs
1 tsp sweet paprika
¼ cup Parmesan cheese, shredded

Salt and chili pepper to taste
3 fresh eggs
2 zucchinis, cut into strips

½ cup mayonnaise
1 garlic clove, minced
Juice and zest from ½ lemon

DIRECTIONS

Preheat oven to 425°F. Line a baking sheet with foil. Mix the pork rinds, paprika, Parmesan cheese, salt, and chili pepper in a bowl. Beat the eggs in another bowl. Coat zucchini strips in eggs, then in Parmesan mixture, and arrange on the baking sheet. Grease with cooking spray and bake for 15 minutes until crispy.

In a bowl, combine the mayonnaise, lemon juice, and garlic and gently stir until everything is well incorporated. Add in the lemon zest and stir again. Serve the zucchini strips with the garlic mayo dip.

Baked Cheese & Spinach Balls

Ready in about: 30 minutes | Serves: 4 | Per serving: Kcal 160, Fat: 15g, Net Carbs: 0.8g, Protein: 8g

INGREDIENTS

⅓ cup ricotta cheese, crumbled
¼ tsp nutmeg
¼ tsp black pepper
3 tbsp heavy cream

½ tsp garlic powder
½ tbsp onion powder
2 tbsp butter, melted
⅓ cup Parmesan cheese, shredded

2 eggs
1 cup spinach, chopped
1 cup almond flour

DIRECTIONS

Place all ingredients in a food processor. Process until smooth. Place in the freezer and allow it to stand for about 10 minutes. Remove and make balls out of the mixture. Arrange them on a lined baking sheet. Bake in the oven at 350°F for about 10-12 minutes. Serve with tomato dip.

Spicy Chicken Cucumber Bites

Ready in about: 5 minutes | Serves: 6 | Per serving: Kcal 170, Fat 14g, Net Carbs 0g, Protein 10g

INGREDIENTS

2 cucumbers, cut into 1-inch slices
2 cups leftover chicken, diced

¼ jalapeño pepper, minced
1 tbsp Dijon mustard

⅓ cup mayonnaise
Salt and black pepper to taste

DIRECTIONS

Cut mid-level holes in cucumber slices with a knife and set aside. Combine chicken, jalapeno pepper, mustard, mayonnaise, salt, and pepper and mix well. Fill cucumber holes with the mixture and serve.

Duo-Cheese Chicken Bake

Ready in about: 30 minutes | **Serves**: 4 | **Per serving**: Kcal 216, Fat 16g, Net Carbs 3g, Protein 14g

INGREDIENTS

2 tbsp olive oil	1 lb ground chicken	1 cup ranch dressing
8 oz cream cheese	1 cup buffalo sauce	3 cups mozzarella cheese, grated

DIRECTIONS

Preheat oven to 350°F. Lightly grease a baking sheet with a cooking spray. Warm the oil in a skillet over medium heat and brown the chicken for a couple of minutes per side. Take off the heat and set aside.

Spread cream cheese at the bottom of the baking sheet and top with chicken. Pour buffalo sauce over, add ranch dressing, and sprinkle with cheddar cheese. Bake for 23 minutes until cheese has melted and golden brown on top. Remove and serve with veggie sticks or low carb crackers.

Cheesy Cauliflower Bake with Mustard Sauce

Ready in about: 30 minutes | **Serves**: 6 | **Per serving**: Kcal 363, Fat 35g, Net Carbs 2g, Protein 6g

INGREDIENTS

2 heads cauliflower, cut into florets	1 tsp red pepper flakes	1 tbsp lemon juice
¼ cup butter, melted	1 cup heavy cream	2 tbsp scallions, chopped
Salt and black pepper to taste	1 tsp Dijon mustard	3 tbsp Pecorino cheese, grated

DIRECTIONS

Preheat oven to 400°F. Combine the cauli florets, butter, salt, pepper, and red pepper flakes in a bowl until mixed. Arrange cauliflower florets on a baking dish. Sprinkle with the Pecorino cheese and bake for 25 minutes until the cheese has melted and golden brown on the top.

Mix the heavy cream and Dijon mustard in a small pan over medium heat and simmer for 2-3 minutes. Turn off the heat, season with salt and pepper, and stir in the lemon juice. Transfer the cauliflower to a plate and spoon the mustard sauce over. Garnish with scallions and serve.

Crispy Chorizo with Cheese Topping

Ready in about: 30 minutes | **Serves**: 6 | **Per serving**: Kcal 172, Fat: 13g, Net Carbs: 0g, Protein: 5g

INGREDIENTS

7 oz Spanish chorizo, sliced	4 oz cream cheese, softened	¼ cup fresh parsley, chopped

DIRECTIONS

Preheat oven to 325°F. Line a baking dish with waxed paper. Bake chorizo for 15 minutes until crispy. Remove and let cool. Arrange on a serving platter. Top with cream cheese. Serve sprinkled with parsley.

Mixed Roast Vegetables

Ready in about: 40 minutes | **Serves**: 4 | **Per serving**: Kcal 65, Fat 3g, Net Carbs 8g, Protein 3g

INGREDIENTS

2 lb butternut squash, cut into chunks	1 lb Brussels sprouts	4 cloves garlic, peeled only
¼ lb pearl onions, peeled	1 sprig rosemary, chopped	3 tbsp olive oil
2 rutabagas, cut into chunks	1 sprig thyme, chopped	Salt and black pepper to taste

DIRECTIONS

Preheat oven to 450°F. Pour the butternut squash, pearl onions, rutabagas, garlic cloves, and Brussels sprouts in a bowl. Season with salt, black pepper, olive oil, and toss. Pour the mixture on a baking sheet and sprinkle with the chopped thyme and rosemary. Roast the vegetables for 15–20 minutes. Once ready, remove and spoon into a serving bowl. Serve with oven-roasted chicken thighs.

Cheesy Green Bean Crisps

Ready in about: 30 minutes | **Serves**: 6 | **Per serving**: Kcal 210, Fat 19g, Net Carbs 3g, Protein 5g

INGREDIENTS

¼ cup Pecorino cheese, grated
¼ cup pork rind crumbs

1 tsp garlic powder
Salt and black pepper to taste

2 eggs
1 lb green beans, thread removed

DIRECTIONS

Preheat oven to 425°F and line a baking sheet with foil. Mix the cheese, pork rinds, garlic powder, salt, and black pepper in a bowl. Beat the eggs in another bowl. Coat green beans in eggs, then cheese mixture, and arrange evenly on the baking sheet. Grease lightly with cooking spray and bake for 15 minutes to be crispy. Transfer to a wire rack to cool before serving. Serve with sugar-free tomato dip.

Bacon-Wrapped Jalapeño Poppers

Ready in about: 30 minutes | **Serves**: 6 | **Per serving**: Kcal 206, Fat 17g, Net Carbs 0g, Protein 14g

INGREDIENTS

12 jalapeno peppers

¼ cup shredded Colby cheese
6 oz cream cheese, softened

6 slices bacon, halved

DIRECTIONS

Cut the jalapeno peppers in half, and then remove the membrane and seeds. Combine cheeses and stuff into the pepper halves. Wrap each pepper with a bacon strip and secure with toothpicks.

Place the filled peppers on a baking sheet lined with a piece of foil. Bake at 350°F for 25 minutes until bacon has browned and crispy and cheese is golden brown on the top. Remove to a paper towel-lined plate to absorb grease, arrange on a serving plate, and serve warm.

Garlicky Cheddar Biscuits

Ready in about: 20 minutes | **Serves**: 4 | **Per serving**: Kcal 153, Fat 14.2g, Net Carbs 1.4g, Protein 5.4g

INGREDIENTS

⅓ cup almond flour
2 tsp garlic powder
Salt to taste

1 tsp baking powder
5 eggs
⅓ cup butter, melted

1 ¼ cups sharp cheddar cheese, grated
⅓ cup Greek yogurt

DIRECTIONS

Preheat oven to 350°F. Mix the almond flour, garlic powder, salt, baking powder, and cheddar cheese in a bowl. In a separate bowl, whisk the eggs, butter, and Greek yogurt and then pour it into the dry ingredients.

Stir well until a dough-like consistency has formed. Fetch half tbsp of the mixture onto a greased baking sheet with 2-inch intervals between each batter. Bake for 12 minutes golden brown. Serve chilled.

Herb Cheese Sticks

Ready in about: 15 minutes | **Serves**: 4 | **Per serving**: Kcal 188, Fat 17.3g, Net Carbs 0g, Protein 8g

INGREDIENTS

1 cup pork rinds, crushed
1 tbsp Italian herb mix

1 egg
1 lb swiss cheese, cut into sticks

DIRECTIONS

Preheat oven to 350°F. Line a baking sheet with parchment paper. Combine pork rinds and herb mix in a bowl to be evenly mixed and beat the egg in another bowl. Coat the cheese sticks in the egg.

Next, generously dredge in pork rind mixture. Arrange on the baking sheet. Bake for 4 to 5 minutes, take out after, let cool for 2 minutes, and serve with marinara sauce.

Coconut Ginger Macaroons

Ready in about: 20 minutes | **Serves**: 6 | **Per serving**: Kcal 97, Fat 3.5g, Net Carbs 0.3g, Protein 6.8g

INGREDIENTS

2 fingers ginger root, pureed
6 egg whites

1 cup finely shredded coconut
¼ cup swerve sugar

¼ tbsp chili powder
Angel hair chili to garnish

DIRECTIONS

Preheat the oven to 350°F. In a heatproof bowl, whisk ginger, egg whites, coconut, swerve sugar, and chili powder. Bring 1 cup of water to boil in a pot over medium heat and place the heatproof bowl on the pot. Do not let the bowl touch the water. Continue whisking the mixture until it is glossy, 4 minutes.

Spoon the mixture into a piping bag after and pipe out 40 to 50 little mounds on a lined baking sheet. Bake the macaroons in the middle part of the oven for 15 minutes. Once they are ready, transfer them to a wire rack, garnish them with the angel hair chili, and serve.

Cheesy Cauliflower Fritters

Ready in about: 35 minutes | **Serves**: 4 | **Per serving**: Kcal 69, Fat: 4.5g, Net Carbs: 3g, Protein: 4.5g

INGREDIENTS

1 lb grated cauliflower
½ cup Parmesan cheese, grated
1 onion, chopped

½ tsp baking powder
½ cup almond flour
2 eggs

½ tsp lemon juice
2 tbsp olive oil
⅓ tsp salt

DIRECTIONS

Place the cauliflower in a bowl and season with salt. Add in the other ingredients. Mix with your hands to combine. Place a skillet over medium heat and heat olive oil. Shape patties out of the cauliflower mixture. Fry in batches for about 3 minutes per side until golden around the edges and set. Serve.

Italian-Style Chicken Wraps

Ready in about: 20 minutes | **Serves**: 4 | **Per serving**: Kcal 174, Fat: 10g, Net Carbs: 0.7g, Protein: 17g

INGREDIENTS

¼ tsp garlic powder
8 oz provolone cheese

8 raw chicken tenders
Salt and black pepper to taste

8 prosciutto slices

DIRECTIONS

Pound the chicken until half an inch thick. Season with salt, black pepper, and garlic powder. Cut the provolone cheese into 8 strips. Place a slice of prosciutto on a flat surface. Place 1 chicken tender on top.

Top with a provolone strip. Roll the chicken and secure with previously soaked wooden skewers. Preheat grill to high. Grill the wraps for 3 minutes per side. Serve with creamy blue cheese dip.

Tabasco Deviled Eggs

Ready in about: 30 minutes | **Serves**: 6 | **Per serving**: Kcal 178, Fat: 17g, Net Carbs: 5g, Protein: 6g

INGREDIENTS

6 eggs
2 tbsp green tabasco sauce

¼ cup mayonnaise
¼ tsp mustard powder

¼ tsp smoked paprika
Salt to taste

DIRECTIONS

Boil the eggs in salted water for 10 minutes. Place the eggs in an ice bath and let cool for 10 minutes. Peel and slice in half lengthwise. Scoop out the yolks to a bowl and mash with a fork. Whisk together the tabasco sauce, mayonnaise, mashed yolks, mustard powder, and salt in a bowl. Spoon this mixture into the egg whites. Arrange them on a serving platter and scatter with smoked paprika.

Nutty Avocado Crostini

Ready in about: 15 minutes | **Serves**: 4 | **Per serving**: Kcal 195, Fat 12.2g, Net Carbs 2.8g, Protein 13.7g

INGREDIENTS

8 zero carb bread slices
4 nori sheets
1 avocado, pitted and chopped

⅓ tsp salt
1 tsp lemon juice
1 ½ tbsp coconut oil

⅓ cup walnuts, chopped
1 tbsp poppy seeds

DIRECTIONS

In a bowl, mash the avocado with a fork. Add in salt and lemon juice and stir. Place the bread slices on a baking sheet and toast under the broiler for 3-4 minutes until golden. Remove and brush them with coconut oi and spread the mashed avocado on top. Garnish with the poppy seeds and walnuts, Serve.

Parmesan Cookies

Ready in about: 25 minutes | **Serves**: 6 | **Per serving**: Kcal 115, Fat 3g, Net Carbs 0.7g, Protein 5g

INGREDIENTS

1 ⅓ cups coconut flour
1 ¼ cup grated Parmesan cheese
Salt and black pepper to taste

1 tsp garlic powder
⅓ cup butter, softened
⅓ tsp sweet paprika

⅓ cup heavy cream
⅓ tsp cumin seeds

DIRECTIONS

Preheat oven to 350°F. Mix the coconut flour, Parmesan cheese, salt, pepper, garlic powder, and paprika in a bowl. Add in the butter and mix well. Top with the heavy cream and mix again until a smooth, thick mixture has formed. Add 1 to 2 tablespoon of water at this point, if it is too thick.

Place the dough on a cutting board and cover with plastic wrap. Use a rolling pin to spread out the dough into a light rectangle. Cut cookie squares out of the dough and arrange them on a baking sheet without overlapping. Sprinkle with cumin seeds. Bake for 20 minutes. Serve chilled.

Spicy Stuffed Eggs with Herbs

Ready in about: 30 minutes | **Serves**: 4 | **Per serving**: Kcal 112, Fat 9.3g, Net Carbs 0.4g, Protein 6.7g

INGREDIENTS

12 large eggs
6 tbsp mayonnaise
Salt and chili pepper to taste

1 tsp mixed dried herbs
½ tsp Worcestershire sauce
¼ tsp Dijon mustard

½ tsp sweet paprika
2 tbsp fresh parsley, chopped

DIRECTIONS

Pour salted water into a saucepan and bring to boil on high heat. Add the eggs and cook for 10 minutes. Remove to an ice bath and let cool. Peel and slice in half lengthways and place the yolks in a bowl.

Use a fork to crush them. Add in the mayonnaise, salt, chili pepper, dried herbs, Worcestershire sauce, mustard, and paprika. Mix until a smooth paste has formed. Then, spoon the mixture into a piping bag and fill the egg white holes with it. Garnish with parsley and serve immediately.

Buttered Broccoli

Ready in about: 10 minutes | **Serves**: 6 | **Per serving**: Kcal 114, Fat: 7.8g, Net Carbs: 5.5g, Protein: 3.9g

INGREDIENTS

1 broccoli head, florets only

Salt and black pepper to taste

¼ cup butter

DIRECTIONS

Place the broccoli in a pot filled with salted water and bring to a boil. Cook for about 3 minutes until crisp-tender. Drain the broccoli and transfer to a plate. Melt the butter in a microwave. Drizzle the butter over and season with some salt and black pepper. Serve.

Parsnip & Carrot Fries with Aioli

Ready in about: 40 minutes + chilling time | **Serves:** 4 | **Per serving:** Kcal 155, Fat 7.4g, Net Carbs 7.4g, Protein 2.1g

INGREDIENTS

Aioli

4 tbsp mayonnaise

2 garlic cloves, minced

3 tbsp lemon juice

Fries

4 medium parsnips, julienned
3 large carrots, julienned

2 tbsp olive oil
2 tbsp chopped parsley

Salt and black pepper to taste

DIRECTIONS

Preheat oven to 400°F. Spread the parsnips and carrots on a baking sheet. Drizzle with olive oil, sprinkle with salt and pepper, and rub the seasoning onto the veggies. Bake for 35 minutes until golden brown.

Make the aioli by mixing the mayonnaise with garlic, salt, black pepper, and lemon juice. Keep in the fridge until ready to use. Remove the fries from the oven, garnish with parsley, and serve with aioli.

Cocoa Nuts Goji Bars

Ready in about: 5 minutes | **Serves:** 6 | **Per serving:** Kcal 170, Fat 11g, Net Carbs 6g, Protein 2g

INGREDIENTS

1 cup raw almonds
1 cup raw walnuts
¼ tsp cinnamon powder

¼ cup dried goji berries
1 ½ tsp vanilla extract
2 tbsp unsweetened chocolate chips

2 tbsp coconut oil
1 tbsp golden flax meal
1 tsp erythritol

DIRECTIONS

Combine the walnuts and almonds in the food processor and process until smooth. Add the cinnamon powder, goji berries, vanilla extract, chocolate chips, coconut oil, golden flax meal, and erythritol. Process further until the mixture begins to stick to each other, about 2 minutes.

Spread out a large piece of plastic wrap on a flat surface and place the dough on it. Wrap and use a rolling pin to spread it out into a thick rectangle. Unwrap the dough and cut it into bars. Serve.

Dill Pickles with Tuna-Mayo Topping

Ready in about: 40 minutes | **Serves:** 12 | **Per serving:** Kcal 118, Fat: 10g, Net Carbs: 1.5g, Protein: 11g

INGREDIENTS

18 oz canned and drained tuna
6 large dill pickles

¼ tsp garlic powder
⅓ cup sugar-free mayonnaise

1 tbsp onion flakes

DIRECTIONS

Combine the mayonnaise, tuna, onion flakes, and garlic powder in a bowl. Cut the pickles in half lengthwise. Top each half with tuna mixture. Place in the fridge for 30 minutes before serving.

Mozzarella & Prosciutto Wraps

Ready in about: 15 minutes | **Serves:** 6 | **Per serving:** Kcal 163, Fat: 12g, Net Carbs: 0.1g, Protein: 13g

INGREDIENTS

6 thin prosciutto slices
18 basil leaves

18 ciliegine mozzarella balls
2 tbsp extra virgin olive oil

DIRECTIONS

Cut the prosciutto slices into three strips each. Place basil leaves at the end of each strip. Top with a ciliegine mozzarella ball. Wrap the mozzarella in prosciutto. Secure with toothpicks. Arrange on a platter, drizzle with olive oil, and serve.

Asiago-Mushroom Balls

Ready in about: 20 minutes | Serves: 4 | Per serving: Kcal 370; Fat: 30g, Net Carbs: 7.7g, Protein: 16.8g

INGREDIENTS

2 tbsp butter, softened
2 tbsp olive oil
2 garlic cloves, minced
2 cups mushrooms, chopped

4 tbsp blanched almond flour
4 tbsp ground flax seeds
4 tbsp hemp seeds
4 tbsp sunflower seeds

1 tbsp cajun seasoning
1 tsp mustard
2 eggs, whisked
½ cup asiago cheese, shredded

DIRECTIONS

Set a pan over medium heat and warm the olive oil. Add in mushrooms and garlic and sauté until tender. Remove to a plate and let cool for a few minutes. Place the asiago cheese, almond flour, hemp seeds, mustard, eggs, sunflower seeds, flax seeds, mushrooms, and cajun seasoning in a bowl.

Create 4 burgers from the mixture. To the same pan, add and warm the butter and fry the burgers for 7 minutes. Flip them over with a wide spatula and cook for 6 more minutes. Serve with guacamole.

Garlic & Basil Mashed Celeriac

Ready in about: 30 minutes | Serves: 4 | Per serving: Kcal 94, Fat 0.5g, Net Carbs 6g, Protein 2.4g

INGREDIENTS

2 lb celeriac, chopped
4 cups water
2 oz cream cheese

2 tbsp butter
⅓ cup sour cream
½ tsp garlic powder

2 tsp dried basil
Salt and black pepper to taste

DIRECTIONS

Bring the celeriac and water to boil over high heat on a stovetop for 5 minutes and then reduce the heat to low to simmer for 15 minutes. Drain the celeriac through a colander after.

Then, pour the celeriac in a large bowl and add the cream cheese, butter, sour cream, garlic powder, dried basil, salt, and black pepper. Mix with a hand mixer on medium speed until well combined. Serve.

Taco Lettuce Rolls

Ready in about: 10 minutes | Serves: 6 | Per serving: Kcal 370; Fat: 30g, Net Carbs: 4.9g, Protein: 19.5g

INGREDIENTS

½ lb gouda cheese, grated
½ lb feta cheese, crumbled
1 tsp taco seasoning mix

2 tbsp olive oil
1 ½ cups guacamole
1 cup buttermilk

6 radishes, thinly sliced
12 lettuce leaves

DIRECTIONS

Mix both types of cheese with taco seasoning mix. Set a pan over medium heat and warm the olive oil. Spread the shredded cheese mixture all over the pan. Fry for 5 minutes, turning once. Arrange some of the cheese mixture on each lettuce leaf, top with buttermilk, guacamole, and radishes. Roll up them folding in the ends to secure. Serve on a large platter with tour favorite dip.

Spiced Gruyere Crisps

Ready in about: 10 minutes | Serves: 4 | Per serving: Kcal 205; Fat: 15g, Net Carbs: 2.9g, Protein: 14.5g

INGREDIENTS

2 cups Gruyere cheese, shredded
½ tsp garlic powder

¼ tsp onion powder
1 rosemary sprig, minced

½ tsp chili powder

DIRECTIONS

Preheat oven to 400°F. Mix the Gruyere cheese with the seasonings. Take 1 tablespoon of cheese mixture and form small mounds on a lined baking sheet. Bake for 6 minutes. Leave to cool. Serve.

Roasted Stuffed Piquillo Peppers

Ready in about: 20 minutes | **Serves**: 4 | **Per serving**: Kcal 132, Fat: 11g, Net Carbs: 2.5g, Protein: 6g

INGREDIENTS

8 canned roasted piquillo peppers
Filling

3 slices prosciutto, cut into strips

8 oz goat cheese, crumbled
3 tbsp heavy cream

3 tbsp fresh parsley, chopped
½ tsp garlic, minced

1 tbsp olive oil
1 tbsp fresh mint, chopped

DIRECTIONS

Mix all filling ingredients in a bowl. Place in a freezer bag, press down and squeeze. Cut off the bottom. Drain and deseed the peppers. Squeeze about 2 tbsp of the filling into each pepper. Wrap a prosciutto slice onto each pepper. Secure with toothpicks. Arrange them on a serving platter. Enjoy!

Party Pâté & Almond Truffles

Ready in about: 15 minutes + chilling time | **Serves**: 4 | **Per serving**: Kcal 274, Fat: 25g, Net Carbs: 1.5g, Protein: 11g

INGREDIENTS

4 oz bacon, finely chopped
4 oz duck pâté

¼ cup almond flour
1 tsp Dijon mustard

6 oz cream cheese

DIRECTIONS

Place a pan over medium heat. Brown the bacon for 5 minutes. Remove to a plate lined with kitchen paper to drain off the excess fat. Combine the pâté and almond flour a bowl and mix until smooth.

Whisk the cream cheese and mustard in another bowl. Make 8-10 balls out of the pâté mixture. Make a thin cream cheese layer over. Coat with bacon, arrange on a plate, and chill for 30 minutes. Serve.

Roasted String Bean & Mushroom Plate

Ready in about: 32 minutes | **Serves**: 4 | **Per serving**: Kcal 121, Fat 2g, Net Carbs 6g, Protein 6g

INGREDIENTS

2 cups string beans, cut in halves
1 lb cremini mushrooms, quartered
3 tomatoes, quartered

2 cloves garlic, minced
3 tbsp olive oil
3 shallots, julienned

½ tsp dried thyme
Salt and black pepper to taste

DIRECTIONS

Preheat oven to 450°F. In a bowl, mix the strings beans, mushrooms, tomatoes, garlic, olive oil, shallots, thyme, salt, and pepper. Pour the vegetables in a baking sheet and spread them all around. Place the baking sheet in the oven and bake the veggies for 20-25 minutes. Serve.

Buttery Herb Roasted Radishes

Ready in about: 25 minutes | **Serves**: 6 | **Per serving**: Kcal 160, Fat 14g, Net Carbs 2g, Protein 5g

INGREDIENTS

2 lb small radishes, greens removed
3 tbsp olive oil

Salt and black pepper to taste
3 tbsp unsalted butter

1 tbsp chopped parsley
1 tbsp chopped tarragon

DIRECTIONS

Preheat oven to 400°F and line a baking sheet with parchment paper. Toss radishes with oil, salt, and black pepper. Spread on baking sheet and roast for 20 minutes until browned. Heat the butter in a large skillet over medium heat to brown and attain a nutty aroma, about 2-3 minutes.

Take out the radishes from the oven and transfer to a serving plate. Pour over the browned butter atop and sprinkle with parsley and tarragon. Serve with roasted rosemary chicken.

Smoked Mackerel Patties

Ready in about: 20 minutes + cooling time | Serves: 6 | Per serving: Kcal 324, Fat 27.1g, Net Carbo 2.2g, Protein 16g

INGREDIENTS

1 turnip, diced
Salt to taste
½ tsp chili pepper

3 tbsp olive oil + for rubbing
4 smoked mackerel steaks, flaked
2 eggs, beaten

2 tbsp mayonnaise
1 tbsp pork rinds, crushed

DIRECTIONS

Bring the turnip to boil in salted water in a saucepan over medium heat for 8 minutes or until tender. Drain the turnip through a colander, transfer to a mixing bowl, and mash the lumps. Let cool.

Add in the mackerel, eggs, mayonnaise, pork rinds, salt, and chili pepper and mix well. Make 6 compact patties. Heat olive oil in a skillet over medium heat and fry the patties for 3 minutes on each side until golden brown. Remove onto a wire rack to cool. Serve with sesame lime dipping sauce.

Swiss Chard Pesto & Scrambled Eggs

Ready in about: 15 minutes | Serves: 4 | Per serving: Kcal 495; Fat: 45g, Net Carbs: 6.3g, Protein: 19.5g

INGREDIENTS

3 tbsp butter
8 eggs, beaten

¼ cup almond milk
Salt and black pepper to taste

Swiss chard pesto

2 cups swiss chard
1 cup Parmesan cheese, grated

2 garlic cloves, minced
½ cup olive oil

2 tbsp lime juice
½ cup walnuts, chopped

DIRECTIONS

Set a pan over medium heat and warm the butter. In a bowl, mix the eggs, black pepper, salt, and almond milk. Pour them in the pan and cook while stirring gently, until eggs are set but still tender and moist.

In your blender, place all the ingredients for the pesto, excluding the olive oil. Pulse until roughly blended. While the machine is still running, slowly add in the olive oil until the desired consistency is attained. Serve alongside warm scrambled eggs.

Spinach & Ricotta Gnocchi

Ready in about: 13 minutes | Serves: 4 | Per serving: Kcal 125, Fat 8.3g, Net Carbs 4.1g, Protein 6.5g

INGREDIENTS

3 cups spinach, chopped
1 cup ricotta cheese, crumbled
1 cup Parmesan cheese, grated

¼ tsp nutmeg powder
1 egg, cracked into a bowl
Salt and black pepper to taste

1 ½ cups almond flour
2 ½ cups water
2 tbsp butter

DIRECTIONS

To a bowl, add the ricotta cheese, half of the Parmesan cheese, egg, nutmeg powder, salt, spinach, almond flour, and black pepper. Mix well. Make gnocchi of the mixture using 2 tbsp and set aside.

Bring the water to a boil over high heat on a stovetop, about 5 minutes. Place one gnocchi onto the water. If it breaks apart, add some more flour to the other gnocchi to firm it up.

Put the remaining gnocchi in the water to poach and rise to the top, about 2 minutes. Remove the gnocchi with a perforated spoon to a serving plate.

Melt the butter in a microwave and pour over the gnocchi. Sprinkle with the remaining Parmesan cheese and serve with green salad.

BRUNCH & DINNER

Homemade Pizza Crust

Ready in about: 8 minutes | **Serves**: 8 | **Per serving**: Kcal: 234; Fat 16.7g, Net Carbs 7.9g, Protein 12.4g

INGREDIENTS

3 cups almond flour
3 tbsp butter, then melted

⅓ tsp salt
3 large eggs

DIRECTIONS

Preheat oven to 350°F. In a bowl, mix the almond flour, butter, salt, and eggs until a dough forms. Mold the dough into a ball and place it in between two wide parchment papers on a flat surface.

Use a rolling pin to roll it out into a circle of a quarter-inch thickness. Slide the pizza dough into the pizza pan and remove the parchment papers. Bake the dough for 20 minutes.

Salami & Prawn Pizza

Ready in about: 35 minutes | **Serves**: 6 | **Per serving**: Kcal 267, Fat 13.3g, Net Carbs 4.3g, Protein 9.5g

INGREDIENTS

1 low carb pizza crust (see "Homemade Pizza Crust")

1 cup sugar-free pizza sauce	16 prawns, deveined and halved	1 tbsp olive oil
2 ¼ cups mozzarella cheese, grated	2 cloves garlic, finely sliced	Salt and black pepper to taste
4 oz Hot Salami, thinly sliced	2 cups baby arugula	10 basil leaves
3 tomatoes, thinly sliced	2 tbsp toasted pine nuts	

DIRECTIONS

Preheat oven to 450°F. With the pizza bread on the pizza pan, spread the pizza sauce on it and sprinkle with half of the mozzarella cheese. Top with the salami, tomatoes, prawns, and garlic, then sprinkle the remaining cheese over it. Place the pizza in the oven to bake for 15 minutes.

Once the cheese has melted, top with the basil leaves. In a bowl, toss the arugula and pine nuts with olive oil and adjust its seasoning to taste. Section the pizza with a slicer and serve with the arugula mixture.

Cheese Sticks with Mustard-Yogurt Dipping Sauce

Ready in about: 40 minutes | **Serves**: 6 | **Per serving**: Kcal: 200; Fat 16.9g, Net Carbs 3.7g, Protein 9.4g

INGREDIENTS

16 oz cheddar cheese with jalapeño peppers

¾ cup Grana Padano cheese, grated	Salt to taste	⅓ tsp dried rosemary
2 tbsp almond flour	¾ tsp red pepper flakes	2 eggs
1 tbsp flax meal	⅓ tsp cumin powder	2 tbsp olive oil
1 tsp baking powder	½ tsp dried oregano	

Dipping sauce

¾ cup jarred fire-roasted red peppers, chopped

1 cup cream cheese	1 tbsp mustard	2 garlic cloves, chopped
⅓ cup natural yogurt	1 chili pepper, deveined and minced	Salt and black pepper to taste

DIRECTIONS

Chop cheddar cheese crosswise into sticks. In a bowl, mix the dry ingredients. In a separate bowl, whisk the eggs. Dip each cheese stick into the eggs and then roll in the dry mixture. Set cheese sticks on a wax paper-lined baking sheet. Freeze for 30 minutes. Mix all ingredients for the dipping sauce until smooth.

In a skillet over medium heat, warm oil and fry cheese sticks for 5 minutes until the coating is golden brown and crisp. Set on paper towels to drain excess oil. Serve with the dipping sauce.

Mexican-Style Frittata

Ready in about: 25 minutes | **Serves:** 6 | **Per serving:** Kcal: 225; Fat 17g, Net Carbs 5.1g, Protein 13.2g

INGREDIENTS

10 eggs
Salt and black pepper to taste
⅓ cup chive and onion cream cheese
3 tbsp butter

1 onion, chopped
1 tsp garlic paste
2 red bell peppers, chopped
½ green bell pepper, chopped

1 tsp chipotle paste
2 cups kale
½ cup cotija cheese, shredded

DIRECTIONS

Preheat oven to 370°F. Mix the eggs with onion-cream cheese, black pepper, and salt. Warm butter in a skillet over medium heat. Sauté the onion for 3 minutes until soft. Add in chipotle paste, bell peppers, and garlic paste and cook for 4 minutes. Place in kale and cook for 2 minutes.

Add in the egg/cheese mixture. Spread the mixture evenly over the skillet and insert it in the oven. Bake for 8 minutes or until the frittata's top becomes golden brown but still slightly wobbly in the middle. Sprinkle with cotija cheese and bake for 3 minutes or until the cheese melts completely. Slice and serve.

Ham & Egg Salad

Ready in about: 20 minutes | **Serves:** 4 | **Per serving:** Kcal: 284; Fat 21.3g, Net Carbs 6.8g, Protein 16.7g

INGREDIENTS

4 eggs
1 cup mayonnaise
1 green onion, sliced diagonally

½ tsp mustard
1 tsp lime juice
Salt and black pepper to taste

1 small lettuce, torn
½ cup ham, chopped

DIRECTIONS

Boil the eggs in salted water for 10 minutes. Remove and run under cold water. Peel and chop them. Remove to a mixing bowl together with the mayonnaise, mustard, black pepper, ham, lime juice, and salt. Lay on a bed of lettuce. Scatter the green onion over and serve.

Mediterranean Cheese Balls

Ready in about: 5 minutes | **Serves:** 6 | **Per serving:** Kcal 217; Fat: 18.7g, Net Carbs: 2.1g, Protein: 10g

INGREDIENTS

4 oz prosciutto, chopped
4 oz goat cheese, crumbled

½ cup aioli
½ cup black olives, pitted and chopped

½ tsp red pepper flakes
2 tbsp fresh basil, finely chopped

DIRECTIONS

In a bowl, mix aioli, prosciutto, goat cheese, red pepper flakes, and black olives. Form 10 balls from the mixture. Roll them in the basil. Arrange on a serving platter and serve immediately.

Pork & Vegetable Tart

Ready in about: 45 minutes | **Serves:** 6 | **Per serving:** Kcal 415; Fat: 26.3g, Net Carbs: 4.2g, Protein: 35g

INGREDIENTS

2 lb ground pork
1 onion, chopped
1 bell pepper, chopped

Salt and black pepper to taste
2 zucchinis, sliced
2 tomatoes, sliced

¼ cup whipping cream
8 eggs
½ cup Monterey Jack cheese, grated

DIRECTIONS

Preheat oven to 360°F. In a bowl, mix onion, bell pepper, ground pork, pepper, and salt. Layer the mixture on a greased baking dish. Spread zucchini slices on top, followed with tomato slices. Bake for 30 minutes.

In a separate bowl, combine cheese, eggs, and whipping cream. Top the tart with the creamy mixture and bake for 10 minutes until the edges and top become brown. Let cool slightly, slice, and serve.

Chipotle Pizza with Cotija & Cilantro

Ready in about: 15 minutes | **Serves**: 2 | **Per serving**: Kcal 397, Fat: 31g, Net Carbs: 8.1g, Protein: 22g

INGREDIENTS

Pizza crust

4 eggs, beaten
¼ cup sour cream
2 tbsp flaxseed meal
1 tsp chipotle pepper

¼ tsp cumin
½ tsp dried ground coriander
¼ tsp salt
1 tbsp olive oil

2 tbsp tomato paste
2 oz Cotija cheese, shredded
1 tbsp fresh cilantro, chopped

DIRECTIONS

Mix eggs, sour cream, flaxseed meal, chipotle pepper, cumin, coriander, and salt in a bowl. Set a pan over medium heat and warm ½ tablespoon oil. Ladle ½ of crust mixture into the pan and evenly spread out. Cook until the edges are set, flip, and cook on the second side. Repeat with the remaining crust mixture.

Warm the remaining ½ tablespoon of oil in the pan. Spread each pizza crust with tomato paste, then scatter over the cotija cheese. In batches, bake in the oven for 8-10 minutes at 425°F until all the cheese melts. Garnish with cilantro and serve.

Broccoli Cheese Soup

Ready in about: 20 minutes | **Serves**: 4 | **Per serving**: Kcal 296; Fat 14.1g, Net Carbs 7.4g, Protein 14.2g

INGREDIENTS

2 tbsp butter
½ cup leeks, chopped
1 celery stalk, chopped
1 serrano pepper, finely chopped

1 tsp garlic puree
½ lb broccoli florets
3 cups chicken stock
1 cup coconut milk

1 tsp mustard powder
6 oz Monterey Jack cheese, grated
Salt and black pepper to taste
2 tbsp fresh parsley, chopped

DIRECTIONS

Set a pot over medium heat and melt butter. Add in serrano pepper, celery, and leeks and sauté for 5 minutes until soft. Stir in garlic puree and mustard powder for 1 minute. Pour in chicken stock and coconut milk. Bring to a boil and reduce the heat. Allow simmering for 10 minutes. Add in the broccoli.

Cook for another 5 minutes. Remove from the heat and fold in the cheese. Stir to ensure the cheese is melted, and you have a homogenous mixture. Adjust the seasoning, top with parsley, and serve warm.

Cheesy Herb Omelet

Ready in about: 10 minutes | **Serves**: 2 | **Per serving**: Kcal 431; Fat: 33.1g, Net Carbs: 2.7g, Protein: 30.3g

INGREDIENTS

4 slices cooked bacon, crumbled
4 eggs, beaten

1 tsp basil, chopped
1 tsp parsley, chopped

Salt and black pepper to taste
½ cup cheddar cheese, grated

DIRECTIONS

In a frying pan, cook the bacon until sizzling, about 5 minutes. Add in eggs, parsley, black pepper, salt, and basil. Scatter the cheese over half of the omelet and, using a spatula, fold in half over the filling. Cook for 1 extra minute or until cooked through and serve immediately.

Broccoli Rabe Pizza with Parmesan

Ready in about: 40 minutes | **Serves**: 2 | **Per serving**: Kcal 673, Fat 47g, Net Carbs 10.7g, Protein 32.6g

INGREDIENTS

1 cauliflower pizza crust
2 tbsp olive oil
2 parsnips, chopped

Salt and black pepper to taste
2 cups broccoli rabe
2 hard-boiled eggs, chopped

½ cup largely diced bacon
1 cup grated Parmesan cheese
2 tbsp chopped basil leaves

Preheat oven to 400°F. Drizzle the parsnips with some olive oil and sprinkle with salt and pepper. Place on a baking sheet. Bake for 20 minutes; set aside. Toss the broccoli rabe with 2 tablespoons of olive oil in a bowl, season with salt and pepper, and drain any liquid from the bowl. Bake the crust for 7 minutes.

Let cool for a few minutes and brush with the remaining olive oil. Scatter the parsnips all over, top with the broccoli rabe, bacon, and eggs, and sprinkle with Parmesan cheese. Bake for 6-8 minutes until the cheese is melted. Garnish with basil and section with a pizza cutter. Serve with sundried tomato salad.

Roasted Vegetable & Goat Cheese Pizza

Ready in about: 45 minutes | **Serves**: 4 | **Per serving**: Kcal 315, Fat 16g, Net Carbs 7.3g, Protein 12g

INGREDIENTS

1 cauliflower pizza crust	1 red bell pepper, cut into pieces	Salt and black pepper to taste
1 sweet onion, cut into chunks	1 medium zucchini, cut into pieces	½ cup pesto sauce
1 eggplant, cut into chunks	2 tbsp olive oil	½ cup goat cheese, crumbled

DIRECTIONS

Preheat oven to 425°F. Bake the pizza crust in a greased baking sheet for 7 minutes. Let cool. In a bowl, mix the onion, eggplant, red bell pepper, and zucchinis with olive oil, salt, and pepper. Pour the mixture into a baking sheet and spread it well around. Bake for 30 minutes, stirring at 10 minutes intervals.

Remove the veggies and set aside. Spread the pesto on the pizza crust. Arrange the roasted veggies on top and sprinkle with goat cheese. Bake the pizza for 5-6 minutes until the cheese is melted. Serve.

Chorizo Scotch Eggs

Ready in about: 35 minutes | **Serves**: 4 | **Per serving**: Kcal 247; Fat 11.4g, Net Carbs 0.6g, Protein 33.7g

INGREDIENTS

4 whole eggs	1 lb chorizo sausages, skinless	¼ tsp onion powder
1 egg, beaten	¼ cup Grana Padano cheese, grated	¼ tsp chili pepper
½ cup pork rinds, crushed	1 garlic clove, minced	Salt and black pepper to taste

DIRECTIONS

Cook the eggs in boiling salted water over medium heat for 10 minutes. Rinse under running water and remove the shell; reserve. Preheat oven to 370°F. In a mixing dish, mix the other ingredients, except for the beaten egg and pork rinds. Take a handful of the mixture and wrap around each of the boiled eggs.

With fingers, mold the mixture until sealed to form balls. Dip the balls in the beaten eggs, coat with rinds, and place in a greased baking dish. Bake for 25 minutes, until golden brown and crisp. Serve chilled.

Italian-Style Roasted Butternut Squash Cups

Ready in about: 40 minutes | **Serves**: 4 | **Per serving**: Kcal 155; Fat: 12.7g, Carbs 6.2g, Protein: 4.6g

INGREDIENTS

2 lb butternut squash, sliced	½ cup buttermilk	Celery salt to taste
2 tbsp coconut oil, melted	1 cup ricotta cheese, crumbled	¼ tsp onion flakes
¼ cup fresh basil, chopped	2 tsp powdered unflavored gelatin	½ tsp fennel seeds
1 cup heavy cream	1 tbsp fresh rosemary, chopped	½ tsp cayenne pepper

DIRECTIONS

Preheat oven to 360°F. Place the squash slices in a baking dish and sprinkle with coconut oil and celery salt. Toss to coat. Roast for 30 minutes. Het a pan on low heat, add in the rest of the ingredients.

Cook until heated through, about 3-4 minutes. Transfer to a food processor, add in the roasted squash, and pulse to obtain a smooth and creamy mixture. Fold in pureed squash and stir to mix well. Ladle the mixture into ramekins. Refrigerate overnight. Flip the ramekin onto serving plates.

Sopressata & Cheese Bake

Ready in about: 1 hour | **Serves**: 4 | **Per serving**: Kcal 334; Fat: 23g, Net Carbs: 6.2g, Protein: 25.5g

INGREDIENTS

8 eggs
Salt to taste
1 cup cheddar cheese, grated
½ cup goat cheese

1 bell pepper, chopped
1 poblano pepper, chopped
½ tsp dried dill weed
1 tsp mustard

4 slices soppressata, chopped
4 slices pancetta, chopped
6 cups hot water

DIRECTIONS

Preheat oven to 360°F. Beat the eggs in a bowl, add cheddar, mustard, and salt and mix to incorporate everything. Place the mixture in a greased casserole. Stir in the remaining ingredients.

Set a roasting pan with hot water in the middle of the oven. Insert the casserole dish into the roasting pan. Bake for around 1 hour. Let cool for some minutes before cutting into squares. Serve while warm!

Tuna & Monterey Jack Stuffed Avocado

Ready in about: 20 minutes | **Serves**: 4 | **Per serving**: Kcal: 286; Fat 23.9g, Net Carbs 9g, Protein 11.2g

INGREDIENTS

2 avocados, halved and pitted
4 oz Monterey Jack cheese, grated

2 oz canned tuna, flaked
2 tbsp chives, chopped

Salt and black pepper to taste
½ cup curly endive, chopped

DIRECTIONS

Preheat oven to 360°F. Set avocado halves in an ovenproof dish. In a mixing bowl, mix Monterey Jack cheese, chives, black pepper, salt, and tuna. Stuff the cheese/tuna mixture in avocado halves. Bake for 15 minutes or until the top is golden brown. Serve with curly endive for garnish.

Bacon Loaded Eggplants

Ready in about: 35 minutes | **Serves**: 4 | **Per serving**: Kcal 245; Fat 12.8g, Net Carbs 9.5g, Protein 15.6g

INGREDIENTS

2 eggplants, cut into halves
1 onion, chopped

4 bacon slices, chopped
4 eggs

Salt and black pepper to taste
¼ tsp dried parsley

DIRECTIONS

Preheat oven at 380°F. Scoop flesh from eggplant halves to make shells. Set the eggplant boats on a greased baking pan. Heat a skillet over medium heat and stir-fry the bacon for 5 minutes until crispy. Remove to a plate. Add the onion and eggplant flesh to the skillet and sauté for 5-7 minutes until tender.

Season with salt, pepper, and parsley and stir in the bacon. Divide the mixture between the eggplant shells. Crack an egg in each half, sprinkle with salt and pepper, and bake for 30 minutes or until the boats become tender and the eggs are set. Serve with tomato salad.

Greek Yogurt & Cheese Alfredo Sauce

Ready in about: 10 minutes | **Serves**: 12 | **Per serving**: Kcal 154; Fat: 13g, Net Carbs: 3.3g, Protein: 6.2g

INGREDIENTS

2 tbsp butter
6 oz heavy cream
Salt and black pepper to taste

2 cloves garlic, chopped
¾ cup sour cream
½ cup Gruyere cheese, grated

1 cup goat cheese
½ cup cooked bacon, chopped
1 cup Greek yogurt

DIRECTIONS

Set a pan over medium heat and warm butter. Stir in heavy cream and cook for 2-3 minutes. Sprinkle with black pepper and salt; mix in the Greek yogurt and cook for 2 minutes. Stir in the remaining ingredients to mix well until smooth. Serve.

Ham & Egg Mug Cups

Ready in about: 5 minutes | Serves: 2 | Per serving: Kcal: 244; Fat 17.5g, Net Carbs 2.9g, Protein 19.2

INGREDIENTS

4 eggs
4 tbsp coconut milk

¼ cup ham, cubed
½ tsp chili pepper

Salt and black pepper to taste
2 tbsp chives, chopped

DIRECTIONS

Mix all ingredients, excluding chives. Divide the egg mixture into 2 greased microwave-safe cups. Microwave for 1 minute. Decorate with chives before serving.

Chorizo & Emmental Baked Eggs

Ready in about: 20 minutes | Serves: 4 | Per serving: Kcal 444; Fat: 35.3g, Net Carbs: 2.7g, Protein: 29.8g

INGREDIENTS

2 tbsp olive oil
4 slices chorizo, chopped
½ cup chives, chopped

10 broccoli florets, chopped
1 clove garlic, minced
1 tsp fines herbes

¼ cup vegetable broth
4 eggs
1 ½ cups Emmental cheese, grated

DIRECTIONS

Warm the oil in a pan over medium heat. Add the chorizo and cook for 4 minutes until brown; set aside. In the same pan, add the chives, garlic, and broccoli and sauté for 3 minutes until soft as you stir occasionally.

Stir in broth and fines herbes and cook for 6 more minutes. Make 4 holes in the mixture until you are able to see the bottom of your pan. Crack an egg into each hole. Spread cheese over the top and cook for 6 more minutes. Scatter the reserved chorizo over and serve.

Asian Tofu Egg Soup

Ready in about: 15 minutes | Serves: 4 | Per serving: Kcal 153; Fat: 9.8g, Net Carbs: 2.7g, Protein: 15g

INGREDIENTS

4 cups chicken stock
1 tbsp tamari sauce
2 tbsp coconut oil, softened

2 eggs, beaten
2 tbsp fresh cilantro, chopped
1-inch piece ginger, grated

Salt and black pepper to taste
4 spring onions, chopped
½ lb extra-firm tofu, cubed

DIRECTIONS

Set a large saucepan over medium heat. Add in tamari sauce, chicken stock, coconut oil, and ginger and bring to a boil. Reduce the heat and simmer for 10 minutes. Place in tofu and simmer for 1-2 minutes.

Gradually pour in the eggs as you stir gently until the eggs are cooked. Adjust the seasoning with salt and pepper. Divide into soup bowls and serve sprinkled with fresh cilantro.

Raspberry & Rum Omelet

Ready in about: 10 minutes | Serves: 1 | Per serving: Kcal 488, Fat: 42g, Net Carbs: 8g, Protein: 15.3g

INGREDIENTS

2 eggs
2 tbsp heavy cream
½ tsp ground cloves

1 tbsp coconut oil
2 tbsp mascarpone cheese
6 fresh raspberries, sliced

½ tsp powdered swerve sugar
1 tbsp rum

DIRECTIONS

Beat the eggs with ground cloves and heavy cream. Set pan over medium heat and warm oil. Place in the egg mixture and cook for 3 minutes. Set the omelet onto a plate.

Top with raspberries and mascarpone cheese. Roll it up and sprinkle with powdered swerve. Pour the warm rum over the omelet and ignite it. Let the flame die out and serve.

Caprese Stuffed Tomatoes

Ready in about: 35 minutes | **Serves**: 4 | **Per serving**: Kcal 306; Fat: 27.5g, Net Carbs: 4.4g, Protein: 11.3g

INGREDIENTS

4 tomatoes
4 slices fresh mozzarella cheese
¼ cup sour cream

1 egg, whisked
1 clove garlic, minced
4 tbsp fresh scallions, chopped

Salt and black pepper to taste
2 tbsp butter, softened

DIRECTIONS

Preheat oven to 360°F. Lightly grease a rimmed baking sheet with cooking spray. Horizontally slice tomatoes into halves and get rid of the hard cores. Scoop out pulp and seeds.

In a bowl, mix egg, salt, butter, black pepper, garlic, sour cream, and scallions. Split the filling between tomatoes, cover each one with a mozzarella slice and bake in the preheated oven for 30 minutes. Place on a wire rack and allow to cool for 5 minutes. Serve alongside fresh rocket leaves.

Vanilla-Coconut Cream Tart

Ready in about: 30 minutes + cooling time | **Serves**: 6 | **Per serving**: Kcal 305, Fat: 30.6g, Net Carbs: 9.7g, Protein: 4.6g

INGREDIENTS

½ cup butter
⅓ cup xylitol
¾ cup coconut flour
⅓ cup coconut shreds, unsweetened

2 ¼ cups heavy cream
3 egg yolks
⅓ cup almond flour
¾ cup water

½ tsp ground cinnamon
½ tsp star anise, ground
½ tsp vanilla extract
2 tbsp coconut flakes

DIRECTIONS

Warm butter in a pan over medium heat. Stir in xylitol and cook until fully dissolved. Add in coconut shreds and coconut flour and cook for 2 minutes. Scrape the crust mixture into a baking dish. Refrigerate.

In the same pan, warm 1 ¼ cups of heavy cream over medium heat. Fold in egg yolks and mix thoroughly. Mix in water and almond flour until thick. Place in cinnamon, vanilla, and anise star. Cook until thick.

Let cool for 10 minutes; sprinkle over the crust. Place in the fridge for 2 hours. Beat the remaining heavy cream until stiff peaks start to form. Spread the cream all over the cake. Top with coconut flakes to serve.

Cauli Mac & Cheese

Ready in about: 15 minutes | **Serves**: 4 | **Per serving**: Kcal 357; Fat: 32.5g, Net Carbs: 10.9g, Protein: 8.4g

INGREDIENTS

1 head cauliflower, cut into florets
2 tbsp ghee, melted
Salt and black pepper to taste

½ cup crème fraiche
½ cup half-and-half
1 cup cream cheese

½ tsp turmeric powder
1 tsp garlic paste
½ tsp onion flakes

DIRECTIONS

Preheat oven to 450°F. Shake cauliflower florets with melted ghee, salt, and black pepper. Arrange on a greased baking sheet and roast for 15 minutes. In a saucepan over medium heat, pour the remaining ingredients and heat through, stirring frequently. Reduce heat to low and simmer for 2-3 minutes until thickened. Coat the cauliflower florets in the cheese sauce and serve immediately in serving bowls.

Eggs in a Mug

Ready in about: 5 minutes | **Serves**: 2 | **Per serving**: Kcal 197; Fat: 13.8g, Net Carbs: 2.7g, Protein: 15.7g

INGREDIENTS

4 eggs
¼ cup coconut milk
¼ cup cheddar cheese, grated

1 garlic clove, minced
¼ tsp dried dill
¼ tsp turmeric powder

Salt to taste
¼ tsp red pepper flakes

DIRECTIONS

In a mixing bowl, mix the eggs, cheddar cheese, red pepper, garlic, coconut milk, turmeric powder, and salt. Divide the mixture between 2 microwave-safe mugs. Place in the microwave for 40 seconds. Stir well and continue microwaving for 70 seconds. Sprinkle with dried dill and serve.

Spicy Cheese Chips

Ready in about: 18 minutes | **Serves**: 2 | **Per serving**: Kcal: 100; Fat 8g, Net Carbs 0g, Protein 7g

INGREDIENTS

3 cups cheddar cheese, grated
⅓ tsp salt

½ tsp garlic powder
½ tsp cayenne pepper

½ tsp dried rosemary
⅓ tsp chili powder

DIRECTIONS

Preheat oven to 420°F. Line a parchment paper on a baking sheet. Mix the grated cheddar cheese with spices in a bowl. Create 2 tablespoons of cheese mixture into small mounds on the baking sheet. Bake for about 15 minutes; allow to cool to harden the chips.

Cheese, Ham and Egg Muffins

Ready in about: 20 minutes | **Serves**: 6 | **Per serving**: Kcal: 268; Fat 18.3g, Net Carbs 0.7g, Protein 26.2g

INGREDIENTS

24 slices smoked ham
6 eggs, beaten

Salt and black pepper to taste
¼ cup fresh parsley, chopped

¼ cup ricotta cheese
¼ cup Brie, chopped

DIRECTIONS

Set oven to 390°F. Line 2 slices of smoked ham into each greased muffin cup, to circle each mold.

In a mixing bowl, mix the rest of the ingredients. Fill ¾ of the ham lined muffin cup with the egg/cheese mixture. Bake for 15 minutes. Serve warm!

Cheese & Pumpkin Chicken Meatballs

Ready in about: 35 minutes | **Serves**: 4 | **Per serving**: Kcal 378; Fat: 24.5g, Net Carbs: 4.7g, Protein: 36g

INGREDIENTS

1 egg, beaten
1 ½ lb ground chicken
½ cup pumpkin, grated

2 garlic cloves, minced
1 onion, chopped
1 tbsp Italian mixed herbs

Salt and black pepper to taste
2 tbsp olive oil
1 cup cheddar cheese, shredded

DIRECTIONS

Preheat oven to 360°F. Combine all the ingredients, excluding the cheddar cheese. Form meatballs from the mixture and set them on a parchment-lined baking sheet. Bake for 25 minutes, flipping once. Spread cheese over the balls and bake for 7 more minutes or until all cheese melts. Serve.

Baked Chicken Legs with Cheesy Spread

Ready in about: 45 minutes | **Serves**: 4 | **Per serving**: Kcal 119; Fat: 10.5g, Net Carbs: 1.1g, Protein: 5.1g

INGREDIENTS

4 chicken legs
¼ cup goat cheese

2 tbsp sour cream
1 tbsp butter, softened

1 onion, chopped
Sea Salt and black pepper to taste

DIRECTIONS

Preheat oven to 360°F and season the legs with salt and black pepper. Roast in a greased baking dish for 25-30 minutes until crispy and browned. In a mixing bowl, mix the rest of the ingredients to form the spread. Scatter the spread over the chicken and serve with green salad.

Chili Egg Pickles

Ready in about: 20 minutes | **Serves**: 4 | **Per serving**: Kcal: 145; Fat 9g, Net Carbs 2.8g, Protein 11.4g

INGREDIENTS

8 eggs
½ cup onions, sliced
2 cardamom pods

½ tsp chili powder
1 tsp fennel seeds
2 clove garlic, sliced

1 cup vinegar
1 ¼ cups water
1 tbsp salt

DIRECTIONS

Boil eggs in salted water until hard-cooked, about 10 minutes. Rinse them under running water, peel, and discard the shells. Place the peeled eggs onto a large jar. Set a pan over medium heat. Stir in all remaining ingredients and bring to a boil. Reduce heat to low and allow to simmer for 6 minutes. Spoon the mixture into the jar. Store in the refrigerator for up to 2 to 3 weeks.

Egg & Cheese Stuffed Peppers

Ready in about: 35 minutes | **Serves**: 4 | **Per serving**: Kcal 359; Fat: 29.7g, Net Carbs: 6.7g, Protein: 17.7g

INGREDIENTS

4 bell peppers, tops sliced off and deseeded
6 oz cottage cheese, crumbled
6 oz blue cheese, crumbled
½ cup pork rinds, crushed

2 cloves garlic, smashed
1 ½ cups pureed tomatoes
1 tsp dried basil

1 tbsp olive oil
½ tsp chili pepper
2 eggs, beaten

DIRECTIONS

Preheat oven to 360°F. In a bowl, mix garlic, cottage cheese, pork rinds, blue cheese, eggs, tomatoes, chili pepper, and basil. Stuff the peppers and place them in a greased casserole dish. Pour in 1 cup of water. Drizzle with olive oil. Bake for 30 minutes until the peppers are tender. Serve with mixed salad.

Gingery Tuna Mousse

Ready in about: 20 minutes + chilling time | **Serves**: 4 | **Per serving**: Kcal 100; Fat: 5.8g, Net Carbs: 4.1g, Protein: 8g

INGREDIENTS

1 ½ tsp gelatin, powdered
3 tbsp water
2 oz ricotta cheese
3 tbsp mayonnaise

1 tsp mustard
3 oz canned tuna, flaked
¼ cup onions, chopped
1 garlic clove, minced

½ tsp salt
¼ tsp black pepper
⅓ tsp ginger, grated

DIRECTIONS

Mix gelatin in water and let sit for 10 minutes. Set a pan over medium heat and warm ricotta cheese. Place in gelatin and mix to blend well; let the mixture cool. Place in the other ingredients and stir. Split the mixture among 4 mousse molds and refrigerate overnight. Invert the molds over a platter to serve.

Jamon & Queso Balls

Ready in about: 15 minutes | **Serves**: 8 | **Per serving**: Kcal: 168; Fat 13g, Net Carbs 2.5g, Protein 10.3g

INGREDIENTS

1 egg
6 slices jamon serrano, chopped
6 oz cotija cheese

6 oz Manchego cheese, grated
Salt and black pepper to taste
¼ cup almond flour

1 tsp baking powder
1 tsp garlic powder

DIRECTIONS

Preheat oven to 420 °F. Whisk the egg in a bowl. Place in the remaining ingredients and mix well. Split the mixture into 16 balls. Set them on a baking sheet lined with parchment paper. Bake for 13 minutes or until they turn golden brown and become crispy. Serve.

Carrot & Cheese Mousse

Ready in about: 15 minutes + cooling time | **Serves**: 6 | **Per serving**: Kcal 368, Fat: 33.7g, Net Carbs: 5.6g, Protein: 13.8g

INGREDIENTS

1 ½ cups half & half
½ cup cream cheese, softened
½ cup erythritol

3 eggs
1 ¼ cups canned carrots
½ tsp ground cloves

½ tsp ground cinnamon
¼ tsp grated nutmeg
A pinch of salt

DIRECTIONS

Heat a pan over medium heat, mix erythritol, cream cheese, and half & half and warm, stirring frequently. Remove from the heat. Beat the eggs; slowly place in ½ of the hot cream mixture to the beaten eggs.

Pour the mixture back to the pan. Cook for 3 minutes, until thick. Kill the heat; add in carrots, cinnamon, salt, nutmeg, and cloves. Blend with a blender. Let cool before serving.

Italian Cakes with Gorgonzola & Salami

Ready in about: 25 minutes | **Serves**: 4 | **Per serving**: Kcal 240, Fat: 15.3g, Net Carbs: 10g, Protein: 16.1g

INGREDIENTS

3 slices salami
4 eggs, beaten

½ cup coconut flour
1 cup gorgonzola cheese, crumbled

A pinch of salt
½ tsp grated nutmeg

DIRECTIONS

Set a frying pan over medium heat. Add in salami and cook as you turn with tongs until browned. Place on paper towels to absorb the excess fat. Chop the salami and stir with the other ingredients to mix.

Grease cake molds. Fill them with batter (¾ full). Set oven to 390°F and bake for 15 minutes. Serve.

One-Pot Cheesy Cauliflower & Bacon

Ready in about: 15 minutes | **Serves**: 4 | **Per serving**: Kcal 323, Fat: 24g, Net Carbs: 7.4g, Protein: 18.8g

INGREDIENTS

2 tbsp butter
½ lb bacon, cut into strips
1 head cauliflower, cut into florets

¼ cup sour cream
¾ cup heavy whipping cream
1 tsp garlic puree

2 tbsp apple cider vinegar
½ cup queso fresco, crumbled

DIRECTIONS

Set a frying pan over medium heat and melt the butter; brown the bacon for 3 minutes. Set aside. Add in cauliflower and cook until tender, about 4-5 minutes.

Add in the whipping and sour cream, then the vinegar and garlic, and cook until warmed fully. Take the reserved bacon back to the pan. Fold in queso fresco and cook for 2 minutes, or until cheese melts.

Cilantro & Chili Omelet

Ready in about: 15 minutes | **Serves**: 2 | **Per serving**: Kcal 319; Fat: 25g, Net Carbs: 10g, Protein: 14.9g

INGREDIENTS

1 tsp butter
1 spring onion, chopped
1 spring garlic, chopped

4 eggs
¼ cup sour cream
1 tomato, sliced

½ green chili pepper, minced
1 tbsp fresh cilantro, chopped
Salt and black pepper to taste

DIRECTIONS

Set a pan over high heat and warm the butter. Sauté garlic and onion until tender, about 3 minutes. Whisk the eggs with sour cream. Pour into the pan and use a spatula to smooth the surface.

Cook until eggs become puffy and brown to bottom. Add cilantro, chili pepper, and tomato to one side of the omelet. Season with black pepper and salt. Fold the omelet in half and slice into wedges.

Chorizo Egg Balls

Ready in about: 10 minutes + cooling time | **Serves**: 6 | **Per serving**: Kcal 174, Fat: 15.2g, Net Carbs: 4.3g, Protein: 5.9g

INGREDIENTS

2 eggs
½ cup butter, softened
8 black olives, pitted and chopped

3 tbsp mayonnaise
Salt to taste
½ tsp crushed red pepper flakes

1 lb cooked chorizo, chopped
2 tbsp chia seeds

DIRECTIONS

In a food processor, place the eggs, olives, pepper flakes, mayo, butter, and salt and blitz until everything is incorporated. Stir in the chorizo. Refrigerate for 30 minutes. Form balls from the mixture. Roll the balls through the chia seeds to coat. Keep in the refrigerator until serving time.

Chicken Meatloaf Cups with Pancetta

Ready in about: 30 minutes | **Serves**: 6 | **Per serving**: Kcal 276, Fat: 18.3g, Net Carbs: 1.2g, Protein: 29.2g

INGREDIENTS

2 tbsp onion, chopped
1 tsp garlic, minced
1 lb ground chicken
2 oz cooked pancetta, chopped

1 egg, beaten
1 tsp mustard
Salt and black pepper to taste
½ tsp crushed red pepper flakes

1 tsp dried basil
½ tsp dried oregano
4 oz cheddar cheese, cubed

DIRECTIONS

In a bowl, mix mustard, onion, ground chicken, egg, pancetta, and garlic. Season with oregano, red pepper, black pepper, basil, and salt. Split the mixture into greased muffin cups. Lower one cube of cheddar cheese into each meatloaf cup. Close the top to cover the cheese.

Bake in the oven at 345°F for 20 minutes, or until the meatloaf cups become golden brown. Let cool for 10 minutes before transferring from the muffin pan. Serve.

Chorizo & Cheese Gofre

Ready in about: 20 minutes | **Serves**: 3 | **Per serving**: Kcal 453, Fat: 37g, Net Carbs: 4.5g, Protein: 25.6g

INGREDIENTS

6 eggs, separate egg whites, and egg yolks
½ tsp baking powder
6 tbsp almond flour
4 tbsp butter, melted

¼ tsp salt
½ tsp dried rosemary
3 tbsp tomato puree

3 oz smoked chorizo, chopped
3 oz cheddar cheese, shredded

DIRECTIONS

In a mixing bowl, mix egg yolks, almond flour, rosemary, butter, baking powder, and salt. Beat the egg whites until pale and combine with the egg yolk mixture. Grease waffle iron and set over medium heat, add in ¼ cup of the batter and cook for 3 minutes until golden. Repeat with the remaining batter.

Place one waffle back to the waffle iron. Sprinkle 1 tbsp of tomato puree to the waffle. Apply a topping of 1 ounce of cheese and 1 ounce of chorizo. Cover with another waffle and cook until all the cheese melts. Do the same with all remaining ingredients. Serve.

Quatro Formaggio Pizza

Ready in about: 15 minutes | **Serves**: 4 | **Per serving**: Kcal 266, Fat: 23.6g, Net Carbs: 6.6g, Protein: 9g

INGREDIENTS

1 tbsp olive oil
½ cup cheddar cheese, shredded
1 ¼ cups mozzarella cheese, grated
½ cup mascarpone cheese

½ cup blue cheese
2 tbsp sour cream
2 garlic cloves, chopped
1 red bell pepper, sliced

1 green bell pepper, sliced
10 cherry tomatoes, halved
1 tsp oregano
Salt and black pepper to taste

In a bowl, mix the cheeses. Set a pan over medium heat and warm olive oil. Spread the cheese mixture on the pan and cook for 5 minutes until cooked through. Scatter garlic and sour cream over the crust. Add in tomatoes and bell peppers; cook for 2 minutes. Sprinkle with pepper, salt, and oregano and serve.

Crêpes with Lemon-Buttery Syrup

Ready in about: 25 minutes | Serves: 6 | Per serving: Kcal 243, Fat: 19.6g, Net Carbs: 5.5g, Protein: 11g

INGREDIENTS

Crêpes

6 oz mascarpone cheese, softened
6 eggs

1 ½ tbsp granulated swerve sugar
¼ cup almond flour

1 tsp baking soda
1 tsp baking powder

Syrup

¾ cup water
2 tbsp lemon juice

1 tbsp butter
¾ cup swerve, powdered

1 tbsp vanilla extract
½ tsp xanthan gum

DIRECTIONS

In a bowl, beat the mascarpone cheese, eggs, swerve sugar, almond flour, baking soda, and baking powder with an electric mixer until well incorporated. Let sit for 5-10 minutes.

Heat pan over medium heat and grease it with butter. Pour in a ladleful of the batter. Swirl the pan quickly to spread the dough all around the skillet and cook the crepe until the edges start to brown, about 2 minutes. Flip over and cook the other side for 2 minutes. Repeat with the remaining batter.

In the same pan, mix swerve sugar, butter, and water. Simmer for 6 minutes as you stir. Transfer the mixture to a blender with a ¼ teaspoon of xanthan gum and vanilla and mix well. Place in the remaining xanthan gum, lemon juice, and allow to sit until the syrup is thick. Pour over the crepes and serve.

Fried Brie Cheese Bites

Ready in about: 15 minutes + chilling time | Serves: 4 | Per serving: Kcal 625; Fat: 53.9g, Net Carbs: 0.7g, Protein: 28.7g

INGREDIENTS

1 cup almond flour
2 eggs, beaten
½ cup vegetable oil

1 cup pork rinds, crushed
12 oz brie cheese, cubed
½ tsp chili pepper

¼ tsp parsley flakes
1 cup hot pepper sauce
1 celery stalk, cut into julienne strips

DIRECTIONS

In a bowl, mix the almond flour with parsley and chili pepper. Pour the pork rinds in another one. Dip the brie cubes into the eggs first and then roll them in the almond flour mixture. Dip again in the eggs and coat with the pork rinds. Put on a plate. Warm the vegetable oil in a pan over medium heat.

Fry the brie cubes in batches until golden brown on all sides, about 5 minutes. Remove to kitchen paper to soak up excess fat. Serve with hot pepper sauce and celery sticks. Serve garnished with parsley, with cranberry sauce on the side for dipping.

Crabmeat & Cheese Stuffed Avocado

Ready in about: 25 minutes | Serves: 4 | Per serving: Kcal 264, Fat: 24.4g, Net Carbs: 11g, Protein: 3.7g

INGREDIENTS

1 tsp olive oil
1 cup crabmeat

2 avocados, halved and pitted
3 oz cream cheese

¼ cup almonds, chopped
1 tsp smoked paprika

DIRECTIONS

Preheat oven to 425°F. In a bowl, mix crabmeat with cream cheese. Fill the avocado halves with crabmeat mixture and top with almonds. Bake for 18 minutes. Decorate with smoked paprika and serve.

Grilled Halloumi Cheese with Eggs

Ready in about: 20 minutes | **Serves:** 4 | **Per serving:** Kcal 542; Fat: 46.4g, Net Carbs: 11.2g, Protein: 23.7g

INGREDIENTS

4 slices halloumi cheese
2 tbsp olive oil
1 tsp dried Greek seasoning blend

6 eggs, beaten
½ tsp sea salt
¼ tsp crushed red pepper flakes

1 ½ cups avocado, pitted and sliced
1 cup grape tomatoes, halved
4 tbsp pecans, chopped

DIRECTIONS

Preheat your grill to medium. Set the halloumi in the center of a piece of heavy-duty foil. Sprinkle oil over the halloumi and apply Greek seasoning blend. Close the foil to create a packet. Grill for about 15 minutes. Then slice into four pieces.

In a frying pan over medium heat, warm the olive oil and cook the eggs. Stir well to create large and soft curds. Season with salt and red pepper flakes. Put the eggs and grilled cheese on a serving bowl. Serve alongside tomatoes and avocado, decorated with chopped pecans.

Goat Cheese Muffins with Ajillo Mushrooms

Ready in about: 45 minutes | **Serves:** 6 | **Per serving:** Kcal 263, Fat: 22.4g, Net Carbs: 6.1g, Protein: 10g

INGREDIENTS

1 ½ cups heavy cream
5 oz goat cheese, crumbled
3 eggs

Salt and black pepper to taste
1 tbsp butter, softened
2 cups mushrooms, chopped

2 garlic cloves, minced
1 tbsp fresh parsley, chopped

DIRECTIONS

Preheat oven to 320°F. Insert 6 ramekins into a large pan. Add in boiling water up to 1-inch depth. In a pan over medium heat, warm heavy cream. Reduce the heat and stir in goat cheese and cook until melted. Remove from the heat. Beat the eggs in a bowl and gradually add the cream mixture.

Sprinkle with pepper and salt. Spoon the mixture into ramekins. Bake for 40 minutes. Melt butter in a pan over medium heat. Add garlic and mushrooms, season with salt and pepper, and sauté for 5 minutes until tender. Spread the ajillo mushrooms on top of each cooled muffin to serve.

Creamy Cheddar Deviled Eggs

Ready in about: 20 minutes | **Serves:** 4 | **Per serving:** Kcal 177; Fat: 12.7g, Net Carbs: 4.6g, Protein: 11.4g

INGREDIENTS

8 eggs
¼ cup mayonnaise
1 tbsp tomato paste

2 tbsp celery, chopped
2 tbsp carrot, chopped
2 tbsp chives, minced

2 tbsp cheddar cheese, grated
Salt and black pepper to taste

DIRECTIONS

Place the eggs in a pot and fill with water by about 1 inch. Bring the eggs to a boil over high heat, then reduce the heat to medium and simmer for 10 minutes.

Remove and rinse under running water until cooled. Peel and discard the shell. Slice each egg in half lengthwise and get rid of the yolks. Mix the yolks with the rest of the ingredients. Split the mixture amongst the egg whites and set deviled eggs on a plate to serve.

Homemade Spanish Salsa Aioli

Ready in about: 10 minutes | **Serves:** 6 | **Per serving:** Kcal 116; Fat: 13.2g, Net Carbs: 0.2g, Protein: 0.4g

INGREDIENTS

1 tbsp lemon juice
1 egg yolk, at room temperature

2 garlic cloves, crushed
Salt and black pepper to taste

½ cup olive oil
¼ cup fresh parsley, chopped

DIRECTIONS

In a blender, place the egg yolk, salt, lemon juice, and garlic and pulse to get a smooth and creamy mixture. Set blender to slow speed. Slowly sprinkle in olive oil and combine to ensure the oil incorporates well. Stir in parsley and black pepper. Refrigerate the mixture until ready.

Cajun Crabmeat Frittata

Ready in about: 25 minutes | **Serves**: 4 | **Per serving**: Kcal 265; Fat: 15.8g, Net Carbs: 7.1g, Protein: 22.9g

INGREDIENTS

2 tbsp olive oil
1 shallot, chopped

4 oz crabmeat, chopped
1 tsp cajun seasoning

6 large eggs, slightly beaten
½ cup Greek yogurt

DIRECTIONS

Preheat oven to 350°F. Set a large skillet over medium heat and warm the oil. Add in shallot and sauté until soft, about 3 minutes. Stir in crabmeat and cook for 2 more minutes. Season with cajun seasoning.

Whisk the eggs with yogurt. Transfer to the skillet. Set the skillet in the oven and bake for about 18 minutes or until eggs are cooked through. Slice into wedges and serve warm.

Prosciutto & Cheese Egg Cups

Ready in about: 30 minutes | **Serves**: 4 | **Per serving**: Kcal 294, Fat: 21.4g, Net Carbs: 3.5g, Protein: 21g

INGREDIENTS

4 slices prosciutto
4 eggs

2 green onions, chopped
½ cup cheddar cheese, shredded

¼ tsp garlic powder
Salt and black pepper to taste

DIRECTIONS

Preheat oven to 390°F. Line the prosciutto slices on greased ramekins. In a bowl, combine the remaining ingredients. Split the egg mixture among the cups. Bake for 20 minutes. Leave to cool before serving.

Chili Chicken Breasts Wrapped in Bacon

Ready in about: 35 minutes | **Serves**: 6 | **Per serving**: Kcal 275, Fat: 9.5g, Net Carbs: 1.3g, Protein: 44.5g

INGREDIENTS

6 chicken breasts, flatten
2 tbsp fresh parsley, chopped
3 garlic cloves, chopped

1 chili pepper, chopped
1 tsp tarragon
Salt and black pepper to taste

1 tsp hot paprika
6 slices bacon

DIRECTIONS

Preheat oven to 390°F. Mix garlic, tarragon, hot paprika, salt, chili pepper, and black pepper in a bowl and rub onto the chicken. Roll the fillets in the bacon slices. Arrange on a greased and bake for 30 minutes. Plate the chicken and serve sprinkled with fresh parsley.

Three-Cheese Fondue with Walnuts & Parsley

Ready in about: 15 minutes | **Serves**: 10 | **Per serving**: Kcal 148; Fat: 10.2g, Net Carbs: 1.5g, Protein: 9.3g

INGREDIENTS

½ lb brie cheese, chopped
⅓ lb Swiss cheese, shredded
½ cup Emmental cheese, grated

1 tbsp xanthan gum
½ tsp onion powder
¾ cup white wine

½ tbsp lemon juice
Black pepper to taste
1 cup walnuts, chopped

DIRECTIONS

In a skillet, thoroughly mix onion powder, brie, Emmental, Swiss cheese, and xanthan gum. Pour in lemon juice and wine and sprinkle with black pepper. Set the skillet under the broiler for 6-7 minutes until the cheese browns. Garnish with walnuts. Serve.

Garlick & Cheese Turkey Slices

Ready in about: 20 minutes | **Serves**: 4 | **Per serving**: Kcal 416; Fat: 26g, Net Carbs: 3.2g, Protein: 40.7g

INGREDIENTS

2 tbsp olive oil
1 lb turkey breasts, sliced
2 garlic cloves, minced

½ cup heavy cream
⅓ cup chicken broth
1 tbsp tomato paste

1 cup cheddar cheese, shredded

DIRECTIONS

Set a pan over medium heat and warm the oil. Add in turkey and fry for 6-8 minutes, stirring often; set aside. Stir the garlic in the pan for 30 seconds. Pour in broth, tomato paste, and heavy cream.

Cook until thickened, about 2-3 minutes. Return the turkey to the pan and spread shredded cheddar cheese over. Let sit for 5 minutes covered or until the cheese melts. Serve instantly.

Pureed Broccoli with Roquefort Cheese

Ready in about: 15 minutes | **Serves**: 4 | **Per serving**: Kcal 294, Fat: 24.7g, Net Carbs: 4.3g, Protein: 9.2g

INGREDIENTS

1 ½ lb broccoli, broken into florets
2 tbsp butter

1 garlic clove, minced
1 cup almond milk

½ cup Roquefort cheese, crumbled
2 tbsp almond flour

DIRECTIONS

Warm the butter in a saucepan over low heat and stir in the almond flour for 2 minutes. Remove from the heat. Using a whisk, slowly stir in the almond milk. Return to the heat and bring to a simmer. Add in the cheese and cook for 1-2 minutes until the cheese melts. Set aside covered.

Place salted water in a deep pan over medium heat. Add in broccoli and boil for 8 minutes. Drain and remove to a food processor. Add in the cheese mixture and blend until smooth and creamy. Serve.

Mini Egg Muffins

Ready in about: 40 minutes | **Serves**: 6 | **Per serving**: Kcal 261; Fat: 16g, Net Carbs: 7.6g, Protein: 21.1g

INGREDIENTS

2 tbsp olive oil
1 onion, chopped
1 bell pepper, chopped

6 slices bacon, chopped
6 eggs, whisked
1 cup gruyere cheese, shredded

Salt and black pepper to taste
¼ tsp rosemary
1 tbsp fresh parsley, chopped

DIRECTIONS

Preheat oven to 390°F. Place cupcake liners to your muffin pan. In a skillet over medium heat, warm the olive oil and sauté the onion and bell pepper for 4-5 minutes as you stir constantly until tender.

Stir in bacon and cook for 3 more minutes. Add in the rest of the ingredients and mix well. Set the mixture to the lined muffin pan and bake for 23 minutes. Let muffins cool before serving.

Cheesy Bites with Turnip Chips

Ready in about: 25 minutes | **Serves**: 4 | **Per serving**: Kcal 177; Fat: 12.9g, Net Carbs: 6.8g, Protein: 8.8g,

INGREDIENTS

1 cup Monterey Jack cheese, grated
½ cup natural yogurt
1 cup Pecorino cheese, grated

2 tbsp tomato puree
½ tsp dried rosemary
½ tsp dried thyme

Salt and black pepper to taste
1 lb turnips, sliced
2 tbsp olive oil

DIRECTIONS

In a mixing bowl, mix cheese, tomato puree, black pepper, salt, rosemary, yogurt, and thyme. Place in foil liners-candy cups and refrigerate until ready to serve.

Preheat oven to 430°F. Coat turnips with salt, black pepper, and oil. Arrange in a single layer on a cookie sheet. Bake for 20 minutes, shaking once or twice. Dip turnip chips in cheese cups.

Herbed Keto Bread

Ready in about: 40 minutes | **Serves**: 6 | **Per serving**: Kcal 115, Fat: 10.2g, Net Carbs: 1g, Protein: 3.9g

INGREDIENTS

5 eggs
½ tsp tartar cream
2 cups almond flour

3 tablespoons butter, melted
3 tsp baking powder
1 tsp salt

½ tsp dried oregano
1 tbsp sunflower seeds
2 tbsp sesame seeds

DIRECTIONS

Preheat oven to 360°F. Combine the eggs with cream of tartar until the formation of stiff peaks happens. In a food processor, place in the baking powder, flour, salt, and butter and blitz to incorporate fully.

Stir in the egg mixture. Scoop the batter into a greased loaf pan. Spread the loaf with sesame seeds, sunflower seeds, and oregano and bake for 35 minutes. Serve with butter.

Juicy Beef Cheeseburgers

Ready in about: 20 minutes | **Serves**: 6 | **Per serving**: Kcal 252; Fat: 15.5g, Net Carbs: 1.2g, Protein: 26g

INGREDIENTS

1 lb ground beef
½ cup green onions, chopped
2 garlic cloves, finely chopped

Salt and black pepper to taste
¼ tsp cayenne pepper,
2 oz mascarpone cheese

3 oz Pecorino Romano cheese, grated
2 tbsp olive oil

DIRECTIONS

In a mixing bowl, mix ground beef, garlic, cayenne pepper, black pepper, green onions, and salt. Shape into 6 balls; then flatten to make burgers. In a separate bowl, mix mascarpone cheese with grated Pecorino Romano cheeses. Split the cheese mixture among prepared patties.

Wrap the meat mixture around the cheese mixture to ensure that the filling is sealed inside. Warm oil in a skillet over medium heat. Cook the burgers for 5 minutes each side. Serve.

Zucchini with Blue Cheese & Walnuts

Ready in about: 15 minutes | **Serves**: 4 | **Per serving**: Kcal 489; Fat: 47.4g, Net Carbs: 6.9g, Protein: 12.7g

INGREDIENTS

2 tbsp olive oil
2 lb zucchinis, sliced
1 ⅓ cups heavy cream

1 cup sour cream
4 oz blue cheese, crumbled
1 tsp Italian seasoning

¼ cup walnut halves
Salt and black pepper to taste

DIRECTIONS

Set a grill pan over medium heat. Season zucchinis with Italian seasoning, salt, and black pepper and drizzle with olive oil. Grill the zucchini until lightly charred. Remove to a serving platter.

In a dry pan over medium heat, toast the walnuts for 2-3 minutes and set aside. Add the heavy cream, blue cheese, and sour cream to the pan and mix until everything is well combined. Let cool for a few minutes and scatter over the grilled zucchini. Top with walnuts and serve.

DESSERTS & DRINKS

Chocolate Marshmallows

Ready in about: 30 minutes | **Serves**: 4 | **Per serving**: Kcal 55, Fat 2.2g, Net Carbs 5.1g, Protein 0.5g

INGREDIENTS

2 tbsp unsweetened cocoa powder
½ tsp vanilla extract

½ cup swerve sugar
1 tbsp xanthan gum

A pinch Salt
2 ½ tsp gelatin powder

Dusting

1 tbsp unsweetened cocoa powder

1 tbsp swerve confectioner's sugar

DIRECTIONS

Line the loaf pan with parchment paper and grease with cooking spray. Mix the xanthan gum with 1 tbsp water and pour it in a saucepan. Stir in the swerve sugar, 2 tbsp of water, and salt. Place the pan over medium heat and bring the mixture to a boil. Reduce the heat and simmer for 7 minutes.

In a small bowl, add 2 tbsp of water and sprinkle the gelatin on top. Let sit there without stirring to dissolve for 5 minutes. While the gelatin dissolves, pour the remaining water in a small bowl and heat in the microwave for 30 seconds. Stir in cocoa powder and mix it into the gelatin.

When the sugar solution has hit the right temperature, gradually pour it directly into the gelatin mixture while continuously whisking. Beat for 10 minutes to get a light and fluffy consistency.

Next, stir in the vanilla and pour the blend into the loaf pan. Let the marshmallows set for 3 hours and then use an oiled knife to cut it into cubes; place them on a plate. Mix the remaining cocoa powder and confectioner's sugar together. Sift it over the marshmallows.

Raspberry Nut Truffles

Ready in about: 6 minutes + cooling time | **Serves**: 4 | **Per serving**: Kcal 251, Fat 18.3g, Net Carbs 3.5g, Protein 12g

INGREDIENTS

1 ½ cups sugar-free raspberry preserves
2 cups raw cashews
2 tbsp flax seed

3 tbsp swerve
10 oz unsweetened chocolate chips

3 tbsp olive oil

DIRECTIONS

Line a baking sheet with parchment paper. Grind the cashews and flax seeds in a blender for 45 seconds until smoothly crushed. Add the raspberry and 2 tbsp of swerve. Process for 1 minute until well combined. Form 1-inch balls of the mixture, place on the baking sheet, and freeze for 1 hour or until firmed up.

Melt the chocolate chips, oil, and 1tbsp of swerve in a microwave for 1 ½ minutes. Toss the truffles to coat in the chocolate mixture, put on the baking sheet, and freeze further for at least 2 hours. Serve.

Lemon Cheesecake Mousse

Ready in about: 5 minutes + cooling time | **Serves**: 4 | **Per serving**: Kcal 223, Fat 18g, Net Carbs 3g, Protein 12g

INGREDIENTS

24 oz cream cheese, softened
2 cups swerve confectioner's sugar

2 lemons, juiced and zested
¼ tsp salt

1 ¼ cups whipped cream

DIRECTIONS

Whip the cream cheese in a bowl with a hand mixer until light and fluffy. Mix in the swerve sugar, lemon juice, and salt. Fold in 1 cup of the whipped cream to evenly combine.

Spoon the mousse into serving cups and refrigerate to thicken for 1 hour. Swirl with the remaining whipped cream and garnish lightly with lemon zest. Let sit in the fridge before serving.

Dark Chocolate Mousse with Stewed Plums

Ready in about: 45 minutes + cooling time | **Serves:** 6 | **Per serving:** Kcal 288, Fat 23g, Net Carbs 6.9g, Protein 9.5g

INGREDIENTS

8 eggs, separated into yolks and whites
12 oz unsweetened chocolate
2 tbsp salt

¾ cup swerve sugar
½ cup olive oil

3 tbsp brewed coffee

Stewed plums

6 plums, pitted and halved
½ stick cinnamon

½ cup swerve sugar
½ cup water

½ lemon, juiced

DIRECTIONS

Melt the chocolate in the microwave for 1 ½ minutes. In a separate bowl, whisk the yolks with half of the swerve until a pale yellow has formed, then beat in salt, olive oil, and coffee. Mix in the melted chocolate until smooth. In a third bowl, whisk the whites with a hand mixer until a soft peak has formed.

Sprinkle the remaining swerve over and gently fold in with a spatula. Fetch a tablespoon full of the chocolate mixture and fold in to combine. Pour in the remaining chocolate mixture and whisk to mix. Pour the mousse into 6 ramekins, cover with plastic wrap, and refrigerate overnight.

The next morning, pour water, swerve sugar, cinnamon, and lemon juice in a saucepan and bring to a simmer for 3 minutes, occasionally stirring to ensure the swerve has dissolved and a syrup has formed.

Add the plums and poach in the sweetened water for 18 minutes until soft. Turn the heat off and discard the cinnamon stick. Spoon a plum with syrup on each mousse ramekin and serve.

Coconut Cheesecake

Ready in about: 30 minutes + freezing time | **Serves:** 12 | **Per serving:** Kcal 256, Fat: 25g, Net Carbs: 3g, Protein: 5g

INGREDIENTS

Crust

2 egg whites
¼ cup erythritol

3 cups desiccated coconut
1 tsp coconut oil

¼ cup melted butter

Filling

3 tbsp lemon juice
6 oz raspberries

2 cups erythritol
1 cup whipped cream

Zest of 1 lemon
24 oz cream cheese

DIRECTIONS

Grease the bottom and sides of a cake pan with coconut oil. Line with parchment paper. Preheat oven to 350°F and mix all crust ingredients. Pour the crust into the pan. Bake for about 25 minutes; let cool.

Meanwhile, beat the cream cheese with an electric mixer until soft. Add the lemon juice, zest, and erythritol. Fold the whipped cream into the cheese cream mixture. Fold in the raspberries gently. Spoon the filling into the baked and cooled crust. Place in the fridge for 4 hours.

Vanilla Ice Cream

Ready in about: 5 minutes + cooling time | **Serves:** 4 | **Per serving:** Kcal 290, Fat 23g, Net Carbs 6g, Protein 13g

INGREDIENTS

½ cup smooth peanut butter
½ cup swerve sugar

3 cups half and half
1 tsp vanilla extract

1 pinch of salt

DIRECTIONS

Beat peanut butter and swerve in a bowl with a hand mixer until smooth. Gradually whisk in half and half until thoroughly combined. Mix in vanilla and salt. Pour mixture into a loaf pan and freeze for 45 minutes until firmed up. Scoop into glasses when ready to eat and serve.

Passion Fruit Cheesecake Slices

Ready in about: 15 minutes + cooling time | **Serves**: 6 | **Per serving**: Kcal 287, Fat 18g, Net Carbs 6.1g, Protein 4.4g

INGREDIENTS

1 cup crushed almond biscuits

½ cup melted butter

Filling

1 ½ cups cream cheese

¾ cup swerve sugar

1 ½ whipping cream

1 tsp vanilla bean paste

4-6 tbsp cold water

1 tbsp gelatin powder

Passionfruit jelly

1 cup passion fruit pulp

¼ cup swerve confectioner's sugar

1 tsp gelatin powder

¼ cup water, room temperature

DIRECTIONS

Mix the crushed biscuits and butter in a bowl, spoon into a spring-form pan, and use the back of the spoon to level at the bottom. Set aside in the fridge. Put the cream cheese, swerve sugar, and vanilla paste into a bowl, and use the hand mixer to whisk until smooth; set aside.

In a bowl, add 2 tbsp of cold water and sprinkle 1 tbsp of gelatin powder. Let dissolve for 5 minutes. Pour the gelatin liquid along with the whipping cream in the cheese mixture and fold gently. Remove the spring-form pan from the refrigerator and pour over the mixture. Return to the fridge.

For the passionfruit jelly: add 2 tbsp of cold water and sprinkle 1 tsp of gelatin powder. Let dissolve for 5 minutes. Pour confectioner's sugar and ¼ cup of water into it. Mix and stir in passion fruit pulp.

Remove the cake again and pour the jelly over it. Swirl the pan to make the jelly level up. Place the pan back into the fridge to cool for 2 hours. When completely set, remove, and unlock the spring-pan. Lift the pan from the cake and slice the dessert.

Berry Tart

Ready in about: 45 minutes | **Serves**: 4 | **Per serving**: Kcal 305, Fat: 26.5g, Net Carbs: 4.9g, Protein: 15g

INGREDIENTS

4 eggs

2 tsp coconut oil

2 cups berries

1 cup coconut milk

1 cup almond flour

¼ cup sweetener

½ tsp vanilla powder

1 tbsp powdered sweetener

A pinch of salt

DIRECTIONS

Preheat oven to 350°F. Place all ingredients except coconut oil, berries, and powdered sweetener, in a blender; blend until smooth. Gently fold in the berries. Grease a baking dish with the oil. Pour the mixture into the prepared pan and bake for 35 minutes. Sprinkle with powdered sugar to serve.

Green Tea Brownies with Macadamia Nuts

Ready in about: 28 minutes | **Serves**: 4 | **Per serving**: Kcal 248, Fat 23.1g, Net Carbs 2.2g, Protein 5.2g

INGREDIENTS

1 tbsp green tea powder

¼ cup unsalted butter, melted

4 tbsp swerve confectioner's sugar

A pinch of salt

¼ cup coconut flour

½ tsp baking powder

1 egg

¼ cup chopped macadamia nuts

DIRECTIONS

Preheat oven to 350°F and line a square baking dish with parchment paper. Pour the melted butter into a bowl, add sugar and salt, and whisk to combine. Crack the egg into the bowl.

Beat the mixture until the egg has incorporated. Pour coconut flour, green tea, and baking powder into a fine-mesh sieve, sift into the egg bowl, and stir. Add the nuts, stir again, and pour the mixture into the lined baking dish. Bake for 18 minutes, remove and slice into brownie cubes.

Vanilla Flan with Mint

Ready in about: 60 minutes + cooling time | **Serves:** 4 | **Per serving:** Kcal 269, Fat: 26g, Net Carbs: 1.7g, Protein: 7.6g

INGREDIENTS

⅓ cup erythritol, for caramel
2 cups almond milk
4 eggs

1 tbsp vanilla extract
1 tbsp lemon zest
½ cup erythritol, for custard

2 cup heavy whipping cream
Mint leaves, to serve

DIRECTIONS

Heat erythritol for the caramel in a deep pan. Add 2-3 tablespoons of water, and bring to a boil. Reduce the heat and cook until the caramel turns golden brown. Divide between 4-6 metal tins. Set aside to cool.

In a bowl, mix eggs, remaining erythritol, lemon zest, and vanilla. Add almond milk and beat until well combined. Pour the custard into each caramel-lined ramekin and place it in a deep baking tin.

Fill over the way with the remaining hot water. Bake at 345°F for 45-50 minutes. Take out the ramekins and let cool for at least 4 hours in the fridge. Run a knife slowly around the edges to invert onto a dish. Serve with dollops of whipped cream, scattered with mint leaves.

Granny Smith Apple Tart

Ready in about: 65 minutes | **Serves:** 6 | **Per serving:** Kcal 302, Fat: 26g, Net Carbs: 6.7g, Protein: 7g

INGREDIENTS

6 tbsp butter
2 cups almond flour

Filling

2 cups sliced Granny Smith
¼ cup butter

Topping

¼ tsp cinnamon

1 tsp cinnamon
⅓ cup sweetener

¼ cup sweetener
½ tsp cinnamon

2 tbsp sweetener

½ tsp lemon juice

DIRECTIONS

Preheat oven to 370°F and combine all crust ingredients in a bowl. Press this mixture into the bottom of a greased pan. Bake for 5 minutes. Remove and let it cool slightly.

Combine the apples and lemon juice in a bowl and arrange them on top of the cooled crust. Combine the rest of the filling ingredients and brush the mixture over the apples. Bake for about 30 minutes.

Press the apples down with a spatula, return to oven, and bake for 20 more minutes. Combine the cinnamon and sweetener in a bowl and sprinkle over the tart.

Note: *Granny Smith apples have just 9.5g of net carbs per 100g. Still high for you? Substitute with Chayote squash, which has the same texture and rich nutrients, and just around 4g of net carbs.*

Blueberry Tart with Lavender

Ready in about: 35 minutes + cooling time | **Serves:** 6 | **Per serving:** Kcal 198, Fat 16.4g, Net Carbs 10.7g, Protein 3.3g

INGREDIENTS

1 large low carb pie crust
1 ½ cups heavy cream

2 tbsp swerve sugar
1 tbsp culinary lavender

1 tsp vanilla extract
2 cups fresh blueberries

DIRECTIONS

Preheat oven to 400°F. Place the pie crust with its pan on a baking tray and bake in the oven for 30 minutes, until golden brown; remove and let cool. Mix the heavy cream and lavender in a saucepan. Set the pan over medium heat and bring the mixture to a boil. Turn the heat off and let cool.

Strain the cream through a colander into a bowl to remove the lavender pieces. Mix swerve and vanilla into the cream and pour into the cooled crust. Scatter with the blueberries. Refrigerate the pie. Serve.

Chocolate Cakes

Ready in about: 25 minutes | **Serves**: 6 | **Per serving**: Kcal 218, Fat: 20g, Net Carbs: 10g, Protein: 4.8g

INGREDIENTS

½ cup almond flour
¼ cup xylitol
1 tsp baking powder
½ tsp baking soda

1 tsp cinnamon, ground
A pinch of salt
A pinch of ground cloves
½ cup butter, melted

½ cup buttermilk
1 egg
1 tsp pure almond extract

For the Frosting:

1 cup heavy cream

1 cup dark chocolate, flaked

DIRECTIONS

Preheat oven to 360°F. In a bowl, mix the cloves, almond flour, baking powder, salt, baking soda, xylitol, and cinnamon. In a separate bowl, combine the almond extract, butter, egg, and buttermilk. Mix the wet mixture into the dry mix. Evenly spoon the batter into a greased donut pan. Bake for 17 minutes.

Set a pan over medium heat and warm heavy cream; simmer for 2 minutes. Fold in the chocolate flakes; combine until all the chocolate melts; let cool. Spread the top of the cakes with the frosting.

Ice Cream Bars Covered with Chocolate

Ready in about: 20 minutes + freezing time | **Serves**: 15 | **Per serving**: Kcal 345 Fat: 32g, Net Carbs: 5g, Protein: 4g

INGREDIENTS

Ice cream

1 cup heavy whipping cream
1 tsp vanilla extract
¾ tsp xanthan gum

½ cup peanut butter
1 cup half and half
1 ½ cups almond milk

⅓ tsp stevia powder
1 tbsp vegetable glycerin
3 tbsp xylitol

Chocolate

¾ cup coconut oil
¼ cup cocoa butter pieces, chopped

2 oz unsweetened chocolate
3 ½ tsp THM super sweet blend

DIRECTIONS

Blend all ice cream ingredients until smooth. Place in an ice cream maker and follow the instructions. Spread the ice cream into a lined pan, and freezer for about 4 hours.

Combine all chocolate ingredients in a microwave-safe bowl and heat until melted. Allow cooling. Remove the ice cream from the freezer and slice into bars. Dip them into the cooled chocolate mixture and return to the freezer for about 10 minutes before serving.

Eggless Strawberry Mousse

Ready in about: 10 minutes + cooling time | **Serves**: 6 | **Per serving**: Kcal 290, Fat 24g, Net Carbs 5g, Protein 5g

INGREDIENTS

2 tbsp sugar-free strawberry preserves
2 cups chilled heavy cream
2 cups fresh strawberries, hulled

5 tbsp erythritol
2 tbsp lemon juice

¼ tsp strawberry extract

DIRECTIONS

Beat the heavy cream in a bowl with a hand mixer at high speed until a stiff peak forms, about 1 minute. Refrigerate. Puree the strawberries in a blender and pour into a saucepan. Add erythritol and lemon juice, and cook on low heat for 3 minutes while stirring continuously.

Stir in the strawberry extract evenly, turn off the heat and allow cooling. Fold in the whipped cream until evenly incorporated, and spoon into six ramekins. Refrigerate for 4 hours to solidify. Garnish with strawberry preserves and serve immediately.

Chocolate Chip Cookies

Ready in about: 20 minutes | **Serves**: 4 | **Per serving**: Kcal 317, Fat 27q, Net Carbs 8.9g, Protein 6.3g

INGREDIENTS

1 cup butter, softened
2 cups swerve brown sugar

3 eggs
2 cups almond flour

2 cups unsweetened chocolate chips

DIRECTIONS

Preheat oven to 350°F. Line a baking sheet with parchment paper. Whisk the butter and sugar with a hand mixer for 3 minutes or until light and fluffy. Add the eggs one at a time, and scrape the sides as you whisk. Mix in almond flour at low speed until well combined. Fold in the chocolate chips.

Scoop 3 tablespoons each on the baking sheet, creating spaces between each mound, and bake for 15 minutes to swell and harden. Remove, cool, and serve.

Coconut Bars

Ready in about: 40 minutes + freezing time | **Serves**: 4 | **Per serving**: Kcal 215, Fat: 22g, Net Carbs: 1.4g, Protein: 2g

INGREDIENTS

3 ½ oz ghee
10 saffron threads

1 ⅓ cups coconut milk
1 ¾ cups shredded coconut

4 tbsp sweetener
1 tsp cardamom powder

DIRECTIONS

Combine the shredded coconut with 1 cup of the coconut milk. In another bowl, mix together the remaining coconut milk with the sweetener and saffron. Let sit for 30 minutes.

Heat the ghee in a wok. Add the coconut mixtures and cook for 5 minutes on low heat, mixing continuously. Stir in the cardamom and cook for another 5 minutes. Spread the mixture onto a small container and freeze for 2 hours. Cut into bars and enjoy!

Chia & Blackberry Pudding

Ready in about: 10 minutes + chilling time | **Serves**: 2 | **Per serving**: Kcal 169, Fat: 10g, Net Carbs: 4.7g, Protein: 7.5g

INGREDIENTS

1 cup full-fat natural yogurt
2 tsp swerve sugar

2 tbsp chia seeds
1 cup fresh blackberries

1 tbsp lemon zest
Mint leaves, to serve

DIRECTIONS

In a bowl, mix the yogurt and swerve sugar. Stir in the chia seeds. Reserve 4 blackberries for garnish. Mash the remaining ones with a fork. Stir in the yogurt mixture. Put in the fridge for 30 minutes. Divide the mixture between 2 glasses. Top each with a couple of blackberries, mint, and lemon zest. Serve.

Strawberry & Basil Lemonade

Ready in about: 3 minutes | **Serves**: 4 | **Per serving**: Kcal 66, Fat 0.1g, Net Carbs 5.8g, Protein 0.7g

INGREDIENTS

4 cups water
12 strawberries, leaves removed
1 cup fresh lemon juice

⅓ cup fresh basil
¾ cup swerve sugar
Crushed Ice

Halved strawberries to garnish
Basil leaves to garnish

DIRECTIONS

Spoon some crushed ice into 4 serving glasses and set aside. In a pitcher, add the water, strawberries, lemon juice, basil, and swerve. Insert the blender and process the ingredients for 30 seconds.

The mixture should be pink, and the basil finely chopped. Adjust the taste. Drop 2 strawberry halves and some basil in each glass and serve immediately.

Lychee and Coconut Lassi

Ready in about: 30 minutes + cooling time | **Serves**: 4 | **Per serving**: Kcal 285, Fat 26.1g, Net Carbs 1.5g, Protein 5.3g

INGREDIENTS

2 cups lychee pulp, seeded
2 ½ cups coconut milk
4 tsp swerve sugar

2 limes, zested and juiced
1 ½ cups plain yogurt
1 lemongrass, white part only, torn

2 tbsp toasted coconut shavings
A pinch of salt

DIRECTIONS

In a saucepan, add the lychee pulp, coconut milk, swerve sugar, lemongrass, and lime zest. Stir and bring to boil on medium heat for 2 minutes, stirring continually. Then reduce the heat, and simmer for 1 minute. Turn the heat off and let the mixture sit for 15 minutes.

Remove the lemongrass, and pour the mixture into a smoothie maker or a blender, add the yogurt, salt, and lime juice and process the ingredients until smooth, about 60 seconds. Pour into a jug and refrigerate for 2 hours until cold; stir. Serve garnished with coconut shavings.

Strawberry Vanilla Shake

Ready in about: 2 minutes | **Serves**: 4 | **Per serving**: Kcal 285, Fat 22.6g, Net Carbs 3.1g, Protein 16g

INGREDIENTS

2 cups strawberries, stemmed and halved
12 strawberries to garnish
½ cup unsweetened almond milk

2/3 tsp vanilla extract
½ cup heavy whipping cream

2 tbsp swerve sugar

DIRECTIONS

Process the strawberries, milk, vanilla extract, whipping cream, and swerve in a large blender for 2 minutes; work in two batches if needed. The shake should be frosty. Pour into glasses, stick in straws, garnish with strawberry halves, and serve.

Vanilla Chocolate Mousse

Ready in about: 30 minutes | **Serves**: 4 | **Per serving**: Kcal 370, Fat: 25g, Net Carbs: 3.7g, Protein: 7.6g

INGREDIENTS

3 eggs
1 cup dark chocolate chips

1 cup heavy cream
1 cup fresh strawberries, sliced

1 vanilla extract
1 tbsp swerve sugar

DIRECTIONS

Melt the chocolate in a bowl, in your microwave for a minute on high, and let it cool for 10 minutes.

Meanwhile, in a medium-sized mixing bowl, whip the cream until very soft. Add the eggs, vanilla extract, and swerve; whisk to combine. Fold in the cooled chocolate. Divide the mousse between four glasses, top with the strawberry slices, and chill in the fridge for at least 30 minutes before serving.

Blueberry Ice Pops

Ready in about: 5 minutes + cooling time | **Serves**: 6 | **Per serving**: Kcal 48, Fat 1.2g, Net Carbs 7.9g, Protein 2.3g

INGREDIENTS

3 cups blueberries

½ tbsp lemon juice

¼ cup swerve sugar

DIRECTIONS

Pour the blueberries, lemon juice, swerve sugar, and ¼ cup water in a blender, and puree on high speed for 2 minutes until smooth. Strain through a sieve into a bowl, discard the solids.

Mix in more water if too thick. Divide the mixture into ice pop molds, insert stick cover, and freeze for 4 hours to 1 week. When ready to serve, dip in warm water and remove the pops.

Blackcurrant Iced Tea

Ready in about: 10 minutes | Serves: 4 | Per serving: Kcal 22, Fat 0g, Net Carbs 5g, Protein 0g

INGREDIENTS

½ cup sugar-free blackcurrant extract
6 unflavored tea bags
2 cups water

Swerve to taste
Ice cubes for serving

Lemon slices to garnish

DIRECTIONS

Pour the ice cubes in a pitcher and place it in the fridge. Bring the water to boil in a saucepan over medium heat for 3 minutes and turn the heat off. Stir in the sugar to dissolve and steep the tea bags in the water for 2 minutes. Remove the bags after and let the tea cool down.

Stir in the blackcurrant extract until well incorporated, remove the pitcher from the fridge, and pour the mixture over the ice cubes. Let sit for 3 minutes to cool and after, pour the mixture into tall glasses. Add some more ice cubes, place the lemon slices on the rim of the glasses, and serve the tea cold.

Mint Chocolate Protein Shake

Ready in about: 4 minutes | Serves: 4 | Per serving: Kcal 191, Fat 14.5g, Net Carbs 4g, Protein 15g

INGREDIENTS

3 cups flax milk, chilled
3 tsp unsweetened cocoa powder
1 avocado, pitted, peeled, sliced

1 cup coconut milk, chilled
3 mint leaves + extra to garnish
3 tbsp erythritol

1 tbsp low carb Protein powder
Whipping cream for topping

DIRECTIONS

Combine the milk, cocoa powder, avocado, coconut milk, mint leaves, erythritol, and protein powder into a blender, and blend for 1 minute until smooth. Pour into serving glasses, lightly add some whipping cream on top, and garnish with mint leaves.

Chocolate Cheesecake Bites

Ready in about: 4 minutes + cooling time | Serves: 12 | Per serving: Kcal 241, Fat 22g, Net Carbs 3.1g, Protein 5g

INGREDIENTS

10 oz unsweetened dark chocolate chips
½ half and half

20 oz cream cheese, softened

1 tsp vanilla extract

DIRECTIONS

In a saucepan, melt the chocolate with half and a half on low heat for 1 minute. Turn the heat off. In a bowl, whisk the cream cheese, swerve sugar, and vanilla extract with a hand mixer until smooth. Stir into the chocolate mixture. Spoon into silicone muffin tins and freeze for 4 hours until firm.

Cinnamon and Turmeric Latte

Ready in about: 7 minutes | Serves: 4 | Per serving: Kcal 132, Fat 12g, Net Carbs 0.3g, Protein 3.9g

INGREDIENTS

3 cups almond milk
⅓ tsp cinnamon powder

1 cup brewed coffee
½ tsp turmeric powder

1 ½ tsp erythritol
Cinnamon sticks to garnish

DIRECTIONS

In the blender, add the almond milk, cinnamon powder, coffee, turmeric, and erythritol. Blend the ingredients at medium speed for 45 seconds and pour the mixture into a saucepan.

Set the pan over low heat and heat through for 5 minutes; do not boil. Keep swirling the pan to prevent boiling. Turn the heat off, and serve in latte cups, with a cinnamon stick in each one.

Cranberry Chocolate Barks

Ready in about: 5 minutes + cooling time | **Serves**: 6 | **Per serving**: Kcal 225, Fat 21g, Net Carbs 3g, Protein 6g

INGREDIENTS

10 oz unsweetened dark chocolate, chopped
½ cup erythritol
⅓ cup dried cranberries, chopped

⅓ cup toasted walnuts, chopped
¼ tsp dark run

¼ tsp salt

DIRECTIONS

Line a baking sheet with parchment paper. Pour chocolate and erythritol in a bowl, and melt in the microwave for 25 seconds, stirring three times until fully melted. Stir in the cranberries, dark rum, walnuts, and salt, reserving a few cranberries and walnuts for garnishing.

Pour the mixture on the baking sheet and spread out. Sprinkle with remaining cranberries and walnuts. Refrigerate for 2 hours to set. Break into bite-size pieces to serve.

Almond Butter Fat Bombs

Ready in about: 3 minutes + cooling time | **Serves**: 4 | **Per serving**: Kcal 193, Fat 18.3g, Net Carbs 2g, Protein 4g

INGREDIENTS

½ cup almond butter
½ cup coconut oil

4 tbsp unsweetened cocoa powder
½ cup erythritol

DIRECTIONS

Melt butter and coconut oil in the microwave for 45 seconds, stirring twice until properly melted and mixed. Mix in cocoa powder and erythritol until thoroughly combined. Pour into muffin molds and refrigerate for 3 hours to harden.

Almond Milk Hot Chocolate

Ready in about: 7 minutes | **Serves**: 4 | **Per serving**: Kcal 225, Fat 21.5g, Net Carbs 0.6g, Protein 4.5g

INGREDIENTS

3 cups almond milk
4 tbsp unsweetened cocoa powder

2 tbsp swerve sugar
3 tbsp almond butter

Finely chopped almonds to garnish

DIRECTIONS

In a saucepan, add the almond milk, cocoa powder, and swerve sugar. Stir the mixture until the sugar dissolves. Set the pan over low to heat through for 5 minutes, without boiling.

Swirl the mix occasionally. Turn the heat off and stir in the almond butter to be incorporated. Pour the hot chocolate into mugs and sprinkle with chopped almonds. Serve hot.

Raspberry Flax Seed Dessert

Ready in about: 5 minutes | **Serves**: 4 | **Per serving**: Kcal 390, Fat 33.5g, Net Carbs 3g, Protein 13g

INGREDIENTS

2 cups raspberries, reserve a few for topping
1 cup heavy cream
½ cup chia seeds

½ cup flaxseeds, ground
4 tsp liquid stevia

3 cups unsweetened vanilla almond milk
Chopped mixed nuts for topping

DIRECTIONS

In a medium bowl, crush the raspberries with a fork until pureed. Pour in the almond milk, heavy cream, chia seeds, and liquid stevia. Mix and refrigerate the pudding overnight. Spoon the pudding into serving glasses, top with raspberries, mixed nuts, and serve

Berry Merry

Ready in about: 6 minutes | **Serves**: 4 | **Per serving**: Kcal 83, Fat 3g, Net Carbs 8g, Protein 2.7g

INGREDIENTS

1 cup strawberries + extra for garnishing
1 ½ cups blackberries
1 cup blueberries

2 small beets, peeled and chopped
2/3 cup ice cubes

1 lime, juiced

DIRECTIONS

For the extra strawberries for garnishing, make a single deep cut on their sides; set aside. Add the blackberries, strawberries, blueberries, beet, and ice cubes into the smoothie maker.

Blend the ingredients at high speed until smooth and frothy, for about 60 seconds. Add the lime juice, and puree further for 30 seconds. Pour the drink into tall smoothie glasses, fix the reserved strawberries on each glass rim, stick a straw in, and serve the drink immediately.

Cinnamon Cookies

Ready in about: 25 minutes | **Serves**: 4 | **Per serving**: Kcal 134, Fat: 13g, Net Carbs: 1.5g, Protein: 3g

INGREDIENTS

Cookies

2 cups almond flour
½ tsp baking soda

¾ cup sweetener
½ cup butter, softened

A pinch of salt

Coating

2 tbsp erythritol sweetener

1 tsp cinnamon

DIRECTIONS

Preheat oven to 350°F. Combine all cookie ingredients in a bowl. Make 16 balls out of the mixture and flatten them with hands. Combine the cinnamon and erythritol. Dip the cookies in the cinnamon mixture and arrange them on a lined cookie sheet. Cook for 15 minutes, until crispy.

Coffee Fat Bombs

Ready in about: 3 minutes + cooling time | **Serves**: 6 | **Per serving**: Kcal 145, Fat 14g, Net Carbs 2g, Protein 4g

INGREDIENTS

6 tbsp brewed coffee, room temperature
1 ½ cups mascarpone cheese
½ cup melted butter

3 tbsp unsweetened cocoa powder
¼ cup erythritol

DIRECTIONS

Whisk the mascarpone cheese, butter, cocoa powder, erythritol, and coffee with a hand mixer until creamy and fluffy, about 1 minute. Fill into muffin tins and freeze for 3 hours until firm.

Mixed Berry & Mascarpone Bowl

Ready in about: 8 minutes | **Serves**: 4 | **Per serving**: Kcal 480, Fat 40g, Net Carbs 5g, Protein 20g

INGREDIENTS

4 cups Greek yogurt
Liquid stevia to taste

1 ½ cups mascarpone cheese
1 ½ cups blueberries and raspberries

1 cup toasted pecans

DIRECTIONS

Mix the yogurt, stevia, and mascarpone in a bowl until evenly combined. Divide the mixture into 4 bowls, share the berries and pecans on top of the cream. Serve the dessert immediately.

Vanilla Bean Frappuccino

Ready in about: 6 minutes | **Serves**: 4 | **Per serving**: Kcal 193, Fat 14g, Net Carbs 6g, Protein 15g

INGREDIENTS

3 cups unsweetened vanilla almond milk, chilled
2 tsp swerve sugar
1 ½ cups heavy cream, cold

1 vanilla bean
¼ tsp xanthan gum

Unsweetened chocolate shavings to garnish

DIRECTIONS

Combine the almond milk, swerve, heavy cream, vanilla bean, and xanthan gum in the blender and process on high speed for 1 minute until smooth. Pour into tall shake glasses, sprinkle with chocolate shavings, and serve immediately.

Mixed Berry Trifle

Ready in about: 3 minutes + cooling time | **Serves**: 4 | **Per serving**: Kcal 321, Fat 28.5g, Net Carbs 8.3g, Protein 9.8g

INGREDIENTS

½ cup walnuts, toasted
1 avocado, chopped

1 cup mascarpone cheese, softened
1 cup fresh blueberries

1 cup fresh raspberries
1 cup fresh blackberries

DIRECTIONS

In four dessert glasses, share half of the mascarpone, half of the berries (mixed), half of the walnuts, and half of the avocado, and repeat the layering process for a second time to finish the ingredients. Cover the glasses with plastic wrap and refrigerate for 45 minutes until quite firm.

Walnut Cookies

Ready in about: 15 minutes | **Serves**: 12 | **Per serving**: Kcal 101, Fat: 11g, Net Carbs: 0.6g, Protein: 1.6g

INGREDIENTS

1 egg
2 cups ground pecans

¼ cup sweetener
½ tsp baking soda

1 tbsp butter
20 walnuts halves

DIRECTIONS

Preheat oven to 350°F. Mix the ingredients, except the walnuts, until combined. Make 20 balls out of the mixture and press them with your thumb onto a lined cookie sheet. Top each cookie with a walnut half. Bake for about 12 minutes.

Chocolate Bark with Almonds

Ready in about: 5 minutes + cooling time | **Serves**: 12 | **Per serving**: Kcal 161, Fat: 15.3g, Net Carbs: 1.9g, Protein: 1.9g

INGREDIENTS

½ cup toasted almonds, chopped
½ cup butter

10 drops stevia
¼ tsp salt

½ cup unsweetened coconut flakes
4 oz dark chocolate

DIRECTIONS

Melt together the butter and chocolate, in the microwave, for 90 seconds. Remove and stir in stevia. Line a cookie sheet with waxed paper and spread the chocolate evenly. Scatter the almonds on top, coconut flakes, and sprinkle with salt. Refrigerate for one hour.

Raspberry Sorbet

Ready in about: 10 minutes + cooling time | **Serves**: 1 | **Per serving**: Kcal 173, Fat: 10g, Net Carbs: 3.7g, Protein: 4g

INGREDIENTS

¼ tsp vanilla extract
1 packet gelatine, without sugar

1 tbsp heavy whipping cream
⅓ cup boiling water

2 tbsp mashed raspberries
1 ½ cups crushed Ice

DIRECTIONS

Combine the gelatin and boiling water until completely dissolved. Transfer to a blender. Add the remaining ingredients and ⅓ cup of cold water. Blend until smooth and freeze for at least 2 hours.

Creamy Coconut Kiwi Drink

Ready in about: 3 minutes | **Serves**: 4 | **Per serving**: Kcal 351, Fat 28g, Net Carbs 9.7g, Protein 16g

INGREDIENTS

5 kiwis, pulp scooped
2 tbsp erythritol

2 cups unsweetened coconut milk
2 cups coconut cream

7 ice cubes
Mint leaves to garnish

DIRECTIONS

In a blender, process the kiwis, erythritol, milk, cream, and ice cubes until smooth, about 3 minutes. Pour into four serving glasses, garnish with mint leaves, and serve.

Coconut Fat Bombs

Ready in about: 2 minutes +cooling time | **Serves**: 4 | **Per serving**: Kcal 214, Fat 19g, Net Carbs 2g, Protein 4g

INGREDIENTS

2/3 cup coconut oil, melted
1 (14 oz) can coconut milk

18 drops stevia liquid
1 cup unsweetened coconut flakes

DIRECTIONS

Mix the coconut oil with the milk and stevia to combine. Stir in the coconut flakes until well distributed. Pour into silicone muffin molds and freeze for 1 hour to harden.

Dark Chocolate Mochaccino Ice Bombs

Ready in about: 5 minutes + cooling time | **Serves**: 4 | **Per serving**: Kcal 127, Fat: 13g, Net Carbs: 1.4g, Protein: 1.9g

INGREDIENTS

½ lb cream cheese
4 tbsp powdered sweetener

2 oz strong coffee
2 tbsp cocoa powder, unsweetened

1 tbsp cocoa butter, melted
2 ½ oz dark chocolate, melted

DIRECTIONS

Combine cream cheese, sweetener, coffee, and cocoa powder, in a food processor. Roll 2 tbsp of the mixture and place on a lined tray. Mix the melted cocoa butter and chocolate, and coat the bombs with it. Freeze for 2 hours.

14-DAY MEAL PLAN TO LOSE UP TO 20 POUNDS

Drink 7 to 9 glasses of water daily

Day	Breakfast	Lunch	Dinner	Dessert/Snacks	Kkal
1	Morning Berry-Green Smoothie	Bacon-Wrapped Chicken with Grilled Asparagus	Russian-Style Beef Gratin	Passion Fruit Cheesecake Slices	1,672
2	Duo-Cheese Omelet with Pimenta & Basil	Peanut Butter Pork Stir-fry	Green Mackerel Salad	Berry Tart	1,784
3	Egg Tofu Scramble with Kale & Mushrooms	Parmesan Wings with Yogurt Sauce	Spicy Sea Bass with Hazelnuts	Peanut Butter Pecan Ice Cream	1,678
4	Dark Chocolate Smoothie	Chili Turkey Patties with Cucumber Salsa	Grilled Halloumi Cheese with Eggs	Chocolate Bark with Almonds (x2)	1,642
5	Spicy Egg Muffins with Bacon & Cheese	Zoodles with Avocado & Olives	Homemade Classic Beef Burgers	Peanut Butter Pecan Ice Cream	1,705
6	Avocado & Kale Eggs	Mexican Beef Chili	One-Pot Chicken with Mushrooms	Vanilla Chocolate Mousse	1,628
7	Almond Waffles with Cinnamon Cream	Taco Lettuce Rolls	Pumpkin & Meat Peanut Stew	Coconut Fat Bombs (x4)	1,642
8	Giant Egg Quiche	Warm Rump Steak Salad	Egg & Cheese Stuffed Peppers	Raspberry Nut Truffles (x2)	1,610
9	Coconut Flour Bagels	Chicken Paella with Chorizo	Strawberry Salad with Cheese & Almonds	Chocolate Chip Cookies (x2)	1,801
10	Bacon & Cheese Pesto Mug Cake	Broccoli Cheese Soup	Pizza Bianca	Raspberry Nut Truffles	1,650
11	Chorizo & Mozzarella Omelet	Vegetable Burritos	Chicken Breasts with Cheddar & Pepperoni	Mixed Berry & Mascarpone Bowl	1,691
12	Breakfast Buttered Eggs	Power Green Soup + Devilled Eggs with Sriracha Mayo	Spiced Pork Roast with Collard Greens	Strawberry Vanilla Shake	1,632
13	Morning Almond Shake	Creamy Stuffed Chicken with Parma Ham	Chipotle Pizza with Cotija & Cilantro	Chocolate Cakes (x2)	1,612
14	Chocolate Creps with Caramel Cream	Coconut Green Bean & Shrimp Curry Soup	Chicken with Creamed Turnip Greens	Green Tea Brownies with Macadamia Nuts (x2)	1,541

INDEX

RECIPE INDEX